THEATRE
The Dynamics
of the Art

Brian Hansen

The University of New Mexico

PRENTICE-HALL
Englewood Cliffs, New Jersey 07632

Library of Congress Cataloging-in-Publication Data

Hansen, Brian.
    Theatre, the dynamics of the art.

    Includes index.
    1. Theater. I. Title.
PN2037.H367   1986   792   85-12248
ISBN 0-13-912676-7 (pbk.)

Editorial/production supervision: Lori L. Baronian and Marjorie Borden
Interior design: Marjorie Borden
Cover design: Photo Plus Art
Manufacturing buyer: Barbara Kittle
Photo Researcher: Christine Carey

ISBN 0-13-912676-7 01

Prentice-Hall International (UK) Limited, *London*
Prentice-Hall of Australia Pty. Limited, *Sydney*
Editora Prentice-Hall do Brasil, Ltda., *Rio de Janeiro*
Prentice-Hall Canada Inc., *Toronto*
Prentice-Hall Hispanoamericana, S.A., *Mexico*
Prentice-Hall of India Private Limited, *New Delhi*
Prentice-Hall of Japan, Inc., *Tokyo*
Prentice-Hall of Southeast Asia Pte. Ltd., *Singapore*
Whitehall Books Limited, *Wellington, New Zealand*

This book is dedicated
to my parents,
who were always there

Contents

Photograph Credits

Researchers, Inc. Photographs on p. 103 courtesy of the Museum of Modern Art/ Film Stills Archives. Copyright © 1982 Columbia Pictures Industries, Inc. All rights reserved. Photograph on p. 110 courtesy of photographer Carolyn A. McKeone and Freelance Photographer's Guild. Photograph on p. 127 and photograph of The Strolling Players on p. 267 courtesy of photographer Jan A. Wein and Freelance Photographer's Guild. Photograph on p. 131 courtesy of photographer, Peter Vandermaark and Stock, Boston. Photograph on p. 139 courtesy of photographer, David S. Talbott and Actor's Theatre of Louisville, State Theatre of Kentucky. Photograph on p. 159 courtesy of the Harvard Theatre Collection. Photograph on p. 162 courtesy of AC & R Public Relations. Photographs on pp. 171 and 175 courtesy of Roy Hoglund and Brian Hansen. Photograph on p. 179 courtesy of photographer, Gregg Mancuso and Stock, Boston. Photographs on p. 187 are from Verdi's *Macbeth*, University of Texas. Photograph on p. 262 courtesy of Robert C. Ragsdale and The Stratford Shakespearean Festival Foundation of Canada. Photograph on page 269 courtesy of the Yale Repertory Theatre. Photograph on p. 273 courtesy of the American Conservatory Theatre. Photograph on p. 283 courtesy of the German Information Center. Photograph on p. 285 with compliments of the Consulate General of the Polish People's Republic. Interpress Publishers, Poland. Photograph on p. 293 courtesy of photographer Gerhard E. G. Scheidle.

Excerpt from *Buried Child* © Copyright 1977, 1979 by Sam Shepard. Reprinted by permission of the Dramatists Play Service, Inc. and the author **Caution:** *Buried Child* being duly copyrighted, is subject to a royalty. The stock and amateur acting rights are controlled exclusively by the Dramatists Play Service, Inc., 440 Park Avenue South, New York, NY 10016. No stock or amateur production of the play may be given without obtaining in advance the written permission of the Dramatists Play Service, Inc., and paying the requisite fee.

Acknowledgments

Whatever the value of the following, none of it would have been possible without the assistance of others. It is only fair that I identify those whose aid has been crucial. For the initial encouragement, I must thank Nancy Tandberg; without her I would probably not have undertaken this task. Once begun, however, I would have slipped into a paralytic depression if it had not been for the supportive and balanced criticism of David Addington. The line drawings of my colleague Roy Hoglund refreshed me during the writing as they will others during the reading. For his assistance from Tokyo I must thank the well-known photographer Tosiro Morita, several of whose photographs appear in the section on Japanese theatre. Steve Dalphin, Marjorie Borden, Lori Baronian, and the capable staff of Prentice-Hall have supported and encouraged me through rough places and smooth. Cheryl Doles has been more than a typist, combining a cool critical eye with proven friendship. Finally, my wife, Gail Joralemon, has provided support and patience—not to mention proofreading skill—in the fullest range of times and places.

Introduction

Let us begin with a cliché: Theatre is a collaborative art. Like most clichés, this is partly true. A work of theatre *is* often created by artists from other art disciplines. Poets may create the script; architects may design the settings that painters then decorate; choreographers and dancers may create the dance portions, composers and musicians, the music, fashion designers, the costumes. All may then join the director and actor to create the work of art we call theatre. In doing so, they give up their identity as independent artists in other disciplines and become "theatre artists." In the process of creating a different art, they have redescribed their own roles.

So far so good; but this cliché, that theatre results from collaboration, falls short of the whole truth because it does not fully explore the idea. Typically we are afraid to squeeze the last drop of meaning from an apparently simple statement. In this case, the whole truth is far more interesting because it is far more complex.

Theatre *is* a collaborative art.

The collaboration which creates the art of theatre, when examined at all carefully, quickly extends beyond the cooperative effort of the skilled artists who create what happens on stage. In a flash, it spills off the stage into the audience. As we will discover, the audience is one of the most important collaborative partners. Each audience member must enter into the process of creating theatre and—as an active participant—must develop and exercise certain skills.

One of the first casualties of this expanded sense of collaboration is the old idea of the audience member as a dull and passive figure, sitting in the dark and having a play "done to them." Good audiences are active audiences; good audiences make good theatre. One of the aims of this book is to help you develop the audience skills which can make theatre such a meaningful experience.*

But let's not stop there: The idea of collaboration extends far beyond the audience in the theatre. The community that supports the theatre has its part to play. As we look back over the history of mankind, we see that periods of cultural greatness have always been periods of artistic vigor—and one of the most active arts is usually theatre. Why? Why is it that in "golden ages" the collaboration between the art of theatre and the supporting culture is most obvious? The society creates the proper conditions and theatre arts, in return, provide an art experience that enriches the life of the society. But what are those conditions? Another aim of this book will be to consider the environment which makes this fruitful level of collaboration possible—or likely—or inevitable. From this we can better understand the role of theatre in our own culture.

Finally, there is the level of collaboration at which any human culture creates and sustains any of the performing arts, indeed, *any* important institution. This book is based on the assumption that some identifiable form of theatre experience is found in every human culture, and has been since the dawn of our species. If this assertion forces us to redefine what we mean by "theatre," we will do so. And, as a result, we will discover that—far from being an expendable and largely trivial ornament to a few well-heeled cultures—theatre is as much a part of a cultural heritage as religion, agriculture, or speech. This so because theatre—like the arts in general—serves as important function for our species. The nature of that function and the mechanisms by which that function is achieved are issues that will appear repeatedly in the pages that follow.

The picture that will emerge is not a series of still photographs of

*Indeed, perhaps the time has come to coin a new verb, "audiencing," which would be to "audiences" what "acting" is to "actors" and "playwriting" is to "playwrights."

great periods, great plays, great productions, and great performers. They will all be there, of course, but they will not hold center stage. Instead, they will be imbedded in a changing net of relationships. This web will extend from the forgotten past to the unimagined future; it will embrace not only the theatrical practices of contemporary Western civilization, but the traditions of Eastern and preindustrial cultures. And you must be alert: Captured in the mesh of our web you may be surprised to find simple, ordinary experiences that you never thought to consider "theatrical."

If we ultimately discover that the complex art of theatre is woven into the larger fabric of human culture, we should not be surprised. All of human experience is of a single piece, though we may choose to examine only one area at a time. The patch called "theatre" may seem an isolated region indeed—until we follow the strands out of its center. At all points the art of theatre is connected with other aspects of human experience. The hard sciences, technology, philosophy, psychology, linguistics, sociology, and so on. And, as in a spider's web, a disturbance in one area is immediately felt everywhere.

While the key concept here is interdependence, the remainder of this book is divided into five parts, each of which explores a different aspect of the basic pattern of interaction. In Chapter 1 we will explore the concept of interaction itself and the levels of interaction, which can be found in any theatre experience. Once this basic pattern is clear, we can move to an exploration of each level separately.

Chapters 2 and 3 take a detailed look at the patterns of actor/ audience interaction as they shape the conventions of theatre, the functions of theatre, and the role of theatre in society. As part of this discussion we will examine the place of theatre in five very different cultures.

In Chapters 4 through 10 we turn our attention to the interaction between the members of the theatre company as they create a theatrical production. We will begin with the actor/actor interaction, but will explore the supportive roles of the playwright, the director, the designers, the critic, and other members of the creative team—including the audience.

Character/character interactions lie at the heart of Chapters 11 through 12. This interaction creates the world of the play, the imaginary construct that allows us to live alternative lives. These worlds have such integrity that they can be described in considerable detail, just as foreign countries can be described. And the special rules of each of these worlds give us the standards in the various dramatic genre: tragedy, melodrama, drama, comedy, and farce.

Finally, in Chapter 13 a range of other interactions are explored. Through them, we see the other possibilities of theatre as it can be used in education, therapy, recreation, and other settings. This chapter must inevitably raise questions about the uses of theatre that may become possible and active in the future.

But we will begin in the present. Let us turn our attention to the center of the theatrical experience. We will start by examining the dynamics of the interdependent relationship that lies at the very core of the theatre experience.

1

Theatre as Interaction

THE THEATRICAL MOMENT

"The Shalako are here! The gods have arrived!"

The restless spectators grow silent and peer into the dark. The ceremonial messengers have already raced through the crowd, carrying the news to the clan houses; their magic has been successful; once again the founder gods have returned to bless the village.

Down the hill from the pueblo administrative offices, beyond full reach of the headlights of the pickup trucks pulled into a circle, six shapes begin to emerge. Slowly they cross the nearly dry stream. They stand expectantly in a loose group at the very place where the villagers first gathered when Zuni pueblo was founded hundreds of years ago. Ten feet tall, with elongated birdlike heads and ceremonial dancing kilts, they simply wait. They are attended by humans and yet they are majestically alone, occasionally clacking their massive beaks and waiting for the correct moment to divide and begin their slow procession in the new houses which have been prepared to receive them . . . and where all night long they will dance the slow, intricate steps that trace out the history of the tribe and assure its continuation.

But for now, the people on the slope and the giant figures simply share the same historic place and stand, the spectators bundled against the cold December air, waiting for the magic time in the night when the special power has accumulated and the process can continue . . . .

Two thousand miles away, another group of people is waiting. These spectators are more physically comfortable; they are indoors, seated in upholstered chairs, and the walls of the theatre muffle—if not exclude—the traffic sounds of New York. They too are in the dark. In the lighted space before them stands a man. They understand that he is supposed to be a doctor—a psychiatrist. He is waiting in his office for the arrival of a most remarkable patient, a young man—almost a boy—who has committed a strange act of violence. Late one night the young patient entered a stable and, using a steel hoof-pick, blinded a number of horses. Why? The psychiatrist is intrigued, and the time has arrived when he can begin his own inquiry into the mind of the troubled youth.

The audience, too, is intrigued. In a world of so much apparently senseless violence, here is a chance to get some answers. What could possibly drive a person to maim defenseless horses? There will be no clumsy interrogation tonight; the questions will be put by an expert, a man trained to understand and cure such abnormal behavior. Tonight it will be science in a struggle with the irrational . . . and is there any question who will win?

And yet there is something troubling. Around the edges of the light there are figures, made larger than life by elevating boots which end in hooves. Their heads, covered with metal masks, are the unmistakable shape of horses' heads. Occasionally, they snort or pound their iron hooves upon the stage. They are unexplained, and the audience has the unsettling feeling that before the night is over, these horse figures will have played a far more important role than they—or the psychiatrist—suspect. The tension in the air is palpable.

Suddenly and silently, at the far side of the circle of light, they see the figure of a slim young man. He stands quietly, his eyes downcast. The psychiatrist looks at him intently, slowly lights a cigarette, and begins his interrogation. . . .

What have these two experiences in common? One is an annual religious event predating history, and the other is a modern play written by a celebrated playwright. And yet they share so many of the same features, we must call them by the same word: theatre. What are the similarities that make them both part of the same, worldwide art form?

DEFINING THEATRE

This whole book is an attempt to define the single word *theatre*. It tries to describe the features of the event in such detail that by the conclusion, you will be so familiar with the enduring aspects of the art form that you will always have a clear understanding of its basic principles. This book is not long; the task seems achievable. But in a more important sense, the task is futile in a book of any length. Futile, that is, if you want a formal, eternal definition.

Theatre is a living art. As such, it continually responds to the world around it. As that world changes, so does theatre. Furthermore, theatre is the product of human imagination; it remains as unpredictable as the minds of those who create it. Change is the order of the day. In fact, this constant interaction between human imagination and a changing cultural environment is suggestive of the ecological balance between living organisms and their biological environment. Just as living organisms must adapt or die out, so must the art of theatre adapt. The wide differences which exist between theatre traditions can be attributed to the same sorts of processes that have created the many species of plant and animal life. And, because species are in constant evolutionary change, no definition of a single species will hold forever. The only constant element seems to be change.

And so it is with the theatre. As we look at examples of theatre throughout the world today we are struck by its great variety: from the ritual of the Australian aborigine to a performance of the Metropolitan Opera; from the dance-drama of Bali to the classroom drama of an English grammar school; from a *kabuki* performance in Japan to a Broadway production of a Neil Simon comedy . . . In each case the style and degree of production vary enormously; the intentions of the playwright and performers may be poles apart; and the expectations of the audience are significantly different.

If you extend the range of theatre events across time, the variety becomes even more striking. The Greek theatregoer of Athens in the fifth century B.C. would hardly recognize an avant-garde production from off-Broadway as the serious, religiously based experience he or she knew from the theatre of Dionysus. A 19th-century patron of the Paris boulevard theatres would have been utterly bored and confused by a 17th-century Japanese *no* drama. One can only guess that the theatregoer of the 30th century will find our theatre as alien to their tastes as we find 10th-century liturgical drama to ours.

So how do we proceed? Let's just accept the fact that the best we can do is make an operational definition of theatre, a definition for today based on the observable properties of the art as we know it today, and which allows our enquiry to continue, even though we recognize in advance that any definition is incomplete and temporary.

One popular method of reaching an operational definition of any kind of human activity is to examine the whole field and search out those characteristics which are *always* present. A strategy for achieving this is to discard every element which is *not* necessary to what people call *theatre*. In his pithy and influential *Toward A Poor Theatre*, the modern director and theoretician Jerzy Grotowski follows this method relentlessly. Do we need theatre buildings, he asks? No; there are many important theatre traditions which do not have buildings called theatres. Do we absolutely need playwrights? No, there have been healthy improvisational theatres which did not work from scripts. Do we absolutely need costumes? No. Makeup? No. Scenery? No. Actors? Audience?

Yes. Yes.

Grotowski concludes, along with many others, that all we really need to create *theatre* is the actor and the audience. Furthermore, these need be only one of each: one actor, one audience member.

THE PERFORMANCE CONTRACT

One actor, one audience member. In our mind's eye we see them facing one another. One on an empty stage, the other in an empty auditorium. Lonely, without costumes, or makeup, or tickets, or a playscript, or any of the other elements of theatre.

But how do we tell which is which? Neither one was born to their roles. And yet as we watch them, the two roles are as clear to us as if they were wearing numbered football jerseys. The actor and the audience member have entered into a social contract as clear and binding as that which identifies parent and child, ruler and subject, hero and outcast. Recognized through a collection of verbal and nonverbal cues and symbols, this unspoken performance contract might be translated into the form on the following page.

Like any two-party contract, this one can be violated by either party at any time. If the audience member's mind is elsewhere and becomes inattentive, the contract is broken. If the actor lacks skill and cannot convey the truth of life in that imaginary world, the contract is broken. When it is broken, the imaginary world crumbles into oblivion. The mutual advantage is lost. This book attempts to describe the means used to create and sustain that performance contract, the mutual advantages gained, and the nature of those imaginary works.

Performance Contract

I, hereafter called "the actor," will pretend to be someone or something other than myself, or myself in a
condition other than my own, in such a way as to
make it clear that I am pretending.

You, hereafter called "the audience," will pretend
that you believe me. You will do all in your power to
believe; I will do every thing I can to allow you to
believe.

Together we will use mutually acceptable means to construct an imaginary world, a world which will exist in
whatever detail we wish for as long as we, sharing the
same time and space, choose to maintain it.

This we shall do for our mutual advantage.

Signed

_____ Actor

_____ Audience

INTERACTION AND THEATRE

An interaction is a continuing relationship between individuals or groups
in which the action of one is influenced by the action of the other, and
vice versa. It may be imagined as an endless chain of events: A does
this, which forces B to do that, which forces A to respond by such-and-
such, whereupon B . . . This design could apply to any number of human
experiences. It could describe an arms build-up between competing
nations. It could also describe a couple falling in love.

This idea of interaction depends upon human communication. Those who study communication as a science describe a communication act as follows: *A* has an idea; *A* encodes the idea; the encoded idea is transmitted through some medium to *B* who then decodes the message. *B* then has a reaction to this idea; this reaction *B* then encodes and transmits back to *A* who decodes it. The loop is then complete; but note that it is only complete when the *B*-to-*A* segment—the feedback segment—is complete. (See Figure 1-1.)

Figure 1-1 All human communication involves the complex processes of encoding, transmitting, and decoding symbols. To be complete, communication must include a feedback step.

The encoded message we call a symbol. A symbol is a sound, a shape, a form, a posture, which people have come to accept as standing for some aspect of human experience. The concept of symbolic communication is immensely complicated, but common experience gives us many familiar examples. For instance, the sounds symbolized by the letters *C-A-T* are themselves a symbol standing for a small, furry mammal kept as a housepet. If *A* says those sounds, and if those sounds travel through the air and are heard by *B*, who decodes them by thinking of the small, furry mammal, the act of communication is well underway. It is completed only when *B* nods to indicate that he understands and *A*, seeing the nod, understands that *B* understands.

This all seems very simple. But notice that the C-A-T sounds only mean *cat* to that minority of humans who are familiar with the symbol system; in short, those who speak English. A person unfamiliar with the symbol system—an Egyptian, for example—might be confused. So might a deaf person. But to a person familiar with the system, the sounds have a precise meaning and can be encoded and decoded with great accuracy. That is because *cat* carries what is called *denotative* meaning. Denotative meaning is that which places the greatest value on clarity and precision. It is "dictionary" meaning; the symbols are widely known and specially selected to minimize confusion. Other symbols which carry denotative meaning include highway signs, mathematical symbols, and such nonverbal symbols as waving goodbye.

But there is another class of symbols which convey a different kind of meaning: *connotative* meaning. Connotative meaning is complex and poetic. Connotative meaning is frequently very important and powerful, but its symbols are not usually found in the dictionary. People often have widely varied responses to this kind of symbol.

To make the matter even more complicated, denotative symbols may be combined to form complex symbols conveying important connotative meaning. For example, the individual words uttered by the character of Hamlet in Shakespeare's play may carry denotative meaning in themselves; however, as they collect into individual speeches, the connotative meaning grows. Ultimately, the *character* of Hamlet himself becomes a symbol. In fact, in nearly 400 years, Hamlet, the tortured Danish prince, has become a symbol of great connotative power in Western civilization—but a symbol composed of a cloud of denotative and connotative meanings.

It is important to remember that both kinds of symbols may be used in theatre. Some of you, familiar with the denotative precision of the symbols used in science and mathematics, may be confused if you seek the same clarity in the arts. By the same token, someone used to the richness of the symbols used in the arts may be bored or unmoved by the denotation of the sciences. Anyone who wants to understand how theatre works as an art form should be aware of the range and complexity of the symbolic communication which is necessary within even a single play or performance.

Bearing this in mind, let us return to the active process that uses these symbols. Specifically, let us return to the interactions which lie at the heart of the performance contract and, therefore, all theatre.

LEVELS OF INTERACTION

Let's return to that one actor and that one audience member in that empty space. One of them, the actor, is pretending to be something other than what he or she is; the other, the audience member, is helping. Together they create the performance contract—which we can now describe as an actor/audience interaction. This is the primary interaction in theatre and the one which separates theatre from all the other arts. In it, the actor and audience work—in a shared time and space—to forge a performance contract and create the world of the play.

With this in mind, we can elaborate somewhat on our basic pattern of human symbolic communication. (See Figure 1-2.)

The symbols used by the actor are easy to recognize. They include the words spoken by characters, their gestures, how they use stage space, the speed and energy with which they speak and move, the emerging plot of the play, and—in a fully produced play—the makeup, costume, scenery, music, and other aspects of production. The full range of meanings are carefully encoded into these symbols and transmitted to the audience by sight and sound. The sensitive audience member then decodes these symbols and, one hopes, understands the intended meaning.

The second half of the interaction may not be so obvious to a casual observer. Maybe this is because we live in a culture in which vigorous audience reaction is not encouraged. We rely on such voluntary responses as laughter, applause, and cheering to indicate approval; booing and hissing may show displeasure. In addition, such involuntary sounds such as weeping, gasps, and—most prized of all by experienced actors—the absolute silence of a totally engrossed audience let the performer know that he or she has completed the communication loop and made contact with the audience.

In other times and cultures, the range of options was far greater. Oriental audiences frequently shout encouragement to actors who are doing well—and give short, critical comments to those who are doing badly. Because Japanese audiences are both mobile and vocal inside the theatre, a Kabuki actor knows he is effective if his performance makes

Figure 1-2 Communication in the theatre—like communication anywhere—is a two-way process.

the audience sit down and stop talking. The tradition of throwing objects at performers has, fortunately, been neglected in recent years. But some 19th-century vaudeville performers had acts of such low quality that they performed behind nets to protect them from vegetables thrown by critical audience members. History records that in ancient Greece one singer, no doubt having trouble with a high note, took a well-thrown fig right in his mouth; the fruit lodged in his throat and he asphyxiated—a classic case of negative feedback.

Some modern audience feedback happens only after the performance. Newspaper critics write reviews; friends advise the actor; even ticket sales become a form of communication, as favorable response may lead to larger audiences, while small audiences may signal to the performer that some aspects of his or her work are not succeeding.

Finally, nothing encourages a performer as much as the knowledge that he or she has a "good" audience, one that is knowledgeable, perceptive, responsive, and appreciative. And an actor who is encouraged frequently gives a better performance. Thus the theatre adage that "good audiences get good shows" is true when we consider the actor/audience interaction from the point of view of the contribution which the audience member makes through feedback.

Although the actor/audience interaction is critical to the theatre event, there are other kinds of interaction which help us understand what happens in theatre and why the art has such special power.

So far, we have spoken as if there were only one actor on the stage portraying only a single character. In some plays this is true; but in most it is not. Usually there are several characters. Often these characters are involved in plots of great complexity in which the characters relate to one another, often under very emotional conditions. In fact, when such a situation occurs in ordinary life, we often describe it as *dramatic*, implying that some aspect of our lives has become as highly charged as the lives of characters on the stage.

But what is it that those characters are doing as they fall in love, fight duels, arrange trysts, argue, scheme, contend, win, and lose? What is happening when King Oedipus asks the oracle at Delphi who is responsible for the pollution of Thebes, is told that *he* is, rejects the idea and sets out to find the man who has killed his own father and married his mother? What do we see as the evidence builds, until Oedipus is forced to acknowledge the truth of his own life and destiny?

We are seeing an interaction. Not the same as the interaction leading to the performance contract, but an interaction nonetheless. Character *A* does something which forces character *B* to respond in some way; as a result, character *A* does something new, character *B* responds by . . . and so it goes. We can refer to this level as *character/character interaction*, and it constitutes the *content* of theatre.

There is an old formula which says that conflict is the basis of all drama. It goes on to say that the conflict can be one of three kinds: person against person, person against nature, and person against himself or herself. This formula is true enough that we will return to it in a later chapter as we discuss the imaginary worlds of the theatre. But in doing so we should point out that this idea of conflict applies best to the drama of derring-do and flamboyant action. *Conflict* is not an accurate word to describe the delicate inner workings of psychological drama, the hypnotic rituals of much avant-garde work, or the quiet intensity of some single-character plays. These are more subtle than the word *conflict* normally implies.

The problem is resolved when we understand that what many call *conflict* is only heightened interaction. Only minor changes are needed: a character interacts with other characters, she interacts with natural elements, and she interacts with herself (becoming, in effect, two or more characters).

This second level of interaction, the character/character interaction, is subject to all the rules of any interaction, including the use of symbols such as speech and gesture to communicate meaning. Let's see if we can capture this level of interaction in a diagram which also includes both actor/audience and character/character interactions. (See Figure 1–3.)

The interactions which make up the character/character level of interaction are, of course, all pretense. They depend entirely on the skill of the actor and the support of the audience if they are to be understood and believed. And yet the interactions which make up the content of any play must have about them the spontaneity, subtlety, and vigor of interactions in real life. In addition, the content interactions must have a clarity which is seldom found in ordinary life. The special characteristics of content interactions and the imaginary world they create are dealt with in considerable detail in Chapters 11 and 12.

The third major level of interaction can be guessed by reference to the previous diagram: if there are actor/audience and character/character interactions described there, the perceptive reader may guess that there is the possibility of interaction between the actors.

Writing in the 4th century B.C., the philosopher Aristotle first

Figure 1-3 Actor/actor interaction parallels the character/character interaction which makes up the content of theatre.

attempted to describe what differentiated theatre from other art forms. He concluded that, unlike lyric and epic poetry, theatre employed "the *mode* of enactment." There is fairly consistent agreement that Aristotle meant that living actors take the stage to perform a play, thereby making of their own bodies and voices the materials of the art. Consider the parallels: in fiction and poetry, the writer arranges words upon paper; in painting, the artist places paint on a canvas; and in music, a composer manipulates sounds to create an artistic effect. Only in theatre, opera, and dance do the performers display their own bodies before a living audience as the materials of their art. Indeed, the primary materials of theatre are the voice, body, and mind of the actor.

It is the *actor/actor interaction* which gives theatre not only its special character as an art form but a special power and immediacy. It is like standing beside Rembrandt as he painted a masterpiece; it is as if we were in conversation with Einstein when he first saw the relationship between mass and energy; it is as if we were in Michelangelo's studio when, having finished his great statue of Moses, he gave it a final blow with his hammer and commanded it to speak!

The actor/actor interaction, carried out before our very eyes, is only the tip of an iceberg of collaboration, or artistic interactions carried out by members of the theatrical company. It is this web of interaction which makes up the business of Chapters 4-9 of this book. There the contribution of each of the theatre specialists is discussed and the creative process of modern Western theatre is described in considerable detail.

Let us now add the actor/actor interaction to our busy diagram. (See Figure 1-4.)

Considered together, the actor/audience, character/character and actor/actor interactions give us a clue as to the special power of theatre as an art form. Like most arts, theatre capitalizes on the natural interest of humans in their own lives—but it does it in three ways, simultaneously. Human interaction is what theatre is about; it is how theatre is done; it is how theatre is perceived. As a species we are compulsively fascinated by human interaction in our ordinary lives, so when three levels of interaction are displayed simultaneously, the attraction is irresistible. This is why every human culture has a theatrical tradition—either formal or informal—and theatrical displays have been a part of human history since we first cautiously rose up on two legs.

It is this three-level richness in human interaction which will always attract people to theatre as an art form. It is also this richness

Figure 1-4 In theatre, three levels of interaction are taking place simultaneously: actor/audience, actor/actor, character/character. These three levels represent the context, the mode, and the content of the art.

which cannot be duplicated by any existing electronic medium. Therefore, there seems little chance that theatre will be replaced—though it will have to remain competitive in other respects.

OTHER LEVELS OF INTERACTION

There are several other levels of interaction which may become important in special situations. For example, the interaction between an actor and the character he or she is playing may become important during rehearsals. This actor/character interaction could develop as the actor discovered parallels between the life of the character and his own. Certain systems of actor training encourage the actor to explore these parallels, delving into his or her personal history for emotional memories and physical images which can enrich the stage life of the character. Thus an actress playing the manipulative Amanda Wingfield in Tennessee Williams' *The Glass Menagerie* may find such a resource in her own mother; as a result, her portrayal of Amanda may resemble her own mother, and Amanda's relationship with her daughter Laura will contain aspects of the actress' relationship with her mother—or the actress with her daughter. The intense self-examination and personal disclosure demanded by this approach have important implications for the psychological health of the actor. We should not be surprised, then, to learn that actor/character interactions provide a fertile area for therapy. Actor/character interactions form the center of psychodrama and sociodrama, two forms of theatre explored in greater detail in Chapter 13.

Another possible level of interaction is audience/audience. This might be subtitled the "social" level of interaction because it encompasses interactions which do not cross the footlights, however important they may be to the audience members. Hence, they operate outside the arena of the art form. Such interactions might include the sense of community that can form when people gather together, and the need to "see and be seen," which is so important to the social worlds of fashion, courtship, and the public display of wealth and power. Of more importance to the art of theatre is the immediate interaction of audience members as they collectively decide what to laugh at, what to praise, and what to mourn in the imaginary world of the play. These last will be discussed more fully in Chapter 10 in which we explore the audience as creative participant.

The perceptive reader is probably asking: "What about audience/character interactions? Is there such a thing?" Before we can answer such a question, we might try to determine what an audience/character interaction would be like. The audience would receive a series of encoded messages from the character; the audience would adjust; then the audience would send a message back to the character. But could the character then adjust or change as a result of the feedback? No. Is it possible for Oedipus to break off his search simply because the audience thinks it unwise? No. The character lives in a hermetically sealed world. Usually, it is only the actor who can interact with the audience. There are plays, it is true, in which the character speaks to the audience and appears to take their opinions into account, but very few in which what the audience says or does *really* changes the way in which the character behaves. In the overwhelming majority of plays, it is the actor who is the intermediary between the world of the character and the world of the audience.

This last fact has attracted considerable attention recently, especially among anthropologists and theatre scholars with a special interest in primitive drama. They point out that the power of the actor to serve as a messenger, as it were, between the world of the living audience and the fictional world of the play parallels the function of the shaman in primitive societies. The shaman is supposed to be especially empowered to move from the world of the living into the world of the spirits and to return with secret information. This suggested similarity in function raises some interesting questions about the function of the actor as a sort of magician in modern society, an idea that has been embraced enthusiastically by some schools of acting training.

PRETENSE AND DECEPTION

Some people are uncomfortable with the element of pretense in theatre; it strikes them as somehow dishonest that people should pretend to be what they are not. Whole cultures have shared this discomfort. The Roman Catholic church during the Middle Ages, the Puritans, and Islam for most of its history have tried to discourage not only acting, but all of theatre, for reasons stemming from this element of pretense. Their argument is some variation on a belief first formulated by Plato in *The Republic.* He said that since theatre is a form of lying it might encourage people to take liberties with the truth in other parts of their lives. Even today there are people who distrust any person or profession that makes "lying" an important part of their everyday work. These are perfectly reasonable objections, and those who raise them deserve serious attention.

We can begin by questioning the truth of their premise; does theatre involve deception? Deception is an attempt to mislead another person as to the truth. This premise implies that if a theatre artist could, he or she would completely mislead the audience into believing that what occurs upon the stage is real life, rather than a representation of real life. But is this the case? The overwhelming evidence is that it is not. As we have seen, the performance contract specifically provides that the audience must themselves pretend to believe. This clearly implies that they do not really believe, and must therefore pretend to do so. In fact, a performance contract cannot be in force unless the audience knows that what it is seeing is pretense. It is that simple. And if an audience knows that what it is seeing is all pretense, there cannot be deception. It is logically impossible for an honest person to say, "What I will tell you next is a lie," and then be accused of misleading the hearer in the next sentence.

As we have seen, the understanding that this is all pretense is built into the performance contract from the very outset. Furthermore, as we shall see, many of the conventions of theatre are actually intended not to deceive the audience, but to remind them that what they are witnessing is only theatre, an art form based on mutual pretense.

FILM, TELEVISION, AND THEATRE

The layperson commonly considers dramatic film and television productions to be a form of theatre. It is easy to understand this widespread misconceptions. Both television and films employ actors, directors, and designers; both rely on writers whose scripts are routinely transferred from one medium to another; film screenings are presented to audiences in special buildings called theatres; television and film both can record live theatre productions for showing at some future time; the acting style in television and film programs is sometimes hard to distinguish from that on stage; and so on. What the layperson frequently overlooks, however, is a fundamental difference between media presentations and live theatre. That difference is the actor/audience interactions.

Consider this obvious fact: in theatre, the audience and the actor share the same time and space. In film and television, they seldom do. Films are shot months or years before they are seen by the public; in addition, they are photographed and edited in places distant from the intended audience. Indeed, they are usually shot entirely out of sequence; they develop a plot only in the editing room. For example, a typical motion picture about Imperial Russia may contain exterior scenes shot in Spain and Bulgaria and interior scenes shot in London.

The first scene shot may have been the execution of the Czar and Czarina; only months later will the actors playing those roles play the wedding scene. The editing of the final version was probably done in Los Angeles; the prints were processed in laboratories in New York. Sixteen months later the audience member sees a screening of the film in Logan, Utah.

Let us suppose the film is excellent. Did the presence of the audience have any influence on the outcome? No, because there was no interaction between the actor and the audience. Time and distance intervened. The film may be an excellent work of art, but the audience is forced to deal with it in much the same way that one experiences a painting. Seen from this perspective, film is not a performing art at all; the performance contract cannot be signed by the audience member because the audience is unable to complete the necessary feedback loop.

Some people prefer film and television to live theatre; others appreciate both. But both camps must understand that the intervention of media has introduced changes which have created a new art form.

Theatre fans love the immediacy of their art form. For them the difference between theatre and film is the difference between seeing an excellent film about a tightrope walker and seeing the event in person. No matter how good the film, the outcome is fixed. The event took place in the past, and what remains is nothing but shadows cast on a wall by specks of silver caught in an emulsion. The enthusiastic fan of live theatre wants to share time and space with the tightrope walker. So, too, do some performers. Some television performers, aware of the benefits provided by a live audience, tape their performances before a live audience. The fact that the audience is present in the studio only serves to underscore the fact that interaction is impossible between the actor and the television viewer.

Whether or not the play contains dangerous elements—stage fights, perhaps, or life-threatening stage magic—there is an element of danger in the live performance of even the most mundane play. The actors are pitting their skills and sensitivity against the endless demands of an art. Each performance is a new experience, and no one can know for certain how it will turn out. Tonight's chemistry may bring about a truly memorable experience—or a disaster.

For the audience, too, there are many unknowns. Tonight's performance contract has never been written before. There is no way of knowing what the interaction will bring. Will the world created by the performers and the audience be a diverting escape from everyday problems? Or will it be a wrenching look at the value of the life that brings those problems?

Every person enters the theatre hoping that his or her life will be changed. Some will be satisfied to emerge refreshed after the passage of a few pleasant hours. Others enter with much higher expectations; they want their lives changed in significant ways. For these people, the adventure is most exciting when the ante is large and the possible outcomes are attractive, or mysterious, or threatening. This theatre-goer becomes a traveler in an unknown country and the actor is the guide: a guide with a band of assistants, with techniques at his or her disposal, and with a wide variety of conventions upon which to draw.

But before we can discuss any of these, we must examine what it is that brings the audience member and the actor together in the first place. To do so, we must ask some difficult questions about the function of the theatre.

Discussion Questions

1. Can you think of activities in your life which have a "performance contract," spoken or implied, attached to them? Consider all the elements.
2. Have you ever experienced a theatre event in which a performance contract was broken? Describe it.
3. Why do we employ at least two kinds of symbols in human communication? What advantages do denotative symbols have? What disadvantages? Answer the same questions for connotative symbols.
4. Why is feedback so important to communication?
5. At what level of interaction (actor/audience; character/character; actor/actor) would the following events take place?

   a. The leading lady is offended by the leading man's breath;
   b. An actor's mother loves the play;
   c. Romeo kisses Juliet;
   d. The blind detective's guide dog keeps walking down to the footlights and barking at the audience;
   e. The actor playing the blind detective loses his temper and kicks the dog;
   f. Hamlet suspects that the ghost is lying to him;
   g. The play wins an award for "best production."

6. Would you consider professional football to be a form of theatre? What about professional wrestling? What about football or wrestling on television?

2

Theatre and Society

INTRODUCTION

Any art lives in a balanced relationship with the society which supports it. This is especially true of theatre, an art which only happens when relatively large numbers of people are assembled in the same space at the same time. And, as we have seen, theatre only happens when all those people understand and accept the performance contract. This much is obvious.

What is *not* so obvious is that there are many unwritten provisions built into the performance contract. Remember the clause which says: "Together we will use mutually acceptable means to construct an imaginary world"? This clause assures that there will be implied rules built into every contract. These unspoken, but well-understood rules vary from culture to culture, sometimes from theatrical production to production.

THE CONVENTIONS OF THE THEATRE

The rules by which actor/audience interactions are established and maintained are called conventions. These conventions are usually unconscious; they are practically never written down. Indeed, conventions are often so completely internalized that neither the actors nor the audience see them for what they are: arbitrary, culture-bound rules governing the details of theatrical performance. This can lead to self-delusion; people who cannot recognize the arbitrary and changing nature of conventions are often tempted to describe them as eternal, natural laws of the drama. For example, when the actor playing the role of a loyal officer in a traditional Peking opera strides onto the stage, he can be immediately recognized as a morally superior person. Why? Because he is wearing bright red makeup on his face. Neither the actors nor the audience find this in the least remarkable. If asked to explain why a loyal officer wears bright red makeup, a Chinese actor or critic might find the question laughable: such characters *always* have bright red faces. Indeed, audiences would probably be confused and upset if the actor did *not* wear red makeup.

Before we become too superior, however, we might quickly review some of the conventions which we experience and accept in American theatre practice. As we do so, try to imagine how bizarre these practices might seem to a perceptive visitor from another culture.

Being in the mood for some *light diversion*, we decide, on the *spur of the moment*, to take in a play. Accordingly, *after dark*, we go to a building which is used for *nothing but theatre*. We are *forced to pay* for the privilege; but we do not do so directly. We buy a *small piece of cardboard* which another person tears in half. We sit in *fixed chairs* with a *large group of strangers*. The electric *lights in the windowless room are then dimmed*. A *piece of cloth* rises, disclosing *another room* in which other people talk and move about *as if they did not know that we were eavesdropping*. But the people in the other room *talk very loudly* and they usually manage to *stand so that we can see their faces*. The room they inhabit is peculiar; all the furniture is along three of the four walls—none of it is placed against the missing fourth wall.

The events in that room are unusual as well: the people *talk only about the subject of the plot; furthermore, they discuss in great detail events which one would have thought they already knew*. The people themselves are not as reasonable as people are in real life; they are *contentious* and *quick to develop conflicts*. Within two hours they get themselves into a serious difficulty which is *resolved only by a surprising event*; this development *frustrates the evil people* and leaves the *good ones in fortunate circumstances*.

At this point, the audience members all *beat the palms of their hands together*; the people in the well-lit room—people who have ignored us for two hours—now face us, smile, and *bend over at the waist*.

The Peking Opera is very dependent upon well-understood conventions. On the right, a high-ranking officer of the state is easily recognized by his elaborate costume: his high moral character is shown by the fact that his facial makeup is bright red.

Of course, you recognize the conventions described here. Some have names: *tickets, exposition, climax, poetic justice, applause, curtain call* and so on. Others are just familiar practices—so familiar in fact, that only an intentionally simple-minded description draws our attention to them. But remember, a classic Greek audience would have been surprised by a performance given at night, or by theatre being presented as a year-round, commercial activity; an Elizabethan audience would be surprised by the fixed chairs, seating on the ground floor, and a curtain; a nineteenth-century American audience might have been offended by being ignored by the actors.

The conventions of theatre are specifically designed to allow the audience to "believe" the truth of the events portrayed. For example, the convention in Western drama today is that only actresses play women's roles. We believe that this is the only "realistic" way to cast a play. Japanese *kabuki* actors and audiences would not agree, however; neither would William Shakespeare. For them, it is (or was) more "realistic" for men or boys to play female roles. These and other conventions, then, serve to convince specific audiences that what is happening on stage captures the essential truth of life offstage.

Other conventions, however, do just the reverse: they remind us that what we are experiencing is "only a play." The lowering of the auditorium lights and the raising of a curtain are ways of telling the audience that the performance is beginning. Similarly, the custom of curtain calls at the conclusion of a play signals the end of the experience. Taken together, these conventions serve to bracket the performance, separating it from the "real life" which surrounds it—in much the same way that the frame of a painting visually separates the painted canvas from the wall on which the painting hangs.

The vast majority of conventions are based in cultural traditions and operate across all theatre productions in a given period. Occasionally, however, an individual playwright or director will create a convention which operates for one production only. An example would be Peter Shaffer's play *Black Comedy*. The major action in this light comedy takes place at night in a house which has suffered a power outage. Much of the humor results from the misadventures of characters who know that no one can see them in the dark. But a play performed in the dark is no fun for an audience; so Shaffer establishes his own convention. The play *begins* in the dark and for a few minutes the surprised audience can only *hear* the actors going about their ordinary business of the play; suddenly, however, the stage lights come up brightly—whereupon the now visible actors begin to stumble around and complain about the dark. Immediately the delighted audience understands the convention which will operate in this play: stage lights mean it is dark in the home; a dark stage symbolizes light.

But such specific conventions are relatively rare. Traditional conventions are far more familiar—and ultimately more interesting if one cares about the larger question of how the art of theatre represents a

Most of the action in Peter Schaffer's *Black Comedy* takes place during a power outtage in a London flat. Schaffer solves the problem by creating a convention. Here we see what the audience sees during a "dark" scene.

specific culture. Any discussion of this kind must start with a single question: what is the function of theatre in this culture?

DOES THEATRE HAVE A FUNCTION?

There are many people who are made uncomfortable by this question. One group—the art-for-art's-sake group—reject the idea that any art has any value outside itself. These artists and critics believe that the art of theatre has, therefore, no function except to "be itself"; that as soon as theatre undertakes extrinsic goals, it becomes therapy, or propaganda, or religious practice, or commerce—or anything instead of an art. To those who hold this point of view, a discussion of the function of theatre is pointless because the concepts of *function* and *art* are mutually incompatible.

Another group finds the question offensive because, as they usually put it, the function of theatre is "entertainment, pure and simple." To these people, entertainment is synonymous with simple diversion, and they believe that larger goals, such as teaching, are not entertaining. Most people would describe as "entertaining" anything which gives them pleasure—and any good theatre artist strives to give pleasure. But people receive pleasure from a wide variety of events, some of them unlikely at first glance. Take tragedy: many people are fascinated and greatly moved by tragic stories and plays. Even though the subject matter may be very unpleasant human experiences, and a sensitive audience may be brought to tears, they would report that they enjoyed the evening's experience. In the same way, other audience members might be entertained by a highly didactic play or one which reminds them of social problems or personal failings.

The theatre lover enthusiastically embraces the idea that theatre should always be entertaining, always enjoyable. At the same time we must remember that a wide variety of theatrical forms can be "entertaining" to various people. Indeed, even the *same* person can have various needs which theatre can fulfill on different occasions.

Another perspective on this question of function has emerged in recent years. This approach builds from an analogy with evolutionary biology. Those who support this line of argument begin by pointing out that, with very minor exceptions, all aspects of animal and plant life aim toward one end: the conferring of competitive advantage to the individual organism. The process may be very complicated, but the successful organism is the one whose genes are passed on to the greatest number of successful offspring. Thus, in times of scarcity, the giraffe with a neck long enough to reach leaves which other animals cannot reach will probably produce more offspring than those with shorter necks. And, thereby, the species of animals called giraffes come to have longer necks than their ancestors. Of course, this general principle applies to the *behavior* of organisms just as much as to their physical characteristics. Indeed, some aspects of the traditional behavior of animal species which were once considered aimless and bizarre are now known to have been carefully developed through generations of natural selection because of the advantage they provide.

It is difficult to extrapolate from the biology of lower animals to the culture of humankind; but the logic remains the same for many human institutions. The development of language, the nuclear family, agriculture, and technology have given humankind an unmatched biological advantage over other animals. Even in those cases where the advantage is not immediately obvious, we can guess that we receive some advantage—especially if the institution appears in all human cultures and all periods. What remains is a systematic effort to determine what advantages our species might receive from the institutionalized form of play called *theatre*.

Such an enquiry could begin in many ways: one approach would be to examine all the stated claims for the function of theatre; another, to examine the early roots of the art in an effort to detect a fundamental pattern and the function of that pattern. We can begin with this last approach.

THE ROOTS OF THEATRE

When we see a performance at the Metropolitan Opera or at one of America's many fine regional theatres, we may be so impressed by the glamor and artistic effectiveness that we lose sight of the fundamental character of the experience. Beneath the layers of artistry, the beautiful costumes, the effective settings, the ornate playhouses, and the professional acting lies the irreducible core of the experience: the actor/audience interaction. By focusing our attention on this core we can trace the primary experience back to its much simpler roots.

Leaving behind the playhouse and the support of a production staff, we visit a ragtag company of touring actors. Discarding the important contribution made by a literary script and a supporting cast, we can further reduce the experience to a single street entertainer. Finally we find ourselves dealing with a very familiar human situation, but one which still displays basic theatrical elements: one person telling a story to another in such a way that he or she *enacts* certain parts. For example, two college students are talking between classes:

STUDENT ONE: Did you see the concert Saturday?
STUDENT TWO: At the Arena? Naw.
       ONE: You should have, man. It was great.
      TWO: Really great, huh?
      ONE: Fabulous!
      TWO: I had to study . . .
      ONE: Jackson Browne was unbelievable! Just . . .
      TWO: Good as his albums?

ONE: Better!
TWO: Better than his albums . . . ?
ONE: Fantastic! He really got into it.
TWO: Oh, yeah?
ONE: Really. They had this spotlight—kind of blue.
TWO: On him?
ONE: On him. All alone. (Student One steps back and pantomimes holding a guitar.) And he just closed his eyes, you know. (He does so.) And he just waited for a long time . . . (does so) . . . and, then . . .

"Fountain of sorrow, fountain of life,
you hear the hollow sound of your own steps in time . . . ' "

(Here Student One repeats the familiar lyric in character, but without really singing it.)

TWO: Far out!

ONE: (Pulling himself out of this portrayal.) I couldn't *believe* it. More than ten thousand people and you could hear a pin drop.

TWO: Far . . .

ONE: I was just watching—and listening—I wasn't even breathing! (Demonstrates with open mouth and wide open eyes the depth of his interest. Pause.)

TWO: Then what happened?

ONE: (Pulling out of his demonstration.) The place just went crazy. Just crazy!

TWO: Fabulous!

ONE: It really was!

TWO: I wish I'd gone . . .

ONE: Fountain of sorrow . . . (Moves away, singing to himself.)

TWO: . . . but I had to work.

This little exchange is not notable for its literary value. But it illustrates how, needing to communicate something important, a college-age person has resorted to enactment. Perhaps his vocabulary failed him; perhaps he knew that his friend would respond more strongly to something other than a literary critique of a rock concert. Whatever the reason, he found a way, within a matter of seconds, to adopt two characters: the singer in question and himself responding to the singer. The portrayal of Jackson Browne need not be world-class mimicry; his description of himself as a listener is probably not a great artistic achievement. Yet both served to kindle excitement in Student Two and achieve what Student One apparently wanted: the respect and envy of his friend.

Certainly Student Two readily adopted the role of audience. He was attentive, enthusiastic, supportive; for his effort he got a pretty good performance. In fact, between them, the two students wrote a rudimentary performance contract.

At this level, then, the mode of enactment and a detectable actor/audience interaction resulted in clear, effective communication. Student Two did not attend the concert, but, to some degree, he benefited from the experience. His eyes and ears and brain were, somehow, extended to participate in an event which was previously closed off to him. Indeed, if all his friends had attended the concert, and all had shared the experience as fully as Student One did, old Student Two might someday come to believe that he *had* attended—in just the same way that thousands of Americans now believe that they *saw* John Kennedy assassinated on television. The fact that this is impossible is ultimately of less importance than the simple truth that people can have their lives significantly enriched by these vicarious experiences. Indeed, the capacity of humans to live several lives for the price of one may lie at the heart of the function of theatre—or, indeed, of any art. Society's collective experience is extended through the contribution of the artist. When we participate in arts experiences, the rest of us are are allowed to experience much more during the span of a single life than would otherwise have been the case. Accordingly, we cannot overlook the contribution of the arts when we recognize humankind's ability to substitute very rapid cultural evolution for the much slower biological variety.

The implications for theatre are profound. Among other things this would mean that theatre as an art form is the institutional elaboration of impulses and practices which are employed every day in informal settings. From this idea, it follows that there is an unbroken spectrum of enactment beginning with two persons in conversation and ending with a Broadway production. It also suggests that the special power of theatre is its capacity to allow a person to vicariously experience the lives of other people. The psychological mechanisms which allow this are not always clear; however, this special power is what society employs when the institution of theatre is put to work for the common good.

THE FUNCTIONS OF THEATRE

Many claims have been made for theatre as a social force. Some are openly stated and believed. Others must be inferred from a number of factors: the conventions of the theatre traditions, the expectations of the audiences, the analyses of theatre historians and anthropologists. Unfortunately, the tradition is usually one of competition between competing single theories; theorists champion a single function and support it against all alternatives. Common sense suggests, however, that several functions can be served at the same time. Consequently, what we may have is a collection of possible functions, each one achieved by somewhat different theatrical means. The theatre artist then makes artistic decisions on the basis of which function he or she seeks to maximize.

In 1976, a group of theatre artists and educators met to reflect on the implications of theatre as a source of social change through education. One outcome of that meeting was an annotated list of the possible functions of theatre.* The list has been expanded and amended somewhat, but it remains the basis of the following:

1. *To provide a public event.* Humankind has an intensely gregarious nature; so much so that to study only a single human in isolation would yield a totally inadequate view of our species. Not only do we usually live in small collectives called families, but we constantly seek out opportunities to gather together into larger groups to see, to share, to communicate, to work or simply to be together. Fairs, quilting bees, service clubs, coffee klatches, scout meetings, and cocktail parties all have, as part of their value, the function of pulling us together into satisfying aggregations. Although it may not be the primary function of any one theatre, public performances can serve the important function of providing the opportunity for social contact.

2. *To demonstrate artistic achievement.* Those who are training in the performing arts must have an opportunity to do so in public. Their growth as artists is dependent upon the experience of working with live audiences. These artists, then, need the opportunity to practice and perfect their skills; it is this opportunity which a live production can provide.

3. *To attract attention to people or issues.* The simple act of performing a play about a subject serves to focus attention on that subject. Sometimes the attention is hardly needed; but a surprising twist can catch the public's attention. The dangers and attractions of adultery is a familiar human concern.

*Report of the Wingspread Conference, American Theatre Association, 1976.

However, in 1881, when Henrik Ibsen wrote *Ghosts*, a play dealing in part
with venereal disease, many of the leading critics in Europe responded with
scathing attacks upon the play and its author. The very act of writing this
play had focused attention on a serious medical problem—and shattered part
of the complacent hypocrisy of the age. Countless other plays have done the
same for other topics: Rolf Hochhuth's *The Deputy* focused attention on the
quality of leadership shown by Pope Pius XII during the Second World War;
The Miracle Worker by William Gibson reminds us of the achievements of

Mrs. Alving (Margaret Tyzack) and Osvald (Nicholas Pennell) in a modern production of Henrik Ibsen's *Ghosts*. A century ago, the subject of the play was taboo in
polite society and Ibsen was viciously attacked for drawing attention to it.

Helen Keller and her teacher, Annie Sullivan; *Fiddler on the Roof* makes us aware of the enduring spirit of the Jewish victims of oppression in the 19th century.

4. *To provide an emotional catharsis.* The Greek word *catharsis* signals the antiquity of this goal. It was the Greek philosopher Aristotle who first suggested that the goal of tragedy was to cleanse or purge an audience of pity and terror by arousing those feelings during a play. The concept has been surrounded by both civilized discussion and violent controversy since at least the Renaissance. A fair interpretation of what Aristotle meant might be this: the Greeks believed that anything in excess was dangerous. The related but reciprocal emotions of pity and terror are especially dangerous to society when they are present in excess; they paralyze an individual, preventing clear thought and blocking effective action. However, when those emotions are aroused in the controlled environment of a play, the audience learns to experience and deal with both. Presumably, during the course of a tragedy, the audience experiences pity at the fate of a tragic hero and terror that the same thing may happen to them. But as a result of catharsis, they leave the theatre strengthened, wiser, and refreshed.

5. *To validate a sense of personal identity and worth.* There is something very reassuring about seeing an enacted representation of one's own history on the stage. The history of theatre is repeatedly marked by plays which serve to remind an audience of who they are and of the special worth they have. Origin myths become the subject of plays, telling again the history of people who relish an account of their special roots. Shakespeare felt the need of his audiences to hear and see the history of their own England played upon the stage. Today in America there are theatres playing expressly for audiences of special subpopulations: gays, Hispanics, children, Viet Nam veterans, etc.

6. *To worship one's gods.* Before dismissing this goal as out of date, one should remember that theatrical performances are part of contemporary religious rites the world over. Native American tribes incorporate theatrical, or para-theatrical, presentations into their ceremonials. And the passion play, or life of Christ, has been performed regularly in Oberammergau, West Germany, since 1643 as an expression of gratitude to God for saving the village from the plague.

7. *To stimulate and shape creative imagination.* The special power of theatre to invigorate the imagination is obvious. In fact, one of the most convincing arguments for including creative drama and children's theatre in the schools has been the positive effect on the imagination of the young.

8. *To Teach.* Informal learning is, of course, a part of nearly every human activity; the theatrical experience undoubtedly shares this capacity for informal—perhaps even unintended—learning. But theatre can also work as an instrument of formal education. Examples abound. In totalitarian countries,

A 1896 photograph of the Zuni Shalako. Even today, in preindustrial societies around the world, theatre activities form a significant part of religious observances.

theatre is regularly used to convey information to the public. Critics of the system might call much of this information "propaganda," but the intention is clearly and officially "to teach." In the United States and Great Britain creative drama is often included in the public school curriculum because of its ability to help teach other subjects. Finally, preindustrial societies frequently depend upon theatre to convey information to the young. They teach about their gods, their origin myths, their taboos, and numberless other bits of information which they consider the very heart of education.

9. *To change or reinforce attitudes.* An attitude is a predisposition toward action: for example, a person who has a positive attitude toward his or her government is more likely to pay taxes than one who does not. That theatre has the ability to influence attitudes has been noted since the earliest times. Plato was unwilling to allow theatre into his perfect republic because of its generally corrupting influence. Totalitarian states have taken a different approach; they allow theatre—but only under close government control. Theatre then becomes a tool aimed at supporting attitudes favorable to the government. In pluralistic societies, groups wishing to change the attitude of the public toward some topic will often arrange for a play to be presented with that as its goal. No better example can be found in American history than *Uncle Tom's Cabin* by Harriet Beecher Stowe. That play was very widely performed in the 1850s and is thought to have served to galvanize American public opinion in the North against the institution of slavery. Whether *Uncle*

The heroine of *Uncle Tom's Cabin* crosses the Ohio River to freedom in the extremely popular dramatization of Harriet Beecher Stowe's famous novel. Scenes of this kind are typical of 19th Century melodrama.

Tom's Cabin actually changed attitudes or simply reinforced existing ones is a question we must leave to the social historians.

10. *To reflect and interpret contemporary life.* Ironically, people often have a clearer sense of the meaning of life in historical periods than in their own. Society must constantly work to clarify and understand the meaning of what is going on around them. Theatre can serve as a very useful tool in this endeavor. Examples abound: the function of much of comedy has always been to establish societal norms by clearly identifying what behaviors are worthy of ridicule. Thus, the very name of Archie Bunker, the leading figure in the television series *All in the Family*, has become synonymous with unacceptably bigoted thinking—an important step forward in an America dealing with major changes in race relations. Such plays as *Sticks and Bones* and *Viet Rock* helped to reflect and interpret American thinking about the Viet Nam War; absurdist plays of the 1950s and 1960s captured an existentialist point of view concerning the very structure of the cosmos; and at a more mundane level, the actions of romantic characters in plays have always served as models —for good or ill—for young people with romance on their minds.

11. *To express social concern and celebrate social achievements.* In recent years, theatre—like journalism—has appeared to many to be interested only in expos-

ing the unpleasant, seamy parts of life. To some degree this is true; in periods in which complacency is a danger, the arts, especially theatre, tend to direct society's attention to what many would prefer to ignore. On the other hand, even in the most critical periods most theatre has celebrated far more than it has criticized. For example, any play in which the good characters prosper is a celebration—albeit unspoken—of the human belief that there is justice in the world and that virtue will be rewarded. Consider the endless succession of dramas about the American West in which we celebrate the triumph of pioneer virtues. Only fairly recently have we been able to deal with portrayals of the bleaker side of life on the frontier. So it has been in all ages. Indeed, the origins of Western drama are deeply rooted in the story of the folk hero, who standing as a surrogate for his or her whole tribe, demonstrates the triumph of the spirit—even when the price paid is life itself.

In the 1960s and 70s many young playwrights took every opportunity to attack America's involvement in Viet Nam. Megan Terry's *Viet Rock* (1966) used elements of rock culture to create a kaleidoscopic—and very negative—picture of the effects of the war.

In the New York Shakespeare Festival's production of *Candide*, Voltaire's 18th Century novel received a very modern treatment. Here Dr. Pangloss explains to his innocent students that everything is for the best in this "best of all possible worlds."

12. *To perpetuate and enrich theatre.* One must never forget that theatre is an art discipline to which many people have made a major personal commitment. In much of the world, it is a profession from which people make a livelihood. It is very important to these people that theatre be continued for its own sake. Thus we sometimes face the contradiction of those who practice an art form with the highest artistic goals giving the crassest reasons for their involvement. It should be borne in mind that a professional actor must be acting in *something* in order to live. If he is not given the chance to attain the loftiest goals in the world, he still tries to keep body and soul together.

These twelve functions of theatre do not capture all the aims which have been advanced. One writer, for example, has recently suggested that the sole aim of theatre is to reduce separation anxiety, a therapeutic function which may work with some individuals in isolated cases but which hardly seems sufficient to maintain an art form which has existed for eons. In addition, some of these dozen functions could be served by another art—or even nonart—activity. Nonetheless, they capture most of the functions claimed for theatre and provide a collection of goals which are consciously or unconsciously adopted by theatre artists worldwide.

THEATRE FORM AND FUNCTION

Think back to the performance contract. Remember the final item, the "mutual advantage" clause? The conventions of a particular theatre are strongly determined by what it is that the parties to the performance contract are trying to achieve. Thus, the form of theatre is the result of its goals or function. It is worth taking the time to consider how the form of a theatrical tradition is influenced by how people want it to function; and how the function can be changed as the form changes. In Chapter 3 we shall examine the theatre of four different social contexts for clues as to what role the art of theatre played in the social fabric of that age.

CONCLUSION

Theatre is a human institution of significant value to the society which employs it. Some societies have elaborate, fine-art theatrical traditions; others have primitive ones. But *all* societies have some tradition because the impulse is universally present in our species.

The irreducible core of theatre is the actor/audience, or context, interaction. We find this interaction present in some of the simplest human communications: when one person decides to enact an experience in order to communicate, and another person assumes the role of audience, the performance contract is in force and a context interaction is present. The unspoken rules for maintaining a performance contract we call *conventions*. These conventions vary from culture to culture, period to period. Individual productions may even create unique conventions which apply to that play only.

The special power of theatre is its ability to allow humans to live other lives vicariously. As a result, individually and collectively, we are able to benefit from experiences which we might never encounter first-hand. Society uses this special power to achieve a number of goals.

These goals—or functions—can vary from culture to culture, period to period, production to production. Also, more than one function can be served simultaneously. The most important point to be borne in mind is that, far from being an aimless diversion, theatre can be an important part of human culture. And, like other aspects of human culture, its overriding goal is to make our species "successful."

Discussion Questions

1. How is the performance contract different from conventions?
2. Detect some conventions of Western theatre which the author did not mention. If you can have conventions which are specific to a certain play, could you have conventions specific to a particular theatre company—or even a particular performance?
3. The question of enactment and performance contract can get complicated. Let's change the circumstances a little in the playlet in this chapter: let's say that the concert has not yet taken place and that Student One has bought a ticket to the concert, but now thinks he has made a mistake. He believes the concert will be a poor one—but is trying to sell his ticket to Student Two by *pretending* that he thinks it will be wonderful. One may be "acting," but do we have a performance contract?
4. Review the twelve functions of theatre again. Try to imagine a theatre experience which would achieve each—making up plays if necessary. Now, repeat the exercise with *non*theatre events. Discuss the advantages of achieving these functions by different means.
5. The concept of evolution, both biological and cultural, is central to this chapter. But such a parallel raises the possibility that theatre will become an "extinct species." What do you think?

3

The Range of Social Contexts

INTRODUCTION

There are many reasons to study the history of theatre; one of the best is to explore the wide range of theatrical possibilities open to human-kind. Even if we cannot fully understand the social environment which evoked those varied theatre traditions, the exercise serves to remind us that the theatre tradition we know best is not the only possible one. We can examine many historical examples, searching for the elements of theatre which seem universal. Then, if we choose, we may select the theatrical conventions which best suit both our needs and those of our culture.

Western theatre had done this with some regularity in the last century. In the first decades of the 20th century there was considerable interest in the oriental theatre, especially the theatre of Japan. During the teens and 20s serious attempts were first made to reconstruct the Elizabethan public playhouse and stage the works of Shakespeare as they might have been in the late 16th century. Finally, since the Second World War there has been significant research into the place of theatre in primitive societies. Indeed, it was this same interest in the primitive roots of theatre which led to much of the highly ritualized experimental theatre of the 60s and 70s.

Since we have already seen that the interaction between the art of theatre and the society which supports it is a reciprocal and changing relationship, we should not be surprised to find that very different periods and cultures have very different theatre traditions. The examples which follow were chosen to illustrate that range. Two, the *Elizabethan age* and *Classical Athens* are periods of amazing achievement, two of the golden ages in Western civilization; another, the theatre of the *Tokugawa Shogunate*, is roughly the same for Japanese culture. *Modern America*, for all its diversity, is a good example of a vigorous period whose long-term importance has yet to be judged. The contemporary *Gimi* culture from the highlands of Papua, New Guinea, probably represents theatre as it existed through the overwhelming majority of our species' time on earth.

THEATRE AMONG THE GIMI*

The Gimi people number no more than 10,000 and live in isolated settlements in the eastern highlands of Papua, New Guinea. Their homeland is quite different from that of the better known tribes of the Sepik River Valley and the islands of the New Guinea archipelago. The rugged mountains are cooler than the lowlands and quite moist. The Gimi economy is based on small gardens of sweet potatoes and other vegetables, and their diet is augmented by birds and small mammals hunted in the forests that cover the beautiful, misty mountains.

As varied and interesting as the scenery surrounding a Gimi settlement may be, it cannot compare with the environment each villager carries in his or her head. Each Gimi tribe member believes that the world is filled with invisible spirits of ancestors, enemies, forest demons, plants, mammals, and birds. Moreover, to keep this invisible world in balance, humans are expected to follow elaborate rules of behavior, rules that dominate every aspect of personal and social life. Most striking among these is the ritualized antagonism between men and women. At puberty, boys are removed from their mothers' houses and expected to live in dormitory-like men's houses. Even after they marry men

*Based upon "Living Theatre in New Guinea's Highlands" by Gillian Gillison, *National Geographic* (August 1983): 147–169.

maintain two residences: the men's house and a home in the circle of women's houses which surround the men's houses. Relations between the sexes is filled with distrust and elaborate taboos.

One of the occasions during which the sexes may mix relatively freely is the festival held every five years or so at which the boys are initiated into manhood and the eligible girls are married. The festival itself includes the preparations, marriages, initiation rites, and extended feasting. It also includes nightlong presentations of short plays.

Dr. Gillian Gillison, who has studied the Gimi for ten years, makes the point that these plays display an artistic achievement as rich and varied as the beautiful wooden carvings which represent the lowland tribes in museums around the world. Unfortunately for art collectors— and the reputation of the Gimis—theatrical performances leave no artifacts behind. There are no theatre buildings, no scripts, no costume collections, nothing except the memory of the participants to keep the theatrical tradition alive. Still, the theatrical productions remain an important part of the cultural heritage of the tribe by transmitting the special traditions of Gimi life.

The preparation for the plays is anything but formal. Members of the tribe organize a play by persuading a few neighbors to join them; they slip away into the forest during the afternoon to rehearse and to improvise effective costumes using leaves, flowers, feathers, berries, moss, bark, and colored clays. That evening they join the crowds gathering in houses around the village, waiting for the most auspicious moment to present their play. Since the plays themselves seldom last more than about ten minutes, the players repeat it at several different houses. In total, a single house may witness ten or more productions during the night, with singing and chanting between each play. Most of the performers participate for the sheer love of it—but some have an ulterior motive. If a young man performs especially well, he may get a woman of marriageable age to fall in love and run away with him. While this would be something of a scandal, it would allow him to avoid paying an expensive bride's price for her.

The content of the plays varies. Sometimes the plots are strictly accurate accounts of well-known myths; at other times the performers take liberties with familiar stories; or they may create original scenes around recent tribal history, including juicy scandals.

Dr. Gillison recounts one playlet in which the women enact the river, accompanying themselves with water-filled sections of bamboo as they dance. They sing:

Shush, shush, shush . . .
Look at me . . .
I am the swollen torrent,
hitting you as I run
down, down, down . . .

They then adopt the role of taro plants, bandicoots, and other denizens of the forest in the time before men and women were separate. Their song and play recall a time of equality between the sexes. Now, however, men are totally dominant, even going so far as to claim to own the game in the forest.

Later, two men with flat masks and vine-wound bodies smeared with clay enter and stagger about the fire circle frightening young and old alike as they enact the roles of two brothers, eternally contending earth spirits, whose uncontrolled savagery demonstrates the need for the rules of behavior which the initiates and the brides are constantly exhorted to follow.

The rite of passage of the initiates is a difficult time for both the boys and their mothers. This pain is expressed in a play about a group of children, orphaned and lost in the forest, who wander helplessly, trying vainly to shoot small game and crying for their parents. Finally, they die and are transformed into pheasant pigeons, a bird well-known for its plaintive, human-like call.

A circle of fate is recounted in another piece: a fierce hunter lies in wait for a flock of cockatoos, but when he shoots at them, they are neither alarmed or harmed. "I shoot at these birds but they do not fear me," he shouts to the audience. "What is this?"

An audience member answers back: "You are shooting at your brothers, don't you know?"

The hunter is trying to kill birds who embody the spirits of his dead ancestors, and therefore they are invulnerable. The audience nods in agreement with the moral: a man and his ancestors are fated to meet.

Sometimes a farcical situation disguises a very serious concern. Gillison describes a scene in which a warrior, a man who must always be on the alert, arrives home to find his wife cooking dinner. At first he does not want to eat, but gradually his wife (played by a young boy) convinces him to consume what she has prepared.

But suddenly his strength fails him and, in a comic interlude, he cannot bend his palm bow far enough to string it. Again and again he tries as the audience howls with laughter. They know that he has been poisoned. They have seen the symbolic poinsettia petals strewn near the fire and realize that the man has violated the serious taboo against eating food prepared by a woman during menstruation. The laughter in no way means that the audience takes the taboo lightly: but it does provide a means of releasing the tension which the delicate topic produces.

The many functions of theatre among the Gimi are clear. At one level, they provide an opportunity for dispersed settlements to come together for serious tribal business. The simple act of gathering together has the effect of giving power and longevity to the tribe; they believe that the life force is released in singing and laughter and that it flies upward into the rafters of the house where it collects to be released later to give vitality to the village.

Beyond this, the plays transmit the history of the tribe to the younger generations. Finally, they enforce the strict rules of behavior; the plays furnish unforgettable illustrations of the price to be paid if the taboos are violated. The power and success of the tribe are celebrated; but tribal failures—including behavioral lapses of its members—are attacked through the corrective power of laughter and ridicule.

The Gimi have no theatres, no scripts, no special costume wardrobes, no directors or playwrights; there is nothing but the magic the Gimi need to pass on their rich culture.

THEATRE IN CLASSICAL ATHENS

Historians may disagree as to the roots of what we now call Western civilization, but few would deny that the first flower of that tradition—the first Golden Age—took place in fifth century B.C. (499–400 B.C.) Athens. It was this single city in this single century that produced the first four great playwrights (Aeschylus, Sophocles, Euripides, and Aristophanes), the first great historian (Herodotus), two of the first three great philosophers (Socrates, Plato, and Aristotle), and a panoply of statesmen, soldiers, poets, artists, and merchants whose contributions leave the mind reeling. It was a century that began in a glorious conflict of national identity and ended in a grinding civil war which left all the belligerents easy prey for outside conquest. Greece was hardly what we today would call a nation; instead, it was a loose confederation of city-states, each one bristling with so much local pride and tribal animosity that true national solidarity was achieved only rarely. The most outstanding occasion of national unity came in response to the series

No actual masks remain from the Greek classical period, but the Greeks themselves were fond of ceramic or stone copies. This replica was discovered in Piraeus in 1959.

of invasions by the Persian Empire, an external threat finally put to rest by the victory of the Greek forces at the battles of Salamis (480 B.C.) and Marathon (490 B.C.). In both of these battles, the city-state of Athens provided the major leadership; and it was Athens that assumed the role of political and cultural leader in the period of greatness afterward, a period that has been given the name of the inspired Athenian leader, Pericles. Periclean Athens was a city supremely confident of its excellence and ready to celebrate every aspect of its cultural life to the fullest.

Religion had always played a powerful role in the private and public life of Athens. Like its commercial life which had always benefitted from its position as a crossroads between the cultures of Egypt, the eastern Mediterranean, and Western Europe, the religion of Greece had grown vital from crossfertilization. The older gods, the pantheon that included Zeus, Hera, and Athena (the city god of Athens itself)—the gods so familiar to the Greeks who had fought at Troy several centuries before—were now joined by a relatively new god, Dionysus. The worship of Dionysus, the god of rebirth, fertility, and wine, was only about a century old in the fifth century B.C., and there remained many relatively new and vital aspects to his worship. One of these was the idea of festivals of original song, dance, and plays presented in his honor.

The most important of these festivals was the Great or City Dionysia celebrated in Athens in the early spring of each year. The striking thing about the City Dionysia was the presentation of plays which occupied several days, sandwiched among the feasting, processions, and other religious observances. The format of the festival changed repeatedly during the fifth century B.C., but at the height of Athens' prosperity and influence, four days of the festival were devoted to theatrical events: three days given over to the presentation of tragedies and one dedicated to comedies.

Theatre historians know surprisingly little about the details of theatrical production in fifth century B.C. Athens, and even less about what preceded it. We do know, however, that the Athenians themselves credited a man named Thespis as the inventor of acting, and gave the date of this innovation as less than 100 years earlier. Historians now believe that Thespis became the "first actor" by adding an element of enactment to a form of choral singing and chanting conducted at places sacred to local culture heroes. The practice must have already been old when Thespis first stepped out of the chorus to portray the heroic figure in question. One thing for certain, these early performances were already a competition; the basis for the word "tragedy" in Greek is "goat song," and seems to refer to the goat which was presented as a prize to

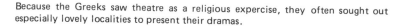

Because the Greeks saw theatre as a religious expercise, they often sought out especially lovely localities to present their dramas.

the winning chorus. This element of competition lasted throughout the fifth century B.C.

To be chosen to compete in the drama competition was itself a great honor, and the cream of the nation's leadership vied for the right. For example, Aeschylus, one of the most revered and successful play-wrights, was also one of Athen's most honored generals; for Aeschylus to win the first prize for tragedy, a feat he accomplished repeatedly, was roughly comparable to having General Dwight Eisenhower win the Pulitzer Price for drama.

Each writer was expected to submit a tetralogy; three tragedies and a satyr play. The tragedies were supposed to relate in some way, because they dealt either with the same heroes or the same themes; the satyr play was a very broad burlesque—usually of the topic that was treated reverently in the trilogy of tragedies. Three of the tetralogies were selected for production and each was assigned to a wealthy citizen who was then expected to pay the cost of the production, excepting the hire of actors and chorus, which was paid for by state funds.

Again, it was considered a great honor to be chosen as the producer of a play in the competition, and no public-spirited citizen would dream of cutting corners when financing the often lavish productions. Four comedies were also selected for presentation, the costs of production also assigned to wealthy patrons. In all, some sixteen plays would be presented during the festival: a trilogy of tragedies and the accompanying satyr play on each of the first three days, and four comedies on the final day.

On the day of production, the Theatre of Dionysus would be filled. Although the population of Athens was much larger than the estimated 16,000 people the theatre could hold, it was expected that all the leading citizens would be in attendance. A small admission fee was charged; if a citizen wished to attend but could not afford the admission fee, public funds were provided. It is also said that prisoners were released for the day in order to attend.

The performances began at dawn and at least one play, *The Agamemnon* by Aeschylus, builds the sunrise into the opening scene, thus taking advantage of a special effect provided gratis by nature. It seems that the plays were presented without serious interruption until early afternoon. This suggests that there must have been a steady coming and going in the audience with picnicking and socializing between the plays—or during slow passages.

There is considerable controversy about how the plays themselves

A modern production of *The Oresteia* of Aeschylus. A chorus, made up of elders
of the city, recoil in horror as Queen Jocasta tells them that she has just arranged
the death of King Agamemnon.

were produced. The consensus supports the idea that the actors—if not
the choruses—were heavily masked and costumed. The traditional argument is that the exaggerated masks and costumes allowed the audience
to see the characters better in the very large theatre; also, megaphone-
like structures built into the masks may have made the actors' voices
more audible. There is even uncertainty as to the number of actors and
chorus members; however, by the end of the century, it is thought that
there were only three actors available. It was up to the playwright to
write works in which the number of speaking characters on stage never
exceeded three and in which an exiting actor would have time to change
mask and costume before re-entering as someone else. Chorus members
numbered twelve or fifteen and were required to sing and chant as well
as dance and perhaps play instruments. All performers were male.

Classic Greek tragedy turned for its thematic material to the
history of the Greek people themselves, including the many unsubstan-
tiated stories we call myths. The major figures are almost always their
great culture heroes, the monumental figures who had consorted with

gods, who had fought in the Trojan War, and who had founded their cities and major dynasties. As we read those plays today, we must remind ourselves that the characters are not empty names from a history book, but the godlike ancestors of the people who were watching the plays.

The plots of the plays are usually quite simple; a major crisis in the life of the hero is recounted; the protagonist faces a dilemma, and we are witness to the manner in which he or she deals with the problem and—usually—their reaction to the resulting disaster. The scenes of dramatic action are alternated with choral odes in which the chorus takes center stage to raise timely questions, to lament the state of the hero or his community, or to praise the appropriate god or goddess— even while beseeching his or her intervention. The chorus usually represents the citizens of the community in which the action takes place, and its presence serves to underline the degree to which the tragic hero's fate is intertwined with that of the common people. Indeed, the outcome of the hero's personal problem is frequently the establishment of some tradition or practice which was familiar to the audience members. As an example, Aeschylus' trilogy *The Oresteia* (the only complete trilogy we have today) deals with the period in Greek history when the rule of law replaced the older idea of revenge. In the first play *Agamemnon*, we see the triumphant return to Greece of Agamemnon, leading general of the combined Greek armies at Troy. He does not know that during his absence his wife, Clytemnestra, has taken a young lover and has spent the years brooding over a number of wrongs her husband has done her. Surprising him in his bath, she and her lover kill Agamemnon and take the throne for themselves. In the second play, *The Libation Bearers*, Agamemnon's son Orestes returns home to find himself facing a cruel dilemma: he is dutybound to revenge his father's death—but to do so, he must kill his mother. Orestes conspires with his sister, Electra, to kill both his mother and her lover. But before he can savor his revenge, he is tortured by the Furies, the horrible monsters who represent guilt in the rich inventory of Greek mythology.

The Furies, the final play in the trilogy, finds Orestes, nearly driven mad by the title characters, seeking sanctuary in the temples of Athena in Athens. There he argues his case first to Athena and then to Apollo himself. Apollo resolves the dilemma by calling off the Furies, and then— to mollify their anger at his interference—assigns them as wards of a new court, one especially designed to deal with blood feuds of this kind in the future. Thus we see a rattling good story leading up to a clear explanation of why civilized nations cannot allow an endless chain of revenge and retribution to undercut the judicial system. Personal tragedy is elevated to civilizing doctrine.

Modern readers of Greek tragedy find it difficult to reconcile their serious and usually reverent tone to the satyr play which ended the day. The satyr play, of which we have only one complete example, was a totally irreverent treatment of the theme of the tragedies. The characters were parodied, the situation was burlesqued, and the language throughout became a bawdy and outrageous reminder of what had preceded it. The name "satyr play" does not have the same Greek meaning as our modern *satire*; instead, it refers to the chorus who were usually dressed as real or mythical animals such as the half-man, half-goat satyr. The modern student may wonder how the Greeks could include such plays in a religious celebration. The answer may be that the ratio between

A satyr attacks a maiden in this vase painting. The action is probably from a play since the satyr is wearing the traditional animal skin, horse tail, and phallus.

tragedy and burlesque tells us something important about Greek thinking; they may have seen the problems of humankind as worthy of three
parts serious concern and one part Bronx cheer.

The final day of the competition, the day devoted to comedy,
shifted the area of focus. Whereas the tetralogies had directed their
attention to the largest problems encountering humankind, problems
related to the ultimate purpose of both the individual and society, the
comedies cheerfully turned to the state of affairs in contemporary
Athens. The only examples we have of comedies of this period all come
from the pen of Aristophanes, but we can infer that his general approach must have been like that adopted by other writers. A typical
comedy by Aristophanes sets up a highly fantastic premise which
satirizes some hot issue in Athens; within that framework, he sets out
to mercilessly mock what he sees as folly among his fellow citizens. For
example, as a true conservative, Aristophanes was deeply distressed by
what he saw as dangerous tendencies in Athenian education. He wanted
to warn his city against the loss of traditional values and deplore the
tendency of the "sophists" to open private schools of philosophy. Since
perhaps the leading sophist was the well-known philosopher Socrates,
Aristophanes chose Socrates as a primary target for brilliant satire in his
play *The Clouds* (423 B.C.). *The Clouds* introduces an old Athenian
father who is being driven to distraction and the poorhouse by the
extravagance of his son. The young man, it turns out, has fallen under
the influence of teachers who have convinced him that it is not necessary
to pay one's debts. As a result, the father is being hounded by creditors.
At this point, the old father has one of those bright ideas which create
great comedy: If the sophists have taught his son that it is not necessary
to pay debts, the father will find a school to learn to escape his debts
too! So he sets off for a school to learn "wrong reasoning." The school
he chooses to attend is run by a fuzzy-headed old philosopher who so
closely resembled Socrates that when the character first entered, according to tradition, the real Socrates stood up so that the audience could
fully appreciate the similarities between the actor's mask and his own
appearance. That first entrance is memorable in another way as well:
the old philosopher is discovered suspended in a basket; after he has
been lowered to the stage floor, he explains that he likes to be nearer
heaven and closer to his intellectual mentors, the clouds. These "clouds"
turn out to be the members of the chorus who then enter—costumed,
one can imagine, in wispy nothings—to sing the praises of "pure"
philosophy. The play continues in this vein until the old father has

learned what he needs to know; that is, he learns that he must not be bullied either by his wastrel son or the fashionable new ideas of the sophists. In the course of the play, there are several points at which the chorus or the major characters address the audience directly, in some cases pointing out individuals and dwelling at some length on their personal habits and social follies. In short, *The Clouds* could be considered a robust comedy demonstrating the essentially healthy state of the Athenian sense of humor, were it not for one fact. *The Clouds* was just one of the series of personal attacks that led up to Socrates' trial in the Athenian Senate, a trial in which he was sentenced to death by drinking hemlock.

Even though there are significant gaps in our knowledge of classical Greek theatre, we can be sure of many important facts: theatre was a highly respected art which combined civic responsibility and religious practice; it developed forms to deal with the wide variety of issues the community thought important; it attracted and held the best minds of the period, both as creative forces and as audiences; in doing so, it built a tradition that was recognized—in its own time as well as in subsequent cultures—as one of the glories of Western civilization.

THEATRE IN ELIZABETHAN ENGLAND

The 16th century was the era in which the English moved quite definitely from the medieval period into the Renaissance. The century began in the social and political chaos following the War of the Roses; it ended in one of the most glorious periods the world has ever seen. A measure of stability was provided by Henry VIII (who reigned from 1509 to 1547), setting the stage for a cultural flowering under his daughter, Elizabeth I (who reigned from 1558 to 1603), for whom the period was named. In theatre, the Elizabethan period is distinguished by such playwrights as William Shakespeare, Ben Jonson, and Christopher Marlowe, and the establishment of a vibrant theatre tradition.

The last third of the 16th century was marked by the centralization of much of English commerce and industry. Displaced peasants moved to the industrial center of the nation to provide a workforce for the first rumblings of the Industrial Revolution; voyages of commerce and exploration set out from a vital seaport which rivaled the foremost in Europe; doctors, attorneys, and would-be politicians flocked to the glittering court of their undisputed queen. The center for all these activities, and the unquestioned capital of an England grown proud and daring, was London. And it was in London, at the end of the 16th century that English theatre became a national industry—as well as an international treasure.

Some may wince to hear the theatre of William Shakespeare described as an industry. But Shakespeare and his associates in the handful of permanent legitimate theatre companies joined the bull- and bear-baiting pits, the cockfight organizers, and numberless other fly-by-night operations to entertain a bustling city. Together, they became what we would call today an *entertainment industry*. Theatre became a service provided, in fixed locations, by artists who made their entire livelihood from their creative work. As professionals, in short.

Before the establishment of full-time professional theatre in London, a development symbolized by the building of the first permanent, freestanding theatre building in 1576, the art of theatre in England had been something of a cottage industry, an art practiced by amateurs on special occasions or by bands of travelling players who moved about the country playing wherever the opportunity arose. These travelling players were, of course, professionals. They might be hired by a nobleman to provide entertainment during a wedding feast in his great hall; they could set up a booth theatre at fairs; they might even be hired by a guild or municipality to give an edge of professionalism to the cycles of religious plays which were given at certain church festivals in small towns. But they had no permanent home, their identity changed as troupes disbanded and reformed in response to changing economic conditions, and they had little prestige. Indeed, they escaped prosecution under the harsh vagabond laws only by the ruse of approaching a powerful nobleman and asking to become his "men." Only then, ostensibly, as his servants, were they allowed to travel about England.

Even then, the travelling players were not totally free to perform. Unless they were playing in the home of a powerful figure, troupes were forced to petition the council of each town for permission to perform there. And so opposed to theatre were many of the conservative municipal leaders that permission was often denied. To many of these respectable English burghers, theatre was a dangerous waste of time, a diversion which kept the godly from attending church, gave apprentices an excuse to avoid work, set poor examples for young people, and attracted crowds which could be fomented to riot. Some even went so far as to attack theatre as a toy of the devil, sent to tempt people to damnation. In the face of this kind of social pressure and financial insecurity, the prospect of settling down as part of an established company,

A company of traveling players, their goods packed in a cart, arrive at an inn. In the background we see how the same company would set up a booth stage in the square of some small town.

in a comfortable theatre in the enlightened capital, must have beckoned the travelling player like a vision of paradise.

Of course, even life in London was not without problems. For one thing, the members of the London City Council shared many of the same attitudes as their country brethren: they were not pleased at the prospect of live theatre corrupting London's citizens, either. As a result, the new theatres had to be built in areas beyond the reach of city ordinances. Generally, this meant just outside the city limits. A theatre district—along with the inevitable bull and bear pits, cockfight emporiums, and brothels—grew up on the south side of the River Thames. Would-be patrons were forced to travel across one of several bridges to reach the theatre, or to be rowed across by obliging watermen in small boats. To save their patrons inconvenience, the theatres would fly flags from staffs on their roofs on performance days when they were playing; a would-be audience member on the far shore could see whether his or her favorite theatre was playing that afternoon before making the trip.

Another problem, only dimly understood by the city officials, often kept theatres closed even outside of town: the plague. It was known that large collections of people helped spread the plague and, as a result, the city council and the queen's Privy Council collaborated to ban all public gatherings during time of plague. To escape financial ruin during these periods, the theatre companies returned to touring the provinces—some even touring Europe.

A key point to keep in mind is that by and large the Elizabethan theatres were supported by box office revenue, not by rich patrons or municipal subsidies. Shakespeare's audiences had to actively seek out his theatre—overcoming a series of obstacles placed in their way—or his company would fold and he would begin looking for another profession.

Tourists, longing for some souvenir of the big city would often buy an engraved panorama of London. This one, done by Visscher in 1616 is notable for the clear picture of the exterior of the Globe Theatre and the Bear Garden. We can see from the flags that both are playing on this day.

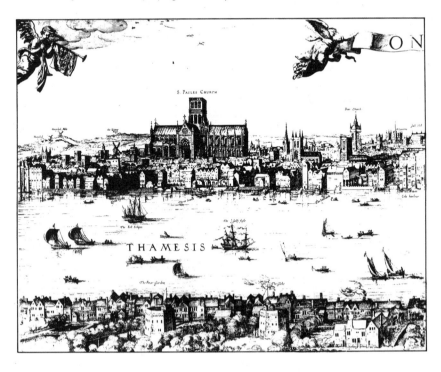

Other playwrights, and nearly all performers, shared this predicament: once they had made a decision to make their living as artists, their entire livelihood depended upon the number of people who were willing to seek out their work and "put their pennies in the box." Therefore, the high quality of the plays written and performed in the Elizabethan period is as much a testimony to the quality and loyalty of Elizabethan audiences as it is to the playwrights and performers.

Those audiences were a remarkable cross-section of the London populace of the time. Eyewitness accounts testify to the fact that, in the public theatres at least, audiences were made up of all classes: shopkeepers rubbed shoulders with gentlemen; laborers and apprentices crowded together with sailors, soldiers, and students; gentlewomen— masked and perfumed against intruding eyes and offending smells— shared the galleries with women of pleasure. These varied audiences crowded into those small theatres more tightly than anything allowed by modern fire laws. They were boisterously responsive, and frequently unruly. The actor who strode onto the stage of the Globe Theatre risked a great deal: his audience expected much and would be as quick to show its displeasure as its acclaim. And, as Shakespeare's plays demonstrate, there was something there for every taste: those who admired great verse would have plenty to jot down in their notebooks to study later—and perhaps to pass off as their own. The poorly educated groundlings could roar at the physical comedy or gape at the derring-do. Men who knew and appreciated good fencing would see blade work of a quality high enough to send them back to their own fencing masters for a refresher course. And the dancing! And the singing! In sum, no person of consequence could afford to miss the theatre—for it was in the theatre that the great issues of the time surfaced and blossomed.

What were those issues? A large percentage of the Elizabethan plays dealt either directly or peripherally with the "outside world." England, an island nation, was becoming a powerful force in the larger world. Plays set in exotic lands had an inherent fascination for London audiences. They flocked to see plays set in Malta, Illyria, Denmark, Italy, and of course the New World. Explorers returning from "the Indies" brought stories of people, animals, plants, whole civilizations which seemed wondrous to the Elizabethans and fueled their curiosity to know more. Playwrights fed that curiosity with an endless list of productions which made up in imagination for what they lacked in scientific accuracy.

Another topic which could be counted upon to hold the attention of Elizabethan audiences was history—preferably their own. Besides extending in space, the curiosity of Elizabethan audiences ranged backward in time to the earliest history, from the times of the legendary kings Gorbuduc and Lear to the more recent British monarchs, through the Greeks and Romans, through the horrifying excesses of the conquering Tamerlane, to the contemporary chronicles of the Italians and Spanish—almost current events to a nation who had only recently warded off an invasion attempt by defeating the Spanish Armada in 1588.

Recent history was the most daring subject. True, a company always ran the risk of offending one of the many powerful circles at court, the city council, or even the strong-minded queen herself. The Lord Chamberlain's office read every play in advance and decided whether public order and decency would be endangered by anything in it. The Lord Chamberlain was quick to censor anything which looked as if it were an unacceptable comment on contemporary politics or the ruling circle. So recent or contemporary history was dangerous ground, indeed. But little else could match the audience-drawing power of a patriotic piece in which the Spanish were described as deceitful curs and the English as virtuous yeomen. And perceptive audiences could be expected to detect a parallel between the events in a play set in distant times and contemporary politics.

But most of all, the Elizabethan audience was interested in people. Recognizable Elizabethans fill those plays—even though they masquerade as kings and queens, historical figures, and foreigners. Elizabethan audiences saw recognizable people pushed to the very edge of their humanity by ambition, or lust, or love, or jealousy, or pride, or any of an endless list of infirmities. They saw people who were larger than life and, as a result, threatened to burst the seams of their social garments. It is as if the Elizabethans, full of themselves and sensing their own potential, were seeking their own limits: trying to define the potential of a human being, to define the term *humanity*. One can only imagine the hush which must have fallen over the Globe Theatre when Richard Burbage, probably the first Hamlet, stepped downstage and speculated:

> What a piece of work is a man! how noble in reason! how infinite in faculty! in form and moving how express and admirable, in action how like an angel, in apprehension how like a god! The beauty of the world! the paragon of animals! (*Hamlet*, II, ii)

When Burbage first spoke these words in public, he was standing within one of the most extraordinary theatrical machines ever devised

—a physical theatre which complemented and inspired the best in the Elizabethan tradition. A professional theatre getting started in a city of 200–300,000 people needs to keep overhead down and variety up. New plays would have to be opened regularly to keep audiences returning, though old favorites could quickly be revived. All of this meant that elaborate productions were virtually out of the question. So were large casts; Elizabethan acting companies usually numbered between ten and fifteen. Each actor was expected to play several roles in each play and to be prepared to play many roles in a variety of others on very short notice. Flexibility became the byword.

The Elizabethan public theatre was surely one of the most flexible in all history. It was a formal theatre, that is, it did not need a totally new setting for each play. Like many traditional theatres throughout history, it had a number of playing areas which could be used without much modification to represent the areas demanded by the script. There is some disagreement among scholars as to the exact configuration of an Elizabethan public theatre, but the major areas seem clear.

The most certain is that there was a platform stage some four or five feet high which thrust into the open center court of a circular building. This platform was considered a neutral space; if a character announced or implied that it was a room in the palace or a field in France or the Roman Senate, it was accepted by the audience to be that place with no further ado. No fuss, and no change of scenery.

Access to the platform was generally by way of two doors, one on each side, which allowed entrances from and exits to the part of the building upstage of the platform, called a *tiring house* (attiring house, or changing room).* These doors stage left and right allowed an actor, or whole groups of actors, to enter on one side of the stage and, passing across it, exit on the other, thus giving a sense of a street, path, or battlefield through which people move. Another point of access to the platform was a curtained alcove, called the *inner below*, which was probably set directly upstage. Because of the curtains, the inner below could be decorated with set pieces designed to give it an identity, and actors could be "discovered" there when the curtain was pulled. A scene which began in the inner below and spilled out onto the platform automatically converted the latter into an extension of the scene in the inner below. By skillfully alternating scenes between the platform and the inner below, a play of considerable scenic diversity could be presented.

But the Elizabethan playwright had even more possibilities. As

*Readers may wish to consult the note on stage geography on page 123.

plays such as *Romeo and Juliet* amply demonstrate, the public theatre had balconies and windows at a second-story level. Most scholars place the working windows on either side of the stage, perhaps over the doors. Some also place a balcony with each window, but most place it in the center. The combining of the balcony and the inner below has suggested that the latter was actually a curtained pavilion jutting some distance onto the platform, the roof of which became a balcony or—in some versions—a second-story stage of considerable size. At the rear (or up-stage) of this balcony was as a second curtained booth called an *inner above* which was used much like its counterpart on the stage floor below it.

Above the inner above was a third-story gallery reserved for the inevitable musicians. Some commentators have suggested that even this was used for certain scenes, possibly including such diversions as displays of gods and goddesses and their subsequent descent to the stage floor (flying) by a winch system.

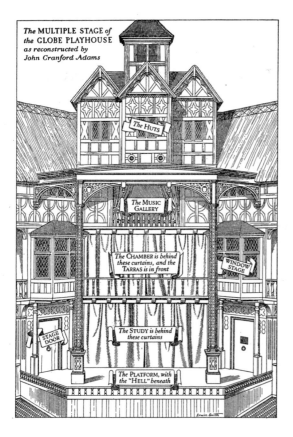

The MULTIPLE STAGE of the GLOBE PLAYHOUSE as reconstructed by John Cranford Adams

The HUTS

The MUSIC GALLERY

The CHAMBER is behind these curtains, and the TARRAS is in front

WINDOW STAGE

STAGE DOOR

The STUDY is behind these curtains

The PLATFORM, with the "HELL" beneath

The John Crawford Adams reconstruction of an Elizabethan public theatre has been questioned in many minor points, but it remains a clear description of the major areas. What he calls "The Study" and "The Chamber" are commonly referred to as the "inner below" and the "inner above."

With this many areas to work with, a playwright or director could create plenty of variety. In addition, the areas could be combined in imaginative ways: Romeo could climb up to the balcony to play a scene with Juliet; defenders could hurl abuse at the attackers of the city gates below; the jutting pavilion could become the prow of a seagoing vessel; ghosts could arrive and depart through *traps* (trapdoors) in the stage floor.

The result was smooth-flowing, dramatic action in which the audience's attention could be moved quickly and easily from character to character, scene to scene, even from plot to plot. This capacity to move the visual focus of an audience is especially valuable when, like the Elizabethans, you are performing outdoors by daylight.

A description of the power of an Elizabethan public theatre is incomplete unless we reflect upon the other half of the equation, the audience spaces. There have been modern attempts to recreate the stage of such a theatre in which scrupulous attention has been paid to the platform, the inner below, the inner above, and so on—but the whole reconstruction has been planted indoors in front of the flat expanse of well-spaced seats which make up the orchestra of a modern theatre. But the Elizabethans favored a projecting playing area in which the audience enveloped the stage. Moreover, they placed two or three galleries around the acting space, and packed people into them more tightly than we can imagine. But imagination will have to do because nowhere today can we visit anything but a close approximation.

So, imagine yourself as an Elizabethan actor—as Richard Burbage, perhaps—standing on the platform of the Globe Theatre before a full house. Almost encircling your feet is a solid sea of humanity. The groundlings standing in the pit watch expectantly, their faces uplifted. Behind them rise three levels of open galleries, the top two divided by partitions into separate rooms in which people both sit and stand. And not one of those people, over a thousand of them according to some estimates, is more than thirty or thirty-five feet away. It is like standing inside a cylinder of attentive humanity. Your every breath can be heard, the merest flick of an eyebrow is shared with all, you have the feeling that the audience can read your thoughts. Until the development of motion pictures and the wide screen closeup, this must have been the most intense scrutiny to which any actor has ever been subjected—and certainly one of the most demanding actor/audience interactions ever devised. The intensity of the interaction between the audience and performer in an Elizabethan public theatre both describes and symbolizes the powerful and valuable interaction between Elizabethan society and its theatre.

The Elizabethan theatre demonstrated many of the same qualities on land as its daring sailors did on the water. It operated at the very limits of everything: it explored new staging methods, new verse forms, new dramatic situations. It thumbed its nose daily at the respectable city council and even dared to cross its queen occasionally. It reveled in being at the center of things; it was not afraid to be a little in harm's way. And its audience loved the daring of this upstart theatre business, supporting it financially, even egging it on to greater aspirations and more forbidden limits. For only thirty years or so the love affair lasted; then it faded away. The Elizabethan outlook somehow hardened into the increasingly cynical worldview of the Jacobeans and in the end both the society and the theatres were pulled down by Cromwell and the Puritans. But while it lasted, what a love affair it was!

THEATRE IN TOKUGAWA JAPAN

The glory which was Elizabethan England flowered under a strong constitutional monarchy. In Japan at roughly the same time a different form of monarchy was developing a very different society and with it, very different forms of theatre.

Periods in Japanese history are frequently named after the surnames of the dynasties which ruled the nation during those times. The Tokugawa period began in 1600 when Tokugawa Ieyasu* established his supremacy over a number of competing military leaders, thus bringing to an exhausted end a period of civil war. The period of peace imposed by Ieyasu and his successors was enforced by the creation of a feudal society with rigid divisions between four clear social classes.

At the very top of the hierarchy was the warrior class (*samurai*) who, though they constituted only about 7 percent of the population, exerted unquestioned control over every aspect of life for all others. In theory the supreme power in Japan was vested in the emperor, but the Tokugawa leadership steadfastly continued the centuries-old tradition of isolating the emperor from temporal affairs, especially the burden of governing, and placing true political power in the hands of a single, strong military figure called a *shogun*. The result, in the 17th century, was a powerful military dictatorship responsible only to the *samurai*

---

*Japanese names, like most of those in Asia, begin with the family name, followed by the individual's personal name.

class and exerting absolute control over a society which was, by any standard, one of the most rigidly structured the world has ever seen.

As in any feudal system, the largest class was the peasants. Nearly 80 percent of the population were farmers; tied to the soil by birth, they tilled the property of the baron who owned the land without any hope of changing their status in life.

Artisans formed a third class. These people included everyone from woodcarvers and screenpainters to swordmakers and teachers. At first the artisans were kept at the castles of the major warlords but, as the power of these regional figures was systematically reduced, the artisans began to gather in the major cities such as Edo—the modern Tokyo.

The fourth and final class was a relative newcomer to the feudal design, the merchant. The towns were swelled by a growing number of

This screen painting by Masanabu Okumura shows a street scene in early 18th Century Edo. Citizens from all walks of life, including a noble lady in a sedan chair, are examining the enticements outside a *kabuki* theatre. The painted signs tell the name of the theatre, show the title of the play that is being performed, and list the scenes. A barker is pointing with his fan to direct the attention of the onlookers to the two illustrations of scenes from the play.

small shopkeepers, moneylenders, traders, commodities speculators and the like. These merchants comprised a lively group essential to the *samurai* but, because they were lowborn and uneducated in the courtly life, they were treated with contempt. They were forced to live only in specially designated parts of the city, they could not marry into the *samurai* class, they were ruinously taxed, and they were prevented from sharing in most of the entertainments open to the *samurai*. Clearly, the needs of the various classes were quite different; it is not surprising that a different kind of theatre came to be favored by each.

No Theatre. In 16th century Japan, *no* theatre was the favored theatrical form of the court and the nobility. Even at that time the form was a venerable one, dating back to at least the late 13th century when the introduction of Zen Buddhism into Japan from China encouraged a major change in the spiritual and aesthetic principles governing much of Japanese life. The Zen emphasis on the impermanence of life, the reverence for nature, and the conviction that "Buddha mind" is lying dormant in all people, awaiting only the cultivation of a teacher to be aroused, had a profound effect on the artistic life of the ruling classes. The distinctive Japanese tea ceremony, combining meditative ritual and artistic utensils in an everyday act, serves as an example of how ordinary existence can be given great spiritual value through simplification and refinement.

In the same spirit, *no* theatre is based upon the idea of great artistic restraint brought to bear on moments of high drama. To a very large degree, a *no* play is an example of how a courtier might be expected to deal with the vicissitudes of life in a world which is at the same time highly structured and secret. A typical *no* play deals with a major figure who while passing near a spiritually important place encounters an attractive or mundane character—only to discover that the stranger is a ghost or demon in disguise. There is a struggle, a dance, or perhaps no more than a meaningful conversation, and the conflict is resolved. The plots of *no* dramas are so very simple and the dialogue so spare that an entire script may fill only a few pages. What cannot be captured in a script, however, and the thing which gives *no* drama its special power, is the way in which each incident, each movement, each word is invested with great power by the attention lavished on it. Every extraneous detail has been removed and the remainder has been extended to the fullest. After centuries of reverent attention to this process, it is not surprising to discover in *no* theatre one of the most artificial and sophisticated theatre forms the world has ever seen.

An early, outdoor production of Japanese *no* theatre. Except that it is placed outdoors, the stage is remarkably similar to its modern descendant. The nobility
watch the production from the shelter of the house at the right; the less fortunate
gather in the courtyard at the front of the stage.

There is considerable controversy about how certain Western
plays, those of Shakespeare, for example, were actually produced. The
original performances were very badly documented and the interruption
of the traditions since then prevents us from reconstructing those early
works. The Japanese reverence for tradition, however, allows us to
know almost exactly how early plays were staged. In the case of *no*
theatre, for example, the productions have not changed greatly since
the 17th century; it is possible to attend productions in modern Tokyo
which would be entirely familiar to the founder of the Tokugawa
shogunate. To be sure, there are changes—the original productions were
held outdoors, and the *no* companies were maintained by the emperor
or wealthy nobles, for example—but in all important respects, today's
no theatre is a meticulous recreation of the original.

The setting is a formal stage, one which serves with only minor
changes for all *no* plays. Since the original plays were staged on the
covered porches of temples, the stage is a more or less faithful recreation of the facade of Buddhist and Shinto temples found all over Japan.
The stage proper is a raised platform eighteen feet square and covered
by a roof; a roof also covers the forty-foot walkway connecting stage
right with a major entrance at the audience's left. Although all important entrances are made down this walkway, there is also a small door

A modern *no* theatre contains all of the elements of its ancient ancestors. A masked actor has just made an entrance down the walkway from stage right. Upstage are the musicians, including two drummers seated on stools. The group at stage left is a chorus.

stage left which is used by chorus and instrumentalists. The stage and walkway are elevated roughly three feet above the audience level. The floor of the stage is designed to amplify the sound of the important stamping footfalls of the actors as they dance. Even the details of finish and painting are traditional: the wood of the stage and pillars supporting the roof are always hand-rubbed cedar; the back wall of the stage house always has a stylized pine tree painted on it; three small pines are always planted along the downstage lip of the walkway.

This commitment to tradition is strongly felt in the costuming. The actors—all of whom are men—wear heavy, elaborate costumes which date in style from the 12th and 13th centuries. All the major characters wear masks; some of the masks used in modern performances are themselves hundreds of years old. The speaking characters seldom number more than three, but a chorus and musicians may bring the total onstage to a dozen or more. The chorus and musicians are unmasked.

The style of acting is perhaps the most memorable aspect of production. To say that it is slow by Western standards is to understate the case: a single gesture can take 20 or 30 seconds to complete; it may take a major figure five minutes to move the 40 feet or so from the main entrance to the stage proper. Their infrequent moments of extremely vigorous dance are given a special power by contrast with the rest of the action in the play. As others have pointed out, *no* is almost a theatre of meditation.

It is also a highly symbolic theatre. The costumes say much about the characters—if an audience knows how to read class differences and emotional states as they are reflected in 13th- and 14th-century clothing. Props are absolutely minimal and are so generalized that they can be used in any production. Finally, the acting remains so symbolic as to be all but inaccessible to the uninitiated; for example, the raising of the hand to cover the masked face of a female character—a gesture which may take 20 seconds to execute—conveys her deep grief.

A program of *no* theatre normally begins at 10:30 in the morning or 4:00 in the afternoon and consists of five or six serious pieces and three short comic ones presented over a period of four or five hours.

A masked demon dances in front of three musicians in this modern *no* production.

Obviously, in such a program, the comic pieces, called *kyogen*, serve a very important function. Not only do they give the audience a chance to release the tension generated by the serious pieces, but, because they frequently mock the material in the serious pieces, they provide a balance in the worldview presented. Kyogen also had the freedom to comment on contemporary conditions; embedded in the humorous situations are comments on faithless lovers, greedy priests, foolish warlords, and a wealth of other observations which had few acceptable outlets in Tokugawa Japan.

In general, then, in *no* drama we see an example of a theatre form developed to meet the needs of an isolated, minority audience with a unified vision of the world and the shared education and experience needed to "decode" a sophisticated message provided by extremely well-trained artists. The world created is a magical/mythical one which reinforced the views of a well-defined ruling class. Since the serious plays are all set in the most remote historical past, there is little chance of any upsetting social commentary. Even if such commentary were possible, the form of *no* theatre is that of meditative theatre, and the form of the experience is far more important than any conventional content.

Kabuki Theatre. *Kabuki* theatre provides a striking contrast to *no*. It is fast moving, colorful, flamboyant, and appeals to a wide range of audiences. And yet, *kabuki* developed in 17th-century Japan in response to other aspects of the same social context as *no*.

As large cities developed in the early years of the Tokugawa shogunate, their growing populations contained large numbers of people—whole classes, in fact—who were only poorly provided for in the feudal scheme of things. Whole sections of those towns, especially Edo, became home to merchants, traders, prostitutes, unattached artists, and lordless warriors—all rootless people who really had no place within the rigid class structure. These districts, each bustling with a vitality of its own, became known as the "floating world," and eventually became the philosophical homes of new art forms. Among these were the rich traditions of colored woodblock printing, the poetic form called *haiku*, and *kabuki*.

From the very outset, *kabuki* (the symbols in Japanese are translated as "song-dance-skill") lacked the carefully cultivated respectability of *no*. According to legend, the founder of *kabuki*, Okuni, a former priestess, began singing and dancing parodies of Buddhist prayers in a

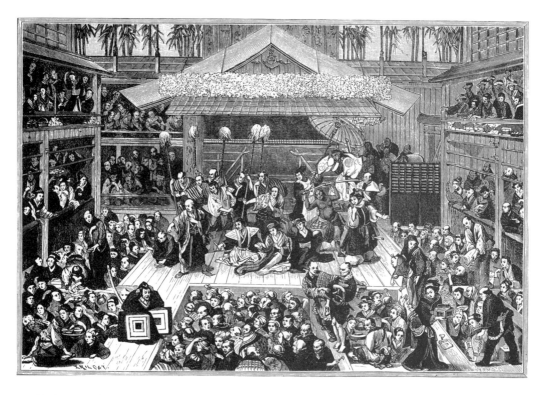

A 19th Century German traveler prepared this picture of the interior of a *kabuki* theatre. While he seems intent on capturing everything that ever happened in such a theatre in one illustration, it does give an idea of one vitality which has marked *kabuki* from its inception.

dry river bed in Kyoto. Later she gathered a company of ladies, made the singing and dancing even bolder, and began a tradition which has for over 400 years combined social controversy and artistic excellence.

Within only a few years, women were banned from the *kabuki* stage as a threat to public decency; it was assumed that all actresses were prostitutes and that their performance was no more than public soliciting. So *kabuki* troupes were reconstituted with all-boy performers —leading to another crackdown by the authorities on the grounds that the performances promoted homosexuality. A compromise was reached in which all roles were played by mature males.

The choice of materials for *kabuki* plays had this same freewheeling disregard for convention; it chose material for dramatic impact rather than social respectability or intellectual content. With the respect for the commonplace and the common people which typifies so much of the art from the "floating world," *kabuki* writers were quick to capitalize on juicy scandals and domestic melodramas, as well as on a wealth of historical tales. Whole plays were borrowed from the puppet theatre and the livelier parts of *no*, and the *kyogen* were shamelessly stolen as well. By the standards of the *no* theatre, the results were coarse, gaudy, overly emotional, and unrestrained. *Kabuki* audiences loved it.

This affectionate relationship with its audience has been a hallmark of *kabuki* since the beginning. The early scripts were really little more than a loose scenario around which the actors were free to improvise. Those early actors chatted with their audiences, received gifts and flowers, and seemed to relish the traditional bustle in the audience. This last was inevitable: performance began at 6:00 A.M. and continued all day; audience members would arrive to see only the play—or even the scene—which interested them, conversing with their neighbors when not enthralled by the action on stage. Today the actors have much less latitude with the script; however, they perform in an atmosphere which might upset Western performers: audiences still come and go during the performance, still talk a great deal, and feel free to shout out compliments or disparaging remarks at key moments. And *kabuki* actors are still objects of adoration. Their fans lavish them with gifts, plead for autographs, and follow them everywhere. Some leading *kabuki* actors even do a brisk business selling small bottles of their bathwater!

For all its comparative freedom, a modern *kabuki* performance is still a fair approximation of its 17th-century ancestor. True, the performances are now performed indoors and have been abbreviated in length to a more manageable four to six hours, and modern stage machinery has made possible some of the most spectacular effects seen anywhere in the world; but the essentials remain much as they were 400 years ago.

The plots of *kabuki* plays can be very complex, including multiple plots and many scene changes, but they often lack the unifying elements which Westerners expect. The plays almost always demonstrate the inherent justice of the universe: the virtuous are rewarded and the villains punished. In addition, thematic material concerning the transitory nature of life and the importance of duty reflect Buddhist and Confucianist religious views. Many of the conflicts result from a clash between love, or some other passion, and duty. A typical *kabuki* play contrives to place a hero in an impossible conflict between emotion and duty as in, say, the love of a young scholar for a *geisha*. In such a case, the outcome is frequently a double love suicide—and an audience in tears.

Mixed in for good measure are supernatural and erotic elements, or just theatrically interesting scenes guaranteed to capture and hold the attention of the audience.

The *kabuki* stage itself is an elaboration on what must have started out much like a *no* stage. The stage platform itself is much wider and deeper than its predecessor, however, and today has many additions which can provide great variety in staging. For example, the modern *kabuki* will have curtains (many of them) which can be used to close off the proscenium arch, revolving stages, and one or two raised walkways connecting the stage with the rear of the auditorium and along which actors can make some of their most effective entrances.

The actors themselves can be very elaborately costumed, sometimes with layers of costumes which are stripped away as new aspects of the characters reveal themselves. The actors are not masked, but heavy, conventionalized makeup conveys to the audience much of what they need to know about the character. Especially effective are the actors

Here a female character—played by a man, of course—exits along the *hanamichi*, the walkway that leads from the stage to the rear of the auditorium. The fact that this *kabuki* play has musicians and chorus on stage indicates that this play has its roots in the *no* theatre tradition.

who play women: their heavy historical makeup and colorful kimonos are complimented by soprano voices and movements so refined that it is said that if a woman *really* wants to know how to conduct herself she should study the actors in *kabuki*.

It is the unabashed theatricality of *kabuki* which has proved so attractive to Western theatre artists. For example, even though they naturally have the capacity to do so, the *kabuki* theatre does not dim the stage lights, change their color, darken the auditorium, or in any other way disguise the fact that the audience is in a theatre. The performance is frankly theatrical in a number of other effective ways. Onstage with the actors are blackclad stage managers who move props, assist the heavily clad actors at key moments, and generally tend to the mechanics of performance; however, because they are black, it is assumed by everyone that they cannot be seen. Like opera singers in the West, *kabuki* actors have developed techniques calculated to draw attention to key moments in the play. They may repeat favorite passages or, at moments of high drama, strike a *mie*, a stationary pose which is held until the audience has had a chance to fully savor the occasion. It is during the *mie* that audiences usually exercise their right to shout out comments.

In the middle of this elaborately choreographed struggle, the hero takes a moment to display a *mie*, the traditional feeze, which allows the audience to fully savor the moment—and to show its approval.

Violent action—especially in picturesque settings—is a mainstay of *kabuki*. Here a skirmish takes place in a snowstorm.

Even today *kabuki* remains popular with all classes of Japanese society; *no* is barely holding its own. The general collapse of the feudal structure of Japanese society in the 19th century was devastating for *no*; its fragile quality had been protected by a social system which prevented it from changing. By contrast, the lusty *kabuki* had remained in constant interaction with a diverse and expanding audience. It provided this audience with a view of the world which they recognized, taught them lessons which they needed, and provided a forum for social comment which they could not find elsewhere. The lesson is clear: the overbred showdog lives best in a pampered environment; the streetwise mutt can prosper anywhere.

THEATRE IN CONTEMPORARY AMERICA

Seldom do we subject our own culture to the kind of examination which we reserve for others; when we do, however, the effort is rewarded by insights which might otherwise have escaped us. We have seen contexts in which theatre was nearly spontaneous and completely amateur and we have seen it as a totally professional and carefully preserved tradition. We have seen it utterly responsive to the interests of all members of the group and we have seen it hermetically sealed from pressures which might force it to change. We have seen it function with light-hearted freedom and we have noted how it can be persecuted for any number of reasons. In the main, however, we have glanced at theatre traditions which treated the potential audience as a single—or possibly dual—force in the interactive process. In strongly unified cultures, this is possible and, from the point of view of the art, perhaps it is even a desirable situation. After all, a society in which all potential audience members share roughly the same values and interests makes an easy target for the theatre artist; the playwrights, the directors, the actors, all have a reasonably good idea of what audiences want and need. In a pluralistic society, however, there can be so much diversity between audience members that a single theatrical tradition is out of the question. In such a case, plural theatre traditions develop to respond to the diverse needs of the society.

The theatrical diversity available in contemporary America is the greatest in the world—and probably the most diverse the world has ever known. The reason is quite simple: diverse needs encourage a diversity of responses. From the variety of simultaneous theatrical traditions we may infer the variety of needs.

Perhaps fifty years ago there was only one perceived center of legitimate theatre in the United States. New York was to America in the thirties what London was to the Elizabethan theatregoers, Paris to Molière, or Athens to Sophocles: it was the only place to be if you were a professional artist or a serious playgoer. Of course, if you were a film-maker you gravitated toward Hollywood; but thousands of aspiring actors, directors, playwrights, and designers moved to New York each year to begin careers in the Broadway theatre world. There really was no other choice.

Today, the picture has changed greatly. First of all, there are only about a third the number of theatres in the midtown Manhattan area called Broadway as there were in, say, 1930. But the total number of theatres in New York is much greater; so is the total number of plays produced in any given year. But the dispersion of the theatres is far more significant than the simple fact that the New York "theatre district" now really extends all over Manhattan and into the adjacent boroughs. The dispersion is nationwide: very fine professional theatres are now found in all major American cities, and many where one would hardly expect them. The Guthrie Theatre in Minneapolis, San Francisco's Actor's Conservatory Theatre, the Actor's Theatre of Louisville, and

Times Square has always been the geographical center of the New York theatre district. This is how it looked on the night that Roosevelt was first elected president. Note that motion picture houses had already begun to fill the area.

many others regularly produce plays of an artistic quality rivaling or exceeding the best Broadway work. Fine professional theatre is also a mainstay of audiences in such unlikely places as Ashland, Oregon; Sarasota, Florida; and Santa Maria, California. With this physical dispersion and increase in both number and quality has come an increase in the number of jobs in live theatre—as well as an increase in the choice of regions in which theatre artists can live and work.

Part of this physical dispersion has been made possible by a range of economic formulas for supporting theatre. The 1930s model was the New York commercial theatre. In this model, an enterprising producer, having come across a script which he or she thinks is a valuable "property," forms a corporation and sells shares in the corporation to fund the production. If all goes well and the play is a hit, it makes back its investment and begins to return profits to the investors (called *angels*).

Today's costs of producing live theatre in New York being what they are, and the chances of attracting spectacular popularity being what *they* are, the angel business is only somewhat less risky than betting on the Irish Sweepstakes. Yet every year hundreds of people—theatre lovers every one—take the gamble and invest in Broadway shows.

But there are fewer commercial plays produced on Broadway each year. And each year the production costs mount, union and zoning problems escalate, and ticket prices—moving upward to keep pace—threaten to make Broadway theatre inaccessible to any but the rich. Clearly, some other system has to be found.*

One answer to the high risk and caution of commercial theatre is the professional, nonprofit theatre. These theatres do not offer a profit motive to investors. Instead, they solicit contributions from philanthropic individuals and foundations to augment the expected gap between box office revenue and expenses. Federal and local tax laws play a significant part in this arrangement: not only are nonprofit corporations freed from paying income taxes but they receive breaks in terms of mailing costs and special help from localities—including, in some cases, reduced rentals on city-owned property. And, of course, the contributions from individuals and foundations offer certain economic advantages to the donors. All in all, the advantages provided to nonprofit theatre companies (and orchestras, galleries, museums, and the like) represent an indirect subsidy to the performing arts. Such a subsidy carries with it the assumption that the theatres are performing a valuable public service and are worthy of support from taxpayers—some of whom may never use the services.

The first theatre groups to break from the commercial model which had prevailed for so long did so shortly after the Second World War. Small groups of actors, playwrights, directors, and designers began to join together to produce their own plays in small theatres away from the expensive Broadway area. This practice thus earned the name of the *off-Broadway movement*. Realizing that this scaled-down level of production made work for many of their members, the performers'

---

*One bright spot in the otherwise gloomy picture of commercial theatre is the so-called dinner theatre. In this configuration a theatre offers dinner and a play as a package. The total operation is, of course, a profit-seeking enterprise; but the economics and audience appeal seem to work out. Dinner theatres are doing well in all parts of the country and—although the plays are seldom challenging and the productions may be marginal—employment is provided for many theatre artists who might be unemployed otherwise. And it must be noted that thousands of people who might not attend their local resident theatre are delighted to experience theatre under these less intimidating circumstances.

unions and craft guilds set up flexible rules allowing participation in off-Broadway productions, and New York City zoning regulations have been favorably modified or ignored. Thus, the off-Broadway formula provided a growing number of showcase productions, productions of plays by playwrights who deserved public attention but whose work did not seem suitable for Broadway. Ironically, these predictions were repeatedly proven dead wrong; time and time again successful off-Broadway productions have been optioned by commercial producers, moved to Broadway, and have proven to be full-scale hits.

By the late 1960s even the off-Broadway formula was proving restrictive. With the tacit approval of the unions, a generation of even smaller theatres (less than 200 seats), even farther from the Broadway mainstream, began to produce plays which would have difficulty in the

The first off-broadway theatres established themselves little more than a mile from Times Square in Greenwich Village. One of the earliest and most successful of these was the Circle in the Square. Here, Dustin Hoffman and Joseph Mayer perform in their 1966 production of *Eh?*.

Probably the most influential of the Off-off Broadway theatres has been the La Mama Experimental Theatre Club. Here Frederich Newman and George Bartenieff portray two of Samuel Beckett's eccentric characters in *Beckett Trilogy*.

increasingly respectable atmosphere of off-Broadway. These theatres became the off-off-Broadway circuit and in them the most experimental, controversial, and politically unpopular plays were produced by artists who were willing to work for nothing—or close to it. Because their budgets were so small and because of their general disinterest in the theatrical polish expected of Broadway theatre, the off-off-Broadway theatres gained a reputation for demanding, but tacky, productions of plays which could never have been produced elsewhere.

The geographic and economic dispersion of American theatre continued along a parallel track with the founding, in the 1960s, of *regional* or *resident* theatres all across the United States. These nonprofit companies increased in number until, today, there are more than 70 members of the League of Resident Theatres. Together they produce over 600 productions per year for audiences of 12 million. As the resident theatres have grown in number and influence they have accepted many responsibilities which used to be the province of Broadway alone. Chief among these is the discovery of new plays; many of the most important plays in recent decades have premiered in resident theatres before going on to commercial success on Broadway.

The picture puzzle of the American theatre still has at least two major pieces missing: community theatre and educational theatre. In cities and towns of all sizes across America there are theatres in which neighbors produce plays on a volunteer basis for the sheer fun of it. Many of these theatres have professional staff leadership but the actors are almost always amateurs and the technical support is volunteer. Community theatres in the United States produce work which ranges from the appallingly inept to the very fine. Their choice of plays tends to lean toward very accessible comedies and close approximations of sure-fire Broadway hits. But some community theatres attempt very difficult work and, as the biennial Festival of American Community Theatre has demonstrated, the best of community theatre need not be embarrassed in any company.

Educational theatre refers to the literally thousands of productions associated with training programs in American high schools, colleges, universities, and conservatories. Again, there is an enormous range in the quality of work presented in educational theatre. A senior class play presented as a combination social occasion and fundraiser by a small rural high school may be highly successful in those terms while lacking —to put the matter delicately—artistic excellence. At the same time, universities which offer specialized training programs in acting, directing, scenic and costume design, and playwriting can often mount productions of amazing quality. A key point is that many audience members' only experience with theatre is through the work of a school program; and the vast majority of young people only experience performance as students.

A final level of diversity in American theatre is harder to document but may be the most important point of all. There is no American theatre per se; there is no single style or subject matter, or group of artists. Instead, there are many styles, many subject matters, many values, many groups of artists. In American commerce, one industry may be busy selling denture adhesive to those who need tight teeth while another business tries to sell Caribbean vacations. So it is with live theatre: one theatre offers a rollicking night out complete with dinner, drinks, and a wild sex farce; another provides audiences a demanding production of *Macbeth*; a third asks audiences to enter a small basement

The larger American Universities have theatre training programs with the resources to produce the most demanding plays. Here we see a scene from The University of Texas at Austin's production of *The Infernal Machine* by Jean Cocteau.

theatre to experience a ringing denunciation of bourgeois values. *And all have audiences.* We have theatres performing in any number of languages: a friend in Los Angeles worked his way through drama school directing productions in Chinese, Italian, and Serbo-Croatian; he did not speak any language except English but he offered his services to the many minority communities to stage their plays—so long as they provided an interpreter.

America has theatres devoted to the special interests and values of many minority cultures: black theatre, gay and lesbian theatre, farmworker's theatre, radical left-wing theatre, anarchist theatre, Jewish theatre—the list continues growing because there is always some group which believes that the existing traditions are not responding to their special needs. Moreover, even the individual has multiple needs which, in a free society, he or she will seek to satisfy. For example, the same person may seek out a serious production of *Hamlet* one night and a romantic comedy the next. A gay person can, after all, be moved with patriotic fervor; a black American might want to roar with laughter at a domestic farce; a Hispanic family can watch the soaps on television and yet wish to celebrate the contribution of their culture to America in live theatre.

And there is the heart of the matter. A large, pluralistic nation such as ours has a range of needs which keeps both the pollster and the artist busy. There are dangers, of course. The centrifugal forces of specialization may tear apart the shared values which bind people together into one culture. But the reverse, a refusal to recognize that there are individual and group differences—and, with them, different needs—would lead to a single, rigid theatre tradition. As we have seen, rigidity can prove deadly, to the art and to the society.

There are many forceful critics of the American theatre scene and their serious concerns demand attention. But one point on which our

The Tyrone Guthrie Theatre in Minneapolis, Minnesota, is home of the Minnesota Theatre Company, one of America's first and most successful resident theatres. This company plays in full repertory; each season, the five plays whose names appear on the colorful banners will be performed in daily rotation.

culture cannot be faulted is the theatrical diversity which we have developed to meet our many needs. It is true that we do not have widespread, direct federal subsidies for the performing arts, as many European nations have; it is true that we do not yet have a single "national theatre," as the British have; it is true that we do not have financial security for artists, or comprehensive training programs, or a systematic program of recognizing our "living national treasures" in the arts, as other nations do. But we have the *potential* for all of this because, in our own ragtag American way, we have a pluralist theatre tradition in healthy interaction with a pluralist society. And the final judgment is not yet in on American theatre in the 20th century.

Discussion Questions

1. Describe censorship as a form of feedback in the interactive model we have been developing. What are the ways in which censorship works? Discuss the values and disadvantages of censorship—in both the short run and the long run.
2. What are some of the signs we look for which indicate a "healthy" theatrical tradition? What are the signs of a poor relationship between society and the theatre?
3. Did you find, as you read the short descriptions of the four foreign theatre traditions, some aspects of theatre which you believe might prove successful with modern American audiences? What are they? How could they be adapted to the theatre tradition you know best?
4. Are there limits to the topics which can and should be explored in live theatre? (The Greeks would have been horrified that we show killing on stage, but nudity and sexual references were expected parts of their theatre.) What would you permit?
5. Are some of the functions of theatre in other times being met by television and film? What could those functions be—and what remains for theatre?

4

The Company

Dr. Lewis Thomas, writer and chancellor emeritus of the Memorial Sloan-Kettering Institute, once asked himself a daring question: Why not consider the whole planet Earth, with its incredible complexity, as if it were that basic building block of biology, a single cell? The idea seemed preposterous at first, but reflection proved that it was not really so farfetched. Thomas's resulting collection of essays, published as *The Lives of A Cell*, won a National Book Award. The book is not only good reading, but serves to remind us of the value of the mental exercise of considering a complicated collection of organisms as if they were actually a single, larger entity. That idea surfaces again and again in this book: you have already been asked to think of the diverse activity called *theatre* as if it had a single continuing function in human culture. Now we will take a moment to consider the theatrical *company* as if it were a single organism.

The theatrical company is that collection of people who gather together to produce a play. The concept is purposely vague. The company could be a group brought together for the production of one play only—as is often done in the American commercial theatre—or it could be a professional repertory company that has worked together on a large number of plays over decades. Who is included? The more exclusive term *cast* includes only the actors. The idea of *company* expands the cast to include the directors, stage managers, and designers. Less frequently, the stagehands, shop crews, promotional and "front-of-house" staff are considered "company"—a producer or director who wishes to promote "company spirit" might include all of these in meetings, communications, praise—and, yes, criticism.

The key aspect in the concept of the company, however, is not so much the personnel included, but what that concept has to say about the creative process employed.

Theatre has always been a highly collaborative art. However, throughout most of its history, it has usually had a simpler form of organization than it has today. There is every reason to believe that, besides writing his plays, Sophocles directed them, coached the singers, and choreographed the chorus. In the same way, Molière directed his own plays and played the major roles. Shakespeare was an actor (though reportedly not a very good one!) and an owner of the company which first produced his plays; there is no question that his opinions were all but law in those premier productions.

But a tradition of a single, strong creative leader does not end the search for the best creative method; there are alternative ways for people to organize themselves to accomplish creative tasks. An authoritarian, hierarchical organization may work well for certain groups (say, a symphony orchestra) but not for others. In the 20th century, a number of different approaches have been explored—all of them aiming to combine efficiency and creativity in a proper balance.

FORMS OF ORGANIZATION

Authoritarian. At one end of a spectrum lies the authoritarian organization. Nowadays, the chief authority is usually a director and, in an ideal example of authoritarian organization, such a director would rule with an iron hand. This hypothetical authoritarian director might commission a playwright to write a play on a particular subject and would not hesitate to change the resulting script to conform to his, or her, expectations; or he might write it himself. He, or she, would then set out to plan the perfect production, doing all the research and preparing detailed notes as to how costumes should look, where actors should stand, how they should deliver each line of dialogue, and so on. Then, calling together the company, he would assign each task and demand that his orders be carried out in perfect accordance with his every wish. No opinions would be solicited; no argument would be allowed. For the actors, this would mean following very detailed orders to the letter; becoming, in effect, puppets who could be depended upon to respond to the director's every wish with precision and absolute dependability. (This last point is not altogether fanciful: Edward Gordon Craig, a famous and respected director, designer, and theoretician, once suggested developing such puppets. Despairing of the quirkiness of actors, their independence, and lack of precision, Craig raged that theatre would never really be an art until actors were replaced by what he called *ubermarionetten*—superpuppets—which could recreate a performance *exactly* as the director envisioned it. Craig died before he had a chance to see the audio-animatrons developed by Disney Studios and widely used at Disneyland, Disney World, and other theme parks.)

The goal of an authoritarian organization is to transfer to the stage exactly the concept which one creative mind has imagined. There have been theatre companies organized with this end in mind—and they have frequently used authoritarian organization to achieve that goal. The authoritarian organizational structure within the company places everyone in a reporting relationship to a supervisor above them and responsible subordinates below them. Thus the organization appears, on paper, to be a nice orderly pyramid with the single, creative leader at the top— anticipating all difficulties.

But *perfect* examples are very difficult to find. Consider the practical difficulties: it is a very rare person, indeed, playwright or director, who can anticipate every detail and solve every problem; sooner or later, probably without much fanfare, some actor or designer is going to anticipate a problem—and solve it—all alone. Indeed, any translation of an idea into a physical thing or event is so complicated that independent decisions are inevitable: the actress cast in a given role has a figure different from the one in a costume sketch, so an accommodating cutter adds another ruffle; a doorknob of the kind required by the director is simply not available and a substitution is made; an actor comes up with an unanticipated reading of a line which is much better than what the director thought she wanted. In numberless ways the hurly-burly of actual production nibbles away at the pure intentions of an authoritarian company. Even Shakespeare's ideas unquestionably changed as they were transferred from the page to the stage. He may have been an owner of his company—but he was not the *only* owner; most of his major actors were part-owners, too, and it's highly likely that *they* had ideas about producing those plays as well.

Supporters of an authoritarian organization value its efficiency and the general unity of the productions which result. However, morale in authoritarian companies can be poor if members do not understand and share the views of the leadership.

Laissez Faire.   This French term is usually used to describe economic systems free from any governmental intervention. Here the term refers to a system of organizing a theatre company so that no one person makes any single decision.

Such a company—again exceedingly rare, if it exists at all—would be at the opposite end of the organizational spectrum from the authoritarian system. A laissez-faire model would require that all decisions be made by consensus—or perhaps majority vote. There would be no single decision maker; there would be no chain of command.

During the 1960s and '70s, there were several groups working to create theatre using this design, or some other method such as reaching decisions by throwing the *I Ching*. The reason most often given for employing a laissez-faire model is that it guarantees that every member of the company understands and agrees on the group's goals. Critics point out that such an approach is very inefficient and that resulting productions are usually lacking in the artistic unity which many people—mostly audiences—value.

Democratic.   A compromise between the two extremes of the authoritarian and laissez-faire attempts to capture some of the best elements of both—without the obvious drawbacks. In this form of organization, the director accepts final responsibility for all artistic decisions, but delegates authority to others in leadership positions. At the same time, the director is open to suggestions from all members of the company, often actively soliciting input from unlikely sources. Naturally, such a director also accepts the obligation to inform the company of major decisions which have already been made, so providing a conceptual framework within which company members may contribute. A more detailed examination of how such a director works is provided in Chapter 7, "The Director."

The democratic approach attempts to use *all* the resources of the company. One way of looking at the problem of group creation is to abandon the old idea that there is an "ideal" production of a play just hovering in the ozone somewhere and waiting to be realized in a perfect production. On the contrary, there are a very large number of productions possible, depending upon the specific cast at hand, the artistic leadership, the political, cultural, and economic environments in which the play will be presented, and so on. The director and producer have decided on the general outline of the production they envision—but it takes enormous work to fill in the very empty spaces within that outline. The excellence of the final production will be determined by the quality of a multitude of relatively small decisions which must be made on a day-to-day basis. How does one guarantee that these decisions will be good ones?

One measure of a good decision is the number of options considered before making it final. A director working alone may be able to dream up, say, ten possible solutions to a problem—from which he or she must choose one. But ten company members, working together, can usually come up with many more than that. (Just how many is an interesting question: ten equally imaginative people, working independently, could come up with 100 solutions—but presumably there would be many duplications, thus giving, say, one-half that number. But ten imaginative people *working as a group* have been shown to inspire one another in such a way that the total number of *usable* options is greatly increased.)

In one sense, the greater number of possible solutions can complicate the director's life—and certain pedestrian directors may object on that point alone. But creative directors usually value the input. They know that in that large collection of solutions may lie a very good one which they had not considered. And, whatever else happens, the director will always have his or her own best solutions to fall back upon, because the final decision is the director's. It is a situation in which there is everything to gain and nothing to lose, unless, of course, everyone making a suggestion has been led to believe that his or her suggestions will be used! But one has to assume that good sense will prevent this confusion, and the resulting frustration.

Another feature of good artistic decisions is a consistent regard for the desired outcomes. Here the director and the rest of the leadership have a responsibility to keep the company working in the same direction. The methods available to a director are many: they include a clear production concept, open communication—including praise for espe-cially valuable contributions—close familiarity with both the work in question and the members of the company, and an accurate sense of how a production will be received by an audience.

THE COMPANY AT WORK

Just as a football team can have a character quite different from the characters of the players who make it up, a company can develop a mode of working that is totally unique. One company can be lively and verbal while another is methodical and quiet. And the character of the company may have little or nothing to do with the character of the play on which it is working. This company character begins to assert itself as early as the first *company meeting*, a meeting frequently de-voted to such rituals as introducing everyone, a general description by the director of his or her concept, a show of the designer's plates, and a pep talk by the stage manager. Often this first meeting is combined with the first reading aloud of the script by the actors. This allows the crews to get to know both the actors and the script, and—everyone hopes—begins to develop a sense of company cohesion.

Regular meetings are scheduled in each area, such as scenery, cos-tume, and props, to allow those task groups to understand where they are in the creative process. Even more frequently, the designers and director meet to report on progress, discuss problems, and chart new directions. These are called *production meetings*, and are absolutely vital if the incredibly complex work of the company is to result in any-thing like a unified production.

Nearly as important as the formal meetings, however, are the in-formal ones. Company members frequently share meals, go out socially after rehearsals, and spend free time together. These informal meetings may not include the entire company; natural subgroups form as friend-ships are made and sustained. These informal exchanges are not usually devoted to the play; indeed, the details of the production may not even arise in conversation.

It would be a foolish director who would try to discourage these informal interactions. They build a sense of cohesiveness within the company, reminding its members that they are part of a group of people who—for the duration of the production period, at least—need one another more than nearly anyone else in the world. Any actor, director, designer, or technician has warmly remembered stories about favorite productions. Usually they were successful ones, but sometimes they were flops. The constant element is the quality of the artistic relationships formed, the crises encountered and overcome, the enduring friendships forged in the white heat of artistic collaboration.

Strangers are frequently surprised by the degree of emotion displayed by the members of a company on closing night. A period of hard work is completed, new tasks are beckoning, the play may even have become a trifle tiresome. One might expect that everyone associated with the production would be pleased to be well rid of it. Instead, the tears, the sad goodbyes, the nostalgic reminiscences, all give testimony to the value that each member has placed on the company. Each has emerged from the experience changed for having been part of a complex organization, an organization which has, for a certain time, become a single entity larger and more productive than any single member.

Discussion Questions

1. Discuss examples of groups you know or have been part of which developed a *group personality*. Describe that personality and say why you think it developed as it did. Don't limit yourself to theatre.

2. What kinds of pressures would encourage a company to move toward an authoritarian organization? A laissez-faire organization?

5

The Actor

An old vaudeville exchange goes like this:

FIRST COMIC: Can you play the violin?
SECOND COMIC: I don't know. I never tried.

Now try this version:

FIRST COMIC: Can you act?
SECOND COMIC: I don't know. I never tried.

Neither version is hilarious; but most people probably find the first much funnier than the second. After all, everyone knows that no one can play a violin without considerable practice. The idea that a person might pick up a violin for the first time and play it well is patently ridiculous.

Many people, however, harbor the idea that they just might be fine *actors*—if only given the chance to try. Why?

Because acting looks so simple. Indeed, the better the acting is, the easier it looks. After all, at first glance it appears that an actor is doing only things that all of us do every day: walking about, talking, listening, eating, arguing, exchanging stories. . . .

Furthermore, we have all heard of people with little or no experience who become "movie stars" overnight after having been discovered sitting at a soda fountain. Some motion picture directors have even developed reputations for using only totally inexperienced actors for particular roles. Of course, upon close examination such stories usually prove to be myths: the overwhelming majority of successful actors, whether in legitimate theatre, film, or television, turn out to be dedicated professionals who were "discovered" only after years, sometimes decades, of training and work in their professions. The success of "naturally talented" amateur film actors who star in one film (and are frequently never seen again) is usually a triumph of directing, filming, and editing, rather than any proof that acting is easy.

And yet the fact remains: Acting looks easy. Why?

As we saw earlier, in performance, there is an unspoken contract between the performer and the audience member ("I will pretend . . . you will pretend to believe me.") in which the two collaborate to create an imaginary world. We saw how this "contract" in a theatre was little more than an elaboration of what almost all of us do regularly in everyday life. In fact, we slip in and out of performance situations so often that, for most of us, the task is fairly simple. Acting seems easy to us because we see in it the general outlines of the "performance contracts" of our ordinary lives.

At a second level, acting involves a version of the performance contract between the actors: one actor adopts a role (either himself or herself in a situation different from his or her real-life condition, or a different person altogether) and the other actors agree to play along. Earlier we called this an actor/actor interaction. The difference between this and actor/audience interaction is that the other partners in this interaction also have imaginary roles. In an actor/audience interaction, the actor makes the greater leap of imagination; in an actor/actor interaction, both participants make an equal leap. The character and intensity of that leap is what the remainder of this chapter is about.

THE ART OF ACTING

Although a great many people have given very serious thought to what constitutes acting, what makes a great actor, what separates good acting from bad, and how actors might be trained, there is anything but unanimity on the subject. A few commentators argue that actors are "born, not made," and that training of any kind is useless. Most experts, however, agree that while certain native gifts may be necessary, rigorous training is essential. Critics have described acting as an example of "animal magnetism" or as a "borderline psychosis." Some have seen the skills involved as strictly external and mechanical; others emphasize elements that can only be spiritual—even mystical. "Psychological gestures," "beats," "trinities," "empathic communication," "chi"—acting criticism and acting texts are often long on poetry, but short on clarity and precision. Acting, in short, is far from a science.

Constantin Stanislavski is usually considered the father of modern actor training. His enormous credibility as a teacher was greatly enhanced by his long and successful career as an actor and director. At right is a famous photograph of him in the role of Satin in the world premier production of Maxim Gorky's *The Lower Depths* (1902).

The person who has had the greatest influence on acting in the 20th century, and a man who devoted his whole life to trying to understand acting so that he might teach it to others, is the Russian actor/director/teacher Constantin Stanislavski (1863–1938). Most modern theories of acting began with his work, even though Stanislavski himself always said that he was doing nothing more than describing what great actors have always done. His aim was to provide some system to what has always been an unruly art.

Even Stanislavski, however, gave credit to the aspects of acting which defy logical description and soar beyond mundane theories. Indeed, he often described his "system" as what one did in those long stretches between moments of inspiration. The aim, of course, is to increase the frequency of the inspiration: those electrifying moments when to some degree even the actor becomes a spectator, a witness to a play taking on a life of its own, those moments when *anything* can happen.

Stanislavski reminded us that no matter how electrifying those few moments of inspiration may be, the stretches between them can be excruciatingly dull in the hands of untrained actors.

WHY DOES THE ACTOR NEED TRAINING?

Most of an actor's training is actually preparation for rehearsal, not performance. Most of the important concepts in acting and actor training pertain to the weeks—perhaps years—of preparation which precede the appearance on stage. It is this preparation which novices know little about and which they conveniently ignore when they fancy that they could be great actors if only given the chance to stride onto the stage.

The discrepancy between time spent preparing and the time spent "acting" is a clue to one of the measures of good acting. Years of preparation may reveal itself in only a split second onstage. Plays may last several hours, but the actor on the stage lives in a continuous present. Like an Olympic diver, all her skill, training, and creativity must be brought to bear in milliseconds of controlled expression. Indeed, nearly everything that an actor does while actually performing happens so quickly and subtly that it is nearly impossible to reflect on the physical and vocal activity itself. In performance, the actor has time and energy only to concentrate on the character's life. This absorption in the role can lead audience members to believe that the actor is unaware of them and is truly living in some imaginary world. This may be an attractive fiction for an actor trying to gain some public notice—but it remains a fiction nonetheless.

Any experienced actor is fully aware of the fact that he or she is performing at all times. To believe otherwise would be a form of madness—and no other actors would play in the same play with a crazy person. What actress playing Desdemona would choose to play opposite an actor who, when the time in Act V comes for Othello to strangle her, believed the situation to be real? No, good actors only *seem* to live the role. All those years of training and weeks of rehearsal are aimed at one goal: to appear to a cooperative audience to be entirely natural and spontaneous. And, as anyone who has tried it knows, achieving that goal can be very difficult indeed. To do it, the serious actor must put all of his or her resources at the service of the dramatic idea.

THE RESOURCES OF THE ACTOR

Consider for a moment the ways in which the audience perceives the play. The most important are clearly sight and hearing: the audience sees what the actor is doing physically and hears what he or she is saying. Of course, there are productions in which other senses come into play. Some modern companies have found ways to physically touch members of the audience, and occasionally a production introduces the sense of smell: food may be served on stage, cigarettes lit, or an actor near the audience may give off a distinctive aroma. And there is always the chance that extrasensory perception, if it exists, may be at work in the communication loop between an audience member and an actor. But there should be little argument that the major means of communication are sight and hearing; and that leaves the actor with his or her body, voice, and mind.

The body and the voice are to the actor what canvas, paint, and brushes are to the painter, and musical instruments are to the musician: the body and voice are the materials of the actor. Add to these a mind with its accompanying memory, imagination, and emotional capacity, and you have everything that an actor carries onto the stage.

The body, the voice, the mind. Everything in acting depends on these. The creative genius of the professional actor is expressed through his or her body, voice, and mind; the training of the actor begins with them.

Methods of training actors vary around the world, and from period to period. In general, those theatres which emphasize stylistic purity and the preservation of historical works begin training at an early age (as early as five years of age in some Asian cultures). In these cultures, the actor spends years developing phenomenal levels of physical and vocal agility and memorizing historical plays. A classical actor in, say, *kabuki* theatre will probably never be asked to interpret an unproduced script; most *kabuki* plays are hundreds of years old and no self-respecting actor would dream of changing any part of them. A major event for a *kabuki* actor would be assignment to a different role within an existing play; most *kabuki* actors play the same roles for their entire life.

A Western actor, by contrast, usually begins training in his or her teenage years and is expected to have greater stylistic flexibility. In the course of a single season, a well-trained Western actor may be assigned roles in plays by Shakespeare, Molière, Eugene O'Neill, and Samuel Beckett. In addition, he or she is expected to deal with previously unproduced scripts or innovative productions of classics. In short, the well-trained Western actor may not have the physical and vocal skills of the Eastern colleague; but she or he must have compensating analytical and imaginative abilities.

The hands of this Thai dancer show the control and expressiveness that can be achieved when the training begins before most Western actors enter kindergarten.

Body. Regardless of the tradition in which he or she works, the actor must have sufficient physical skill to express what is demanded. These expressive demands can vary. For example, *strength* and *endurance* may be important. Some roles are physically demanding; they may require an actor to run, fight, climb, jump over furniture, and fall during the course of an evening (twice a day on Wednesdays and Saturdays when matinee performances are scheduled). Even the film actor may be required to do the most exhausting activities over and over again for the filming of repeated "takes."

More important are the physical skills required to *communicate* simple information. For example, it is necessary for an actor to be able to share clearly with an audience where the character is looking, listening, etc. When one character is speaking, the other actors help focus the audience's attention on that character by focusing their attention on the speaker. A good actor can communicate clearly where his or her attention is focused by physical means.

Another physical attribute of actors is *control.* It is obvious that an actor in legitimate theatre must be able to repeat the same gestures night after night in precisely the same way—making it seem absolutely natural and spontaneous each time, of course. She must be able to light the cigarette between precisely the same words, step through the door on exactly the same count, see the corpse at the moment rehearsed, and do it each performance, perhaps eight a week, for months on end.

Another aspect of control has to do with the "size" of a performance. A stage production in a large theatre cannot be played only for those audience members in the first few rows; the size of the gestures, glances, and other physical attributes of a performance must be able to be seen in the last row of the theatre without being so wildly exaggerated as to be grotesque. The task is a formidable one, but skillful actors achieve the goal regularly. However, weeks later, the same actor may be playing the same role in a film or on television. Here the challenge is precisely the reverse: the portrayal must now be proportionally reduced to accommodate a lens which might be only inches away. The control required to work at this scale is precisely equivalent to that needed in a large theatre. The actor with good physical training will be able to meet the challenge.

No character is interesting without a full portrayal of his or her emotional life. An amazing percentage of what we know about a character is conveyed by physical means. The well-trained actor knows this and works to develop a body that is *totally responsive to emotional*

All the strength, endurance, and control of the actor are brought to bear in moments such as this. The actor with poor physical training is a danger to himself and others.

states. In everyday life we all work to develop techniques to mask our emotional states. (After all, we don't want the boss to know how angry we really are!) But actors must learn to be perfectly "clear" on occasion; their anger must be able to burst through without impediment. At other times, it must be inhibited by the character's social control. But in this case, both the anger *and* the social control must be clearly conveyed to the audience. A difficult challenge, but one which actors relish.

To succeed, the actor must be prepared to respond physically with the whole body. We have all seen poor actors portray anger on the stage: their faces are contorted, they recite angry words, but everything happening in the head is contradicted by what is happening in the rest of the body. The relaxed back, the slack hands, the locked knees! To avoid this mixed message, the actor works hard to develop a body that is completely responsive to emotional states. Of a truly expressive actor you can honestly say, "Even his toes were angry."

To develop the physical skills mentioned above actors may study dance, particularly modern dance, ballet, and jazz. In addition, they may take one or more of the martial arts such as karate, judo, kung fu, aikido, or fencing. Stage combat, whether armed or unarmed, has the double value of developing the actor's body while teaching skills that are frequently needed in plays. Period movement classes teach actors to recreate the movement patterns and social graces of historical periods, with special attention to the use of the costumes and accessories of each culture.

Voice. Modern theories of actor training tend to minimize the separation between the actor's body and the actor's voice. Though they are perceived quite differently by audience members, voice and body are as related in the actor as they are in the character. For that reason, courses in voice for the actor relate the production of sound to the

Vocal training is part of the preparation of any professional actor.

muscular condition of the entire body; the quality of sound is a product of the skillful relaxation of the body's resonant surfaces and cavities, so that even articulation is connected with physical relaxation and flexibility. In short, particularly in the area of vocal production, modern training methods tend to emphasize an "integrated" training program. The aim of such a program is a voice which is *strong, flexible, responsive,* and capable of a range of *special skills.*

Before the advent of electronic means of amplification, a very powerful voice was an absolute necessity for any actor. Nineteenth-century theatres tended to be very large, frequently holding audiences of more than 3,000. In such a large space it is an enormous challenge to be heard at all, let alone be understood. To carry a large role would mean the actor would be working his or her voice with the energy one experiences today only in opera singers. A well-trained voice was crucial. Fortunately, most actors are not forced to work under conditions of that kind today. Still, the vocal demands of performing regularly in relatively large spaces may make demands far beyond what an untrained voice can meet. And an actor with laryngitis is an unemployed actor.

Vocal programs for actors attempt to develop skills that allow an actor to "project" in any reasonable-size theatre. This concept has three aspects. Not only must the sound of the actor's voice be heard in all parts of the theatre, but the words must be understood as well. In addition, the quality of the sound must be appropriate to the role; it will not do for all the speeches to sound shouted. The layperson can hardly begin to understand the skill displayed by a fine actor who manages to play an intimate scene in a large theatre in such a way that every member of the audience can participate in both the meaning and the sense of intimacy.

Like nearly everything else in the theatre, the speech of characters on stage is usually more demanding than speech in everyday life. Stage characters are usually more articulate, more colorful in their speech, and more expressive in their voice than people in ordinary life. This should not surprise anyone; after all, we go to the theatre to see larger-than-life characters live more intensely than the people we know. However, this fact makes special vocal demands on actors. In ordinary conversation a person might use a pitch range of, say, five notes; an actor may be asked to create a character who uses a two-octave range. In the same way, an actor may be asked to provide a much wider range of volume than people in ordinary life.

Just as the body of the actor must be capable of responding to

New York's Carnegie Hall is not as large as some theatres—and its accoustics are legendary. Still, the task of being heard and understood in the last row is an awesome challenge for any beginning actor.

emotional states, so must his or her voice. An amazingly large percentage of the "meaning" conveyed in speech is completely apart from the words employed. Consider the messages we hear which contradict the words, "You naughty boy!" spoken with the laughing lilt which makes it anything but a scolding; "I'm just fine," delivered with a catch in the throat which brings expressions of concern from friends; "I am not a crook!" shouted by a shady politician with a vehemence that raises suspicions nationwide. A good actor's voice can be a transparent medium through which we see and understand the emotional life of the character—in stark contrast to ordinary life, in which we usually work to make our voices a social mask.

The special demands of poetic drama may test the actor in other ways. A single Shakespearean speech may require a character to deliver five to ten lines on one breath—or color the sound in special ways—or laugh and speak simultaneously. Other roles may require special dialects; most professional actors have several dialects ready to use at any time, plus they have an ear good enough to mimic new ones with very little work. All of these techniques must be available to the actor if he or she is to express the fullness of the character's internal life.

That, after all, is the goal of the actor: to be able to express spontaneously and accurately the internal life of the character. To do that, the actor must develop the skill to connect an emotional state to the voice. The subtle power of the voice to communicate emotion can hardly be described, let alone taught. But the serious actor must always work to keep his or her voice responsive to feelings, imagination, and the other workings of the mind.

Mind. The aspect of training which distinguishes the modern actor from his or her predecessor is unquestionably the mental preparation. All actors must have fine memories and good concentration; in addition, the modern actor also must have analytical skills, skills of the imagination, and spontaneity. Particularly in Western drama, the emphasis is upon psychological action: the internal interactions which parallel and sometimes supersede the external action. It was the truth of these internal experiences which Stanislavski emphasized in his theatre and in his training. Subsequent teachers have continued to give great emphasis to the training of the actor's mental equipment.

In the 19th century, the famous American actor Edwin Booth and the equally famous Italian actor Tommasso Salvini toured the United States playing in—among other plays—Shakespeare's *Othello*. One night Booth would play Othello and Salvini would play Iago; the next night they would reverse roles. When one considers that Iago is the longest role Shakespeare ever wrote and Othello is about the third longest (Hamlet is second), the simple feat of memorizing the lines is staggering. But, however remarkable the idea of alternating the two roles was, no contemporary critic thought to comment on the memorization aspects of the feat. The reason was that many actors of that time had memorized both roles—as well as Hamlet. Indeed, the leading actors of the time were usually proficient in as many as a dozen roles—all large— at any one time. They could be proficient in another dozen or so on a few days' notice. Even today, a stage actor is expected to have a good memory. It must be fast; it must be accurate. In the legitimate theatre, an actor with a poor memory is an unemployed actor.

In films and television the need is not nearly as acute. Since films are always shot in very short "takes" and nearly always shot out of sequence, there is little incentive for an actor to memorize the entire part at one time. Stage actors have been known to mock film actors who need "idiot boards" or cue cards out of camera range.

For the legitimate actor, however, the prospect of being onstage for more than two uninterrupted hours is both a cross to bear and the glory of the art. And, of course, it is not just that the actor must memorize the words in the correct order, it is necessary to memorize as well *when* to say them; in short, the cues. Few things can so quickly earn the contempt of one's fellow actors as an uncertain grasp of lines, including an inability to give fellow actors the cues they need.

Another casualty of uncertain lines—and far more important than an annoyed colleague—is the actor's concentration. Attention devoted to trying to remember lines is energy which cannot be dedicated to the actor's primary task—living as fully as possible in the imagined world of the play. One of the basic skills of any actor is the capacity to shut out of his or her field of attention everything not relating to the dramatic action at hand. Like anyone else, an actor has a demanding, complex life offstage, complete with problems and satisfactions. Except in special circumstances, that life must be left in the wings. The actor learns to live exclusively in the play's world for its duration. In addition, the actor must overcome one of the most primary anxieties known to mankind: stage fright. She must train herself to put aside personal concerns and concentrate on a totally artificial situation—while being stared at by hundreds of silent people. The mental discipline needed to do this is difficult to achieve, and actors spend considerable energy developing those concentration skills. Today, many actors practice forms of meditation in order to develop the skill to live totally in the present in the dramatic world of the play while being watched by strangers.

The fallacy still exists that an actor does not *need* analytical skills; after all, the argument goes, between the playwright and the director, the actor is told everything he or she needs to say or do. But this is not quite true. The modern actor especially must be able to read and analyze a playscript accurately, precisely, imaginatively—and sometimes, quickly. Much of the analytical work once done by directors (if at all!) is now expected to be done by the actor himself.

One of the major contributions of Stanislavski and his followers was to see human behavior as purposive—everything people do, however eccentric it may seem to outsiders, is an attempt to achieve particular ends. The same rules apply with even greater rigor to the actions of people in the carefully structured world of the play. Therefore, the actor is trained to ask the following questions from the point of view of the character:

"Who am I?"
"What do I want?" (What is my objective?)
"What am I going to do to achieve it?"
"Where have I come from?"
"Where am I going?"

These questions can only be answered by careful attention to the script and by the application of an analytical process developed through long practice. Gradually, a hierarchy of goals and actions develops for each character: a few lifelong goals become clear, then a midrange goal which operates for the length of the play (a "spine"); then objectives for each scene; and, finally, a series of strategies for achieving goals within each scene. All of these combine to become the *action* of each character. These competing, complementary, or just juxtaposed actions make up the complex life of the play—and, usually, it is the actor who provides the details of that life and thereby gives the work its richness.

As an abbreviated example, imagine a character whose major objective in life is self-definition, to discover who she is. Many things have happened to her, and many things will happen to her in her life. In this segment of that life, however—the segment covered in this play—she must face a major life decision: she must either choose to pursue a promising but uncertain career or marry an attractive young man and give up all thought of a profession. (Our playwright has provided no compromise.) Her decision in this case will certainly define "the kind of person she is." Our heroine will wrestle with this question throughout the play, seeking an answer which should become clear some time before the final curtain. In a particular scene, she may feel that she needs to know how her beloved feels about her prospective profession. She *must* know! But he is being evasive because he doesn't want to say anything which might cause her to love him less.

So the objective of the character in this scene is to get a piece of information. In order to achieve that objective, our heroine may ask the question directly, or employ a number of other tactics. Some of these will be overt and clearly spelled out in the text. Others will be covert or hidden. Action which is not directly illuminated in the dialogue is called *subtext*. Some of the most powerful scenes are those in which the tactics are entirely subtext.

"If I were this character, in this circumstance, how would I react?" This is the question, spoken or implied, to which the actor must constantly address herself. By recalling life experiences, or seeking out new ones, the actor provides the basic information for the process. But it is the actor's imagination which combines that information in ways needed by the play. In matters both large and small the imagination is at work. How would my character light a cigarette? Would he hold a chair for a

---

HOFFMAN'S TRANSFORMATION IN "TOOTSIE"

While he was preparing to film the movie "Tootsie," Dustin Hoffman spent months learning to transform himself into a credible semblance of a woman for the female character he would play, and doing a succession of screen tests to assess how convincing he looked.

At one screen test, he—as Dorothy Michaels, the soap opera star he plays in the film—was improvising in front of the camera when he was asked whether he thought he would ever have children.

In her soft Southern voice, Dorothy said no, she thought she wouldn't be having children. Her interrogator persisted: Why not? "I think it's a little late in the day for that," said Dorothy—and, suddenly overwhelmed, she burst into tears.

"I felt so terrible that I would never have that experience," says Hoffman, his voice still filled with wonderment. "Nothing like that has ever happened to me. I've been acting for—what, nearly 30 years?—and I've never had a moment like that before in my life."

Indeed, Hoffman is a parent several times over: He considers himself the father of his first wife's child by a previous marriage as well as the child they had together, and he has another child with his second wife, who is now pregnant again.

But the role of Dorothy Michaels was a powerful personal experience for Hoffman, plunging him into an intensive self-examination that has changed him in many ways. "I really liked her," he says fervently. "I started to feel about her the way I had never felt about a character before. She made me very emotional, VERY emotional. I still haven't understood it completely."

Reprinted courtesy of *New York Times* News Service, original wire story by Leslie Bennetts, Dec. 26, 1982.

The story on the preceding page illustrates how Dustin Hoffman experienced an important actor/actor interaction during his preparation for his role as Dorothy Michaels in the film *Tootsie*.

lady? Would she hold a baby naturally or clumsily? How would this character respond to news of the death of a loved one? Pursued consistently, this extension of imagination leads the actor to make greater and greater contact with the character. This identification in the realm of feeling has a traditional name: *empathy*. The word literally means "feeling into," and captures the idea that the actor has extended her responses into the character. It also raises the intriguing idea that the character and the actor are interacting. Indeed, actors often report that their lives have been altered as a result of playing specific characters. This level of actor/character interaction is discussed in considerable detail in Chapter 13.

The experienced, well-trained actor has the capacity to explore dramatic situations in still another manner. In the same way that audiences come to the theatre to discover hidden truths about characters during a performance, the director and actor work together to make similar discoveries during rehearsals. A rehearsal technique with strong implications for performance is *improvisation*, a technique which can help actors discover just such hidden truths.

Habit is the enemy of creative insight. So it is that in rehearsal actors and directors may occasionally set up circumstances which demand a spontaneous response: a scene from the play may be paraphrased; a scene that does not exist in the play may be improvised—perhaps two characters who never meet in the play may have an exchange, or characters in the play will be suddenly set in some other circumstances and the actors asked to improvise the resulting scene. The aim is usually not to rewrite the play. Instead, actors and director hope that by changing their circumstances the characters will reveal portions of their personalities which had been hidden. In improvisation, the actors may find themselves listening more closely to what their characters are saying, watching more carefully for external signs of internal interaction; they may, in fact, find their characters saying things which had lurked unspoken in the written script.

Improvisation is not widely used in performance, but the *spontaneity* it fosters is widely appreciated. The dangerous sense that "anything can happen" is one of the primary appeals to live theatre. Actors who are open and responsive to the special circumstances of a particular performance have a quality to which audiences respond; it is also a quality which inspires other actors. So, within limits, the capacity of actors to "change" a performance spontaneously reinforces just those aspects of live theatre which make it attractive in the first place.

THE ACTOR AT WORK

Very few actors work alone. Nearly all work only in the company of other actors, directors, playwrights, designers, and other members of production companies. The various ways in which companies may be organized internally are described in Chapter 4. However, there are two alternative relationships of any company to the larger producing organization. When a contemporary American actor signs a contract to act, he or she will join either a resident company or a production company.

A *resident company* is a group of actors and other artists who live in the same city and work in the same theatre for an extended period of time; their contracts are renewed by the season and they know that they will participate in all, or nearly all, the plays mounted by the theatre in that season. Sometimes the plays are presented serially—that is, one play will open for a run of some weeks; then it will close, to be followed by the next play, and so on. Less frequently, plays will be presented in repertory; a number of plays are readied at one time and presented in a staggered performance schedule which allows a serious patron to see all of the plays in the repertory in a few days. Whichever production scheme a theatre uses, a resident company has many advantages for an actor: he or she is assured of employment for an extended period, a family can put down roots and get to know the community, and the range of plays presented may be a valuable challenge for the actor. The most important value, however, arises from the fact that the members of the company, working closely over an extended period, get to know one another quite well. They come to appreciate each other's strengths and weaknesses; the company can become a well-oiled and supportive organization. Most actors benefit from a close collaboration of this kind.

The more familiar *production company* brings artists together only for a single production and keeps it together only as long as the production runs. In a typical New York show, the actors can gather together to rehearse a new play for four weeks, spend a week or so in previews, open the show and close it a week later. In total, they may have worked together only six or seven weeks—and under the most trying circumstances. Under these conditions, it is a wonder that they can produce the play at all, and no wonder at all that they have little chance to really get to know one another as artists. Working actors may appear in several plays a year under this schedule. If a play is very successful, the actor is usually guaranteed an extended contract. But in exchange for that security he or she must play the same role eight times a week for months or years.

Even when employed, professional actors may find the future so uncertain that they must be constantly on the lookout for other jobs, something that may prevent them from giving full attention to their current job. And they are usually so delighted to have work that they give little thought to the quality of the role or the overall excellence of the script. Sad, but true.

In resident companies, on the other hand, plays are frequently chosen with a particular actor in mind. For example, Shakespeare's company at the Globe was such a resident theatre, and the playwright is thought to have written the roles of Hamlet, Macbeth, and Othello for the special qualities of one of his leading actors, Richard Burbage. Desirable as this may be, the other side of the coin is that some members of a resident company may not be exactly the actors needed for specific roles: as a result, there may be some compromise in the fit between the roles needed and the actors available.

In casting an individual production, however, a director usually has a wide selection of actors from which to choose. The audition procedure can be very exacting.

AUDITIONS AND CASTING

Audition procedures vary widely depending upon the director, the play, the special requirements of the season, the producer, and the actors' union. The director usually has a fairly clear idea of a character's age, size, build, voice type, and other features. The director then sets out to find a single actor—out of perhaps hundreds—who best fits those requirements; the actor sets out to convince the director that he or she is exactly what the director is looking for—or, barring that, to convince that director that her first impression of the role was totally wrong and should be changed to conform to what the actor in front of her does best. To guarantee that all professional actors are given a fair chance at roles, the actor's union, Actors Equity Association, requires that adequate public notice be given of casting and that all interested union members be interviewed. Although the "interviews" may last as little as three minutes each, this interview procedure can take days. The process is so lengthy (and demoralizing for all concerned!) that major theatres may retain a staff member, a casting director, whose sole function it is to find likely candidates for the next step, audition.

In auditions, a director is free to ask an actor to do any number of things from a simple interview, through prepared scenes, to cold readings and improvisations. An extended *interview* allows the director to learn more about the actor as a person. Each actor has already provided the director with a résumé: a short listing of previous roles, a description of his or her training, and a notation of any special skills an actor might have that would not be readily apparent (juggling, karate, musical instruments played, etc.). So, in an interview the director searches for those personal qualities in the actor which might transfer easily and profitably to the character he has in mind. To test the actor's skill, the director may ask her to perform *audition pieces*. These are short monologues or soliloquies which most actors have ready for presentation on short notice. These audition pieces are designed to show the special talents of the actor; all are carefully chosen and polished to perfection.

Even experienced actors may go through an interview process prior to being cast. And the discussions with the director continue throughout the rehearsal period.

In a *cold reading*, the actor is given a copy of the script and asked to read a role (either singly or in a group) from the play. Since the actor may not be familiar with either the play or the role, this is often a harrowing experience. Still, most professional actors are quite good at cold readings; some are absolutely superb! Finally, to test the imagination and spontaneity of the actors, the director may ask each to participate in an *improvised scene* in which the actor is asked to respond with no preparation whatsoever.

The director may continue to call back repeatedly the actors still in contention until he or she has sufficient information to make a decision. Few of the decisions the director will make during the course of production are as important as casting. But, ultimately, a cast list is posted and the cast gathers to begin work.

Rehearsal. The working methods of directors, particularly in the early stages of rehearsal, vary greatly. Depending on the production the group is gathered to prepare, the first work may involve either a great deal of discussion and personal interaction or immediate attention to the work at hand. For example, if the company is preparing a totally improvised piece, they may start with a period of intense introspection, trust exercises, and general orientation to the process of the work at hand. In those companies whose aim is performance of an already finished script, the first work will normally consist of a detailed reading of the script interspersed with discussion of interpretative questions. It is in this period that each actor reaches some preliminary decisions as to the character he or she will be playing. Character relationships are sorted out, the theme of the play is clarified, and the director's *concept* is fully established.

At some point the director usually begins to *block* the show, i.e. establish the general movement patterns of the actors. As the play is blocked, the actors begin to fill out their characterization with *business*, the smaller physical adjustments and manipulation of props required. If the play contains special movement sequences, a specialist may be brought in; a fight director if there are fights, a choreographer if there are dances. If the play contains special vocal problems, experts such as dialect coaches and singing coaches may be employed.

Some directors require that actors arrive at the first rehearsal with the lines memorized; others allow memorization to occur rather late in the rehearsal period. Eventually, however, all the actors must be "off book." Since modern theatres seldom make use of prompters, actors

Rehearsal props: crude approximations of the real things are used until rather late in the rehearsal process. Here Richard Basehart rehearses for the Lincoln Center Repertory Company's 1968 production of Edmond Rostand's *Cyrano de Bergerac*.

must not only be very secure in their lines, but must have some skill in ad libbing out of the inevitable confusion caused by forgotten or misplaced lines.

Because theatres are expensive to rent, rehearsals may be conducted in sparsely furnished rehearsal studios with the furniture indicated by folding chairs, walls and stairs shown by tape on the floor, and all but essential props either mimed or presented by rough rehearsal props. Gradually, however, the *rehearsal props* are replaced by the real thing, and crude rehearsal costumes begin to approximate the actual costumes, which will not arrive until dress rehearsals.

Late in rehearsals, technical rehearsals begin. These are held in the actual theatre on the actual set. As they progress, lights, sound, and properties are added until the show can be run fairly smoothly from beginning to end.

The last and most elaborate rehearsals are *dress rehearsals*. In these, all aspects of production are as they will be when the public experiences the production. The actors are fully costumed and made up. Such consumables as cigarettes and food are provided to be smoked or eaten. The lighting, sound, and setting are defined and provided with detail until the right mood is achieved and the right environment created. During the very last dress rehearsals, some invited audience members may be provided to give the actors some idea of what they may expect from the public: where applause and laughs may occur, how the presence of an audience may affect their nerves.

Performance. Once a play opens, the actor really begins acting; everything preceding this point has been rehearsal. The play is now truly in the hands of the actors. Once the curtain goes up there is really very little a playwright, a designer, or a director can do. The other members of the company may even feel a trifle superfluous as they see well-trained, committed actors take and hold the attention of the audi-

Even in scenes of intense emotion, when it appears that the actors are totally involved with their characters, there is still considerable actor/actor interaction. Here Ian D. Clark and Marie Romain Aloma are seen from the wings during a production of August Strindberg's *Easter* as produced by Theatre Compact.

ence. The playwright may decide to alter a line here, a scene there; a director will take notes during each performance and praise or criticize the actors in an effort to improve their performance. But it is the actor who ultimately steps out of the darkened wings onto the lighted stage and signs the performance contract with the audience.

It would, however, be misleading to suggest that the only interaction during a performance is between the individual actors and the audience and between characters in the play. Even in the midst of the most engrossing, the most intense scene, there is significant actor/actor interaction.

It would be both interesting and amusing for an audience member to hear the silent dialogue that takes place between even deeply involved actors during a performance. It might sound like this:

SHE: The chair is farther downstage than usual; I hope he notices.
HE: Who knocked this chair off its marks? I'll have to cross upstage instead of downstage.
SHE: Good cross!
HE: Stay open, I'll just lean farther into the scene.
SHE: Hey, I like it when you crowd me a little. It makes the fear easier.
HE: Wow, she's really afraid tonight. I'll really browbeat her! I won't quite let her finish her line.
SHE: He's never been this mean to me before. This is great!
HE: My god! She's crying.
SHE: My god! I'm crying.
HE: Wow! She is a fine actress!
SHE: Oh—I do love this play!
HE: God! I love this profession.

At some level, the audience understands and appreciates it when actors are working well and thoroughly enjoying their work—just as actors know when audiences are enjoying the experience. Those moments, while all too rare, are so precious to the actor that much of the grief of a life in theatre can not only be forgiven but cherished. The years of training, the endless memorization, the uncertainty of the profession, the grueling hours, the personal insecurity, all of these fade into insignificance when two actors are connecting with each other, with absorbing characters, and an appreciative audience. In moments like that some actors maintain that the relationship becomes more than interaction—it becomes unity. Actor, character, and audience merge into a single ecstatic whole that has neither parts nor dimension. In those rare moments the actor finds complete justification.

Discussion Questions

1. Do you have friends or acquaintances who are outstanding performers (dare we call them actors?) in ordinary life? In what social situations are these performers most effective? Do people encourage them?

2. What are the materials of the actor?

3. There are books on acting which exhort a would-be actor to "Stop acting!" What do you imagine is meant by this?

4. Some actors are more effective on the screen than on the stage; others are more successful on the stage. Why do you think this is the case?

5. What is meant by the term "social mask"?

6. Obviously an actor does not need to have experienced everything he or she is expected to portray on the stage (what about death?). But is is possible for an actor to have had too little personal experience? Explain.

7. Can you think of other situations which demand the concentration skills of an actor?

8. What is "action" as it is defined by the actor?

9. Note and explain the difference between these two questions as they might be asked by an actor:

   "If I were in these circumstances, how would I react?" and

   "If I were the character in these circumstances, how would I react?"

6

The Playwright

The confusion about what a playwright actually *does* begins with the name. We frequently see the noun incorrectly spelled playwrite. This form emphasizes the mechanical act of putting words on paper—and therein lies the confusion.

Whatever literary skills are demanded, the playwright is less concerned with writing down plays than he or she is in "constructing" plays—hence, the suffix *-wright* is especially descriptive. We find it in such terms as *wheelwright* ("one who makes wheels"), *wainwright* ("one who builds wagons") or *shipwright*. Therefore, it makes better sense to think of a playwright as a theatre craftsperson constructing dramatic ideas than it does to model him or her after a poet or a journalist. Many successful playwrights were, like Shakespeare, superb literary artists whose work would have lived and been admired even if it had never been produced in the theatre. However, many wonderful poets, novelists, and historians have tried to write plays—and failed miserably. They learned that the role of playwright requires some special skills for success—perhaps even a special way of viewing the world.

THE PLAYWRIGHT AND THE COMPANY

Rarely is the playwright a physical member of the theatrical company. There have been playwrights who were fully part of a company: Shakespeare and Molière were members of theatrical troupes and wrote parts with specific actors in mind, including roles for themselves. Even today there are examples of playwrights who have directed or acted in their own plays. But in most cases the playwright is an uncomfortable member of the company at best.

Part of the tension arises from the popular perception that the playwright's task is already completed when the company begins its work. This may not be factually correct, of course; companies have begun rehearsing act 1 when act 3 was still being written. Or massive rewrites may be undertaken while the play is in rehearsal—or even during preview performances. But the feeling remains: the original conceptual work by the playwright is usually long finished by the time the actors see the script. This leads to a second source of conflict between the company and the playwright.

Any playwright has a mental image of how his or her play should look and sound. In some cases, the image is very clear indeed, and has been developed with a huge personal investment over a long period of time. Sadly, the precise details of this very personal image cannot be conveyed in the script; even if they could be, the artistic goals of the directors, designers, and actors might not be those of the playwright. In short, the stage is set for a monumental series of communication failures: anything the company does is bound to be at least slightly different from what the playwright envisioned. If it is less effective, the playwright is disappointed; if it is *more* effective he or she is offended. This is normal. The history of new plays in production is often a volatile one: it includes playwrights raging at directors and actors for destroying a promising script, directors furious at meddling writers who "don't understand the theatre," and explosive scenes which end with the playwright walking out in high dudgeon or being excluded from rehearsals by a director or producer trying to salvage some semblance of a calm working environment. The basic conflict always returns to a fundamental question: who is the creative artist and who is the interpretative artist?

There are, then, two ways of considering the role of the playwright: the more traditional view is that he or she is an original, creative artist whose ideas are fully captured in script form, later to be interpreted by a theatrical company. Two knowledgeable, contemporary scholars state this line of argument very clearly as follows:

> Like symphonies, most plays are written to be performed, but the potential performance is complete in the playwright's words, just as the melody, harmony, rhythm, tempo, and orchestration "are" in the composer's written score. . . . Both symphonies and plays are forever-possible-but-never-to-be-realized performances, "ideal" performances in the philosophical sense, inherent in the score or script and independent of the artists who perform them.*

Such a view makes the playwright the primary artist, and dooms all the other theatre artists to the hopeless task of trying to capture that "ideal" performance on stage.

The alternative is to see the playwright as a crucial member of the collaborative group which creates theatre. In this second view, the playwright is the source of ideas that are ultimately made manifest by actors, directors, designers—indeed, the remainder of the theatrical company.

This book emphatically takes the latter view. In Western theatre, all but a tiny minority of theatrical productions begin with a written script. But all over the world there are plays produced which have no "script"—certainly not one that has been written down and published. Preindustrial societies such as the native American, Australian aboriginal, as well as the folk theatre traditions of Africa, Asia, and Latin America produce plays that are serious works of art—yet have no "script." In these situations the traditions are so well known that every member of the performance company—not to mention the audience—knows "what happens next." The "script" is, in fact, part of the community's oral tradition: there probably never was a single playwright, and none is really needed, as these plays are revived, year after year, as part of the society's cultural tradition.

The simple observation that the playwright is not essential to the art of theatre should not mislead anyone into undervaluing the enormous contribution of playwrights. It is unthinkable that the highly developed theatre traditions of the Orient and the West could have developed as they have without playwrights. Indeed, when the great intellectual and artistic figures of Western civilization are listed, it is humbling to see how many are playwrights: Aeschylus, Sophocles, Euripides, Aris-

---

*Reinert, Otto and Arnott, Peter. *Thirteen Plays: An Introductory Anthology* (New York: Little, Brown, 1978), p. 4.

tophanes, Shakespeare, Racine, Molière, Goethe, Shaw—the list goes on and on. And the huge majority were closely attached to specific producing companies.

Given this fact of history, doesn't it make perfect sense for contemporary playwrights to form even closer associations with theatrical companies? Perhaps. Yet in some important sense, the role of the playwright is better served from outside the company.

It can be useful for a playwright to know well the company for whom he or she writes. Roles can be created to match the talents available to play them; spectacle can be restricted to the scenic resources at hand, themes and language can be shaped to the proven interests of the audience which this company attracts. But these points have their counterbalancing disadvantages: mediocre acting talents may inspire the creation of only mediocre characters; limited technical resources will encourage a reduced vision; predictable audience response may lead to formula plays. When we note that Shakespeare and Molière were members of companies, we ought not forget the numberless, unremembered hacks who were *also* members of companies. Perhaps some of these poor devils would have made a greater creative contribution if they had *not* been so close to the producing artists.

Theatre companies, when all is said and done, can be remarkably isolated and artificial collections of people. Good playwrights write best about things they know best; if they know only about the theatre, their vision of life will be at best only secondhand. As one critic noted after viewing a festival of student films: "They aren't making films about life; they are making films about other films!" Another scholar has said: "You can't make theatre out of theatre."

A major function of the playwright lies in his or her connection not with the company but with the audience. The artist may, in fact, be the "antennae of society," an advance scout whose job it is to detect danger or opportunities before the rest of us can. The playwright serves as an extension of that part of society's collective nervous system which we call the group imagination. His or her job is to imagine what the rest of us cannot or will not—and to share that vision with us through theatrical means. Sometimes the vision the playwright offers is nothing more than a minor twist on familiar events; the result is a diverting novelty with no important consequences. At other times, the vision is one that crowds up out of our darkest unconscious and leaves us shattered, off-balance, or renewed.

THE PLAYWRIGHT AND THE AUDIENCE

The playwright's imagination and expressive skills serve as a catalyst: they trigger reactions at many levels. To the audience, the playwright serves as a storyteller, a guide, a psychiatrist, sometimes an adversary. He or she must be able to tell a story which has clarity, internal probability, interesting characters, suspense, and dramatic structure. In addition, it might have amusing dialogue, arresting ideas, and a well-supported point of view concerning a social problem. Much of this is in the realm of craft and, in general, the craft of the good storyteller must be present even when the playwright aspires to additional roles.

Psychiatrists have often noted that the role of playwright is akin to that of God: with no blasphemy intended, the playwright parallels Genesis by creating an entire world—out of nothing. This world lives in bits and pieces within a playwright's head until, painstakingly, the parts begin to appear on paper. In such a case, the playwright becomes a guide to that world and we, the audience or reader, become tourists. We are led—at first tentatively, then with greater confidence—into a world that appears complete and whole. Like any good guide, the playwright shows us the major sights and helps us understand the rules of this new world, the customs which govern the behavior of people there. He or she, like any good guide, may even lead us around aspects of the new world that might bore, confuse, or upset us for no purpose. At the conclusion of the tour, we return to our own worlds with the same benefits of foreign travel at its best: We understand our own world and ourselves better—because we know of some alternatives.

Sometimes, the world into which we move is our own internal one. The playwright who arranges such a journey assumes a role rather like a psychiatrist: eliciting information from us, asking the provocative questions at the proper time, simply "being there" during the rough moments. At other times, such a playwright may simply present us with an evocative symbol and ask the most demanding question of all: "What do you see?"

Another role which has achieved some popularity in the last century is that of adversary. In this stance the playwright sets out to show the audience things it would not, under normal circumstances, want to see or hear. In fact, such a playwright may be challenging some important value held by the audience—or even its entire view of the world. The strategies employed by adversarial playwrights may vary: after writing several straightforward, hard-hitting, and largely unpopular plays, George Bernard Shaw turned to a series of witty, warm, and thoroughly enjoyable plays which just as effectively savaged the values of his comfortable middle-class audiences. These audience members smiled and laughed through plays which, they later realized, had raised serious doubts about the real world which they themselves had created and sustained.

Some modern playwrights have not shown the same finesse. Handke's *Assaulting the Audience* is a one-act, one-character harangue against everything which a bourgeois audience might find valuable. With a little less venom, the Living Theatre's production of *Paradise Now!* mocked and parodied the middle-class American values the company found so restrictive.

One may reasonably ask why any audience would choose to attend a play in which they are attacked—and attacked in a context in which they will find it difficult to fight back. Clearly, such audiences have compensating reasons for attending: social prestige, an amusing evening of the kind provided by Shaw, loyalty to the theatre company, and others. It may even be that such an audience member already has unspoken doubts and is not so thoroughly committed to the values under attack as the playwright may assume.

Give-and-take between the playwright and the audience is not so immediate or so inevitable as that between the actor and the audience. But interaction does occur. Obviously a decidedly negative response to a play may convince the playwright not to attempt *that* form again. But history provides better examples: In 1879 Henrik Ibsen created a furor with *A Doll's House*. The inciting incident was the final scene, in which a woman leaves her husband and children because her integrity is being stifled. Furious editorials exploded all over Europe as the guardians of conventional thinking thundered that no woman should *ever* leave her family. They even accused Ibsen of being a feminist! Ibsen listened to all of this with Nordic forbearance; then—in 1881—he published *Ghosts*, a play about a woman who does *not* leave her husband. Of course, Ibsen nicely stacked the deck: this woman experiences every humiliation at the hands of her philandering husband and, at the conclusion of the play, is forced to watch her adored son go mad from congenital syphilis. Ibsen's critics got the message.

The history of theatre, like the history of ideas in general, is marked by an interaction between playwrights and their audiences. Successful playwrights are giving audiences what they want and need; to that de-

Henrik Ibsen as he appeared in 1896. Together with August Strindberg, he is credited with changing the direction of Western drama.

gree, playwrights are a product of their audiences. But the best playwrights are also shaping the tastes, interests, values, and—to some degree, at least—the actions of audiences. Hence the influences are reciprocal. In this way, the influence of the playwright can be far greater than any other of the individual theatre artists—if he or she can find a meaningful dramatic idea and translate it into theatrical terms.

THE PLAYWRIGHT AND THE SCRIPT

The idea that the inexperienced reader should be able to make theatrical sense of a playscript is a relatively recent one. It was only toward the second half of the 19th century that important playwrights such as Ibsen, Strindberg, and Shaw—in some cases keenly aware that their plays would not be immediately produced—began to write for a reader's market. As they did, they began to provide much more information than would previously have been provided in a script intended for production. Careful and detailed stage directions, complete descriptions of settings, and penetrating character sketches all allowed a reader to create in his or her mind what would have been obvious had that person been able to attend a full production. The practice continues today. Shakespeare, knowing that he would be in rehearsal to choreograph a fight scene, could include only the cryptic stage direction, "They fight."

By contrast, here is how Noel Coward describes a particularly effective spat in his play, *Private Lives:*

AMANDA: Ridiculous ass.

ELYOT: I beg your pardon?

AMANDA: I said ridiculous ass!

ELYOT: (with great dignity) Thank you very much indeed. (He drinks the brandy and turns upstage and stands in the waist of the piano looking at a magazine.)

(Amanda rises, crosses to the radiogram and changes the record for a particularly noisy one. She returns to the settee and sits.)

You'd better turn that off, I think. It's very late and it will annoy the people upstairs.

AMANDA: There aren't any people upstairs. It's a photographer's studio.

ELYOT: There are people downstairs, I suppose?

AMANDA: They're away in Tunis.

ELYOT: This is no time of the year for Tunis. (He crosses to the radiogram and turns it off, walks back to the piano and continues to look at his magazine.)

AMANDA: (icily) Turn it on again, please.

ELYOT: I'll do no such thing.

AMANDA: Very well, if you insist on being boorish and idiotic. (She rises, crosses to the radiogram and turns it on again even louder than before. She takes a few dance steps to bring her in front of the L end of the settee.)

(Elyot turns the pages of his magazine with increasing speed.)

ELYOT: (slamming the magazine down on the piano) Turn it off. It's driving me mad.

AMANDA: (shouting) You're far too temperamental. Try to control yourself.

ELYOT: (shouting) Turn it off!

AMANDA: I won't.

(Elyot rushes down to the upstage side of the radiogram. Amanda crosses below the tub chair to the downstage side of the radiogram. She arrives as Elyot scratches the sound-box across the record. He steps back. Amanda picks up the record and stands with it in her hand, her back to the radiogram.)

There now, you've ruined the record. (She scrutinizes it.)

ELYOT: Good job, too.

AMANDA: Disagreeable pig.

ELYOT: (taking a step to her, suddenly stricken with remorse) Amanda darling —Sollocks.

AMANDA: (furiously) Sollocks yourself! (She breaks the record over his head.)

ELYOT: (staggering) You spiteful little beast! (He slaps her face.)

(Amanda screams loudly and hurls herself sobbing with rage into the tub chair.)

AMANDA: (wailing) Oh, oh, oh —

ELYOT: (crossing to R of her and kneeling) I'm sorry. I didn't mean it—I'm sorry, darling, I swear I didn't mean it.

AMANDA: Go away, go away, I hate you!

ELYOT: Amanda—listen—listen—

AMANDA: (swinging her R arm and hitting him backhand) Listen indeed; I'm sick and tired of listening to you, you damned sadistic bully. (She rises.)

ELYOT: (rising and walking upstage; with grandeur) Thank you. (He stalks towards the door in stately silence.)

(Amanda throws a cushion out of the tub chair. It misses him. He laughs falsely.)

A pretty display, I must say.

AMANDA: (taking two cushions from the settee and hurling them at him; wildly) Stop laughing like that.

ELYOT: Very amusing indeed.

AMANDA: (losing control) Stop—stop—stop—(she rushes upstage round the L end of the settee throwing another cushion at him. It passes him and hits the lilies on the piano.)

(Elyot pushes Amanda and she knocks over the chair L of the table. She makes a rush at Elyot and he knocks over the chair R of the table.)

I hate you—do you hear? You're conceited, and overbearing, and utterly impossible! (She rushes towards the double doors.)

ELYOT: (meeting Amanda and grasping her by the shoulders; shouting her down) You're a vile-tempered, loose-living, wicked little beast, and I never want to see you again as long as I live. (He pushes her.)

(Amanda staggers back, knocks over the drinks trolley and sits with a bump on the small settee up L. There is a pause. She rises.)

AMANDA: (very quietly) This is the end, do you understand? The end, finally and forever. (She starts for the double doors.)

(Elyot meets her at the doors and grabs her by the arms.)

ELYOT: You're not going like this.

AMANDA: Oh, yes I am.

ELYOT: You're not.

AMANDA: I am; let go of me. (She pushes him in the chest.)

(Elyot staggers backwards downstage. Amanda follows him a few steps.)

(Breathlessly) You're a cruel fiend, and I hate and loathe you. (She turns and rushes to the double doors and opens them. Sibyl and Victor are standing outside the doors.) Thank God I've again realized in time what you're really like. Marry you again, never, never, never—I'd rather die in torment—

ELYOT:. (rushing after Amanda, grabbing her round the waist and pulling her backwards towards the settee) Shut up; shut up; I wouldn't marry you again if you came crawling to me on your bended knees—

(They turn and Amanda goes over backwards onto the settee with Elyot on top of her.)

—you're a mean, evil-minded, little vampire—I hope to God I never set eyes on you again as long as I live.

(Amanda and Elyot roll onto the floor. Amanda, on top, bangs his head on the floor. He hits her behind.)

AMANDA: (rising and crossing L; screaming) Beast; brute, swine; cad; beast; beast; brute; devil—

(Elyot grasps her foot as she passes and she falls. They both rise and stand screaming at each other. Victor and Sibyl enter the room quietly and stand just inside the double doors, staring at Elyot and Amanda in horror. Simultaneously, Elyot dashes to the door down R and Amanda to the door down L as—

THE CURTAIN FALLS*

Coward is also being particularly careful in describing this scene (which he himself originally staged—and in which he played the role of Elyot) because he knows it will be performed by amateur actors who will need all the help he can give. You may be certain that the original manuscript was far more laconic.

Basically, the group for which a playwright writes is not the reader, or even the audience member, but the production company. The playwright is attempting to communicate his or her ideas as clearly and provocatively as possible to the group of people who will bring them to life on stage.

The word *provocatively* is important here. We have already used the word *catalyst* to describe how a playwright functions; like the chemical equivalent, the catalytic power of the playwright is his or her ability to trigger important reactions elsewhere. Some of the most important ones are those triggered in the production company.

A script is necessarily incomplete. It is often no more than an outline for a play. True, it contains all the dialogue, but it gives only the barest

*Reprinted with permission of Samuel French, Inc. Copyright 1930 by Noel Coward.

STAGE GEOGRAPHY

There is a continuing need for consistency in providing directions. Therefore, theatre people have adopted the following rules: stage directions are always given from the point of an actor standing on stage and facing the audience. Therefore, the direction *stage left* (or just *left*) would indicate the side of the stage to the *audience's right; stage right* is the *audience's left*.

Combined with these are the terms *upstage* and *downstage* (or just *up* and *down*). *Upstage* means away from the audience; *downstage* means towards the audience.

These four terms—plus the straightforward *center stage*—allow a playwright or director to describe the plane of the stage floor with enough accuracy to communicate with actors. For example, the stage directions *upstage center* (UC) indicates the position in the center of the stage farthest from the audience; *downstage right* (or *down right*) refers to the area of the stage closest to the audience and farthest to their left. Taken together, the five terms can easily be combined to describe fifteen areas on the stage as shown in the accompanying diagram.

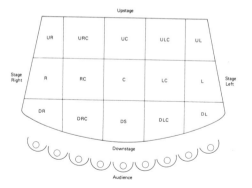

One may well ask what happens when a play is given an *arena* production; with the audience on all sides, the system collapses. So directors and actors have to fall back on field expedients. The most common solution is to simply designate one side of the acting area as *downstage* and work from there; another device is to name all entrances according to the compass (north, south, etc.), or else number them, and give all stage directions in terms of entrances.

The huge majority of scripts, however, describe productions for proscenium arch staging. It is necessary, therefore, for readers to remember always that an experienced playwright is describing the visual aspects of productions *as they relate to the actor standing on the stage facing the audience.*

idea of how that dialogue might be delivered. It may have a verbal description of the stage setting, but the finished setting will convey a great deal more information to the audience than the written description. The power of a good script is the power to inspire a good company to produce a great performance. It may not seem fair—and many writers have raged against the pattern—but the truth remains: playwrights live most authentically through the work of others. They deal with audiences only through intermediaries. To be great, a playwright must first inspire other artists to be great.

In the same way, a symphonic composer has not achieved his or her goal until perhaps one hundred other people have decided to play their individual instruments according to some instructions set down on paper. The conductor waving his or her arms at the front tells them when to follow the next instruction, and how.

The comparison with the score of a symphony has another parallel: it takes considerable skill to look at the notes printed on a page and imagine how the symphony might sound. In much the same way, the script of a play demands certain skills of a reader. We should not be surprised when a person who has only read a play finally sees it performed well and exclaims: "I had no idea that the playwright had all that in mind." Maybe the playwright did *not* have all that in mind—but he or she provided enough provocative material that the remainder of the company could elaborate on the outline of the script. Everyone hopes the playwright was pleased by the result.

THE PROCESS OF THE PLAYWRIGHT

Earlier, we noted that the job of the playwright is to imagine what the rest of us cannot—or will not—and to share that vision with us through theatrical means. The last three words are the ones which mark a person as a playwright; poets, novelists, songwriters, painters, all share a vision of the world—but only a playwright shares it through theatrical means. What are those "theatrical means"?

Back in chapter 1, we noted that theatre employs the mode of enactment—actors and actresses pretend to be people other than themselves, doing what those fictitious people would do. And now we are saying that the script is something akin to a list of instructions to those actors—and other members of the company. The playwright hopes that those "instructions" will be followed; in addition, he or she hopes that those "instructions" will provoke a series of secondary activities which fill out and expand the original idea.

But how does someone go about achieving such an extraordinary task? Fortunately, there are some general observations which any playwright can keep in mind.

Sources. Where does one get an idea for a play? The conventional wisdom is that ideas for works of art appear from nowhere, utterly consuming the artist until he or she expresses them; hence the idea of inspiration as a divine influence "breathed into" an artist.

The truth is, as always, more complicated. Some scriptwriters never have to dream up ideas; some, like writers for television series, work on ideas that others have generated. Others accept commissions to write pieces on historical figures or famous events. Most playwrights, however, find themselves set to work by original ideas arising from unlikely parts of their experience. These ideas are usually incomplete at first and may be totally unfocused. There is just something about an incident, a phrase, a visual image which seizes and holds the attention of the writer; he or she cannot get rid of it. Sometimes the initiating idea is so apparently trivial and the attention it demands so consuming that the playwright is the first to describe her response as obsessive.

A common thread in this process is the kind of incident which starts the sequence: it is almost always strongly embedded in human affairs; it is about people interacting with their world. The would-be playwright is attracted to human action—what people want, why they want it, what obstacles they encounter en route to their goals. Partly, this is a habitual mind set: upon hearing or seeing (or hearing of) a particular human action, the playwright says, "Why would a person do such a thing? What happens next? What do the other people say, and do, and feel?" In short, they begin to spin the incident into a plot.

As an example, the experience that led Peter Shaffer to write his prizewinning play *Equus* came from hearing a very brief account of a teenage boy who had gouged out the eyes of a number of horses. The very brevity of the story was part of the inspiration, since it suggested no reason for this apparently pointless act of cruelty. Like the central figure in his about-to-be-written play—a psychiatrist—Shaffer himself began to probe the realm of apparently pointless violence.

Of course, a would-be novelist might do the same. The difference is that a playwright begins to see and hear the action in the present tense—as an audience might. Sometimes a striking visual image first leaps to mind; sometimes it is a sound, a smell, a texture. But always there are people involved—doing things, asking questions, confronting one another, thwarting, abetting, conspiring. And haunting the play-

EQUUS *(1973)* by Peter Shaffer

Equus seems well on its way to becoming a classic. Since its premiere in 1973, it has received great critical acclaim and popular success. It won a Tony award for "best play" in 1975; it has been made into a film; it continues to be widely produced by both professional and amateur companies. The play has also been at the center of a lively exchange of letters to *The New York Times* on the subject of the assertion that it can be barbarous for a psychiatrist to cure some patients. The groundwork is laid, then, for *Equus* to live forever in college drama anthologies.

That is not why it is included here. Our interest derives from Shaffer's attempt to explore the ecstatic roots of religion and his decision to use theatre in the process. In doing so, he not only reminds us that theatre was there at the beginning, but also shows us how modern theatre techniques still display that ancient magic.

Of course, Shaffer is not always successful. As critics have noted, Dr. Dysarte's dilemma—if it has any ethical validity at all—is almost talked to death; rather than empathize with the good doctor, we are tempted to dismiss him as still another windy, middle-aged neurotic. Alan's psychosis is given more coherence and validity than it deserves, perhaps. Maybe the subject matter is exploited. And, granted, the required nude scene is a throwback to the experimental theatre of the sixties. No matter. Shaffer is reaching for something hidden deep within the collective memory of our species. That takes nerve—and for his courage alone, much may be forgiven him.

At the very least, we are left with a fine example of skillful playcrafting in which the representational and presentational elements of theatre are mixed, storytelling is raised to a high art, ritual is fused with naturalistic acting, and a shared adventure is created.

This last is illustrated by an event actually experienced by this author. The scene was a Friday night performance of *Equus* in a New York theatre. Anthony Hopkins was playing Dysarte under circumstances which were less than ideal. It was a rainy evening, which meant that the curtain was late going up; it also meant that audience members were arriving in rain gear, which they proceeded to shake out and fold in the vestibules at the head of each aisle before crowding into their seats with many muttered apologies and other exchanges with those already in place. And, as always, the street noises of wet New York were adding their distractions to the general confusion. Still, the actors maintained their concentration through the opening minutes of the play. But when the first big scene between Dysarte and Alan was about to begin, Hopkins paused for a moment; he turned to the audience and said, "Why don't we wait—while you settle down." He said it without anger, but with a tone which conveyed the seriousness of the occasion. He was saying, in effect, "There is really no point in going on with this experiment unless the audience is prepared to gives its total concentration, too." He was like a responsible surgeon refusing to undertake a dangerous operation unless the conditions were, if not perfect, at least acceptable. In this case, Hopkins understood his audience very well. The last of the stragglers seated themselves and stowed their gear. Cough drops were inserted into mouths. Noses were blown. And the audience, did, indeed, settle down. Hopkins simply stood, apparently lost in thought, but completely in character during the several minutes that this took. And then the delicate operation continued.

Peter Shaffer is quite exact about the setting for *Equus*. The acting space is a bare wooden square surrounded on three sides with a railing which gives it the feeling both of a boxing ring and a horse showing arena. The whole square is set on a turntable in such a way that the actors can revolve it. He wants the audience to surround this area; in a proscenium theatre, he asks that banks of audience seating be placed upstage of the acting area. The actors who are not in the scene remain in sight, sitting on benches on either side of the acting space.

The first image of the play is a tableau; in a pool of light, Alan Strang, the young man we will meet later, is seen with his cheek against the neck of the horse Nugget. The horses throughout are played by their actors wearing steel

wire hooves and a steel and leather horse mask on their heads. No attempt is ever made to disguise the fact that the horses are being represented by actors.

As the picture of Alan and Nugget fades, the lights reveal Dr. Dysarte downstage. As he smokes, he tells the audience that he was haunted by the image of the boy and the horse. He explains that his life is at a crisis point: he is a staff child psychiatrist in a provincial mental hospital, and he has come to doubt his ability—or even his right—to deal with the emotional and mental problems of children. To illustrate the state in which he finds himself, Dysarte begins to tell the audience about the case of Alan Strang. The remaining action of the play is essentially flashback. Dysarte is both narrator and participant, and moves quickly back and forth between both roles. In addition, Dysarte's scenes with Alan contain secondary flashbacks in which Alan is in both the scene with Dysarte and the earlier scene he is describing.

Dysarte begins with the time when he first learned of the crime and the young man in question; he is approached by Heather Salomon, a children's court magistrate, who presumes on their friendship by asking Dysarte to see the boy and attempt to understand what has driven the lad to blind six horses with a steel hoof pick. She explains that the other judges in her court are so revolted by the crime that without Dysarte's help, Alan will spend a long term in prison—when he is obviously mentally ill. Will Dysarte see him? The doctor is intrigued by the case and persuaded by his friend to make room for the boy in his heavy schedule.

Dr. Dysarte meets Alan for the first time in a scene which is marked by decidedly one-way communication. Dysarte tries to establish some kind of contact; Alan sings television commercial jingles. Beneath it all, however, Alan is hearing at least some of what Dysarte is saying.

Dysarte shares with the audience a dream he had the night following his meeting with Alan. He is the high priest in some primitive, golden age. Dressed in an elaborate costume, including a golden mask, he has an enormously important job: an almost endless line of children is presented to him, held over a stone altar by two assistant priests; his job is to cut the entrails out of the children and drop them to the floor where the future is read from the pattern they make. Dysarte is very good at this, but he is becoming nauseated by the job. He dares not let the assistant priests know his feelings—because if they sense any doubt on his part, he will be disemboweled himself. But the horror is growing and the mask is slipping.

Dysarte learns from the nurses that Alan is having terrible nightmares. Alan has begun to communicate—though in a very elliptical style. Sensing that there may be some tension in the home, Dysarte meets with the parents.

Mrs. Strang is entirely mystified by the crime. She notes that Alan has always loved horses, had pictures of them in his room, and, as a child, had demanded to have horse stories read to him—particularly references from the Bible. Alan spent hours watching television, especially westerns; however, since his father does not approve of television, the son and mother conspired to have him watch at a neighbor's house. Dysarte's suspicions are confirmed: the mother is strongly religious and the father is an atheist. In matters of sex, Alan has little or no education, but his mother has urged him to prepare for a "higher love."

Dysarte strikes a bargain with Alan. He will answer one of Alan's questions for each of his that Alan answers. Alan's questions are penetrating, and the doctor finds himself revealing more than he intended. But finally, Dysarte gets Alan to tell—and to relive—the moment on the beach when, as a small boy, he had seen his first horse in the flesh and had even ridden a little on his back. From the language he uses, it is easy to see that for Alan, the experience was one with strong sexual overtones. And he resents his father for having been the one to pull him roughly from the horse's back and to rage at the young horseman who had provided the ride.

Now we meet Dalton, the owner of the stables. From him, Dysarte learns that Alan was first introduced by Jill Mason, a girl who worked in the stables. Dalton reports that Alan was a good worker, but never rode the horses . . . though the owner was always suspicious that someone was riding them at night.

Dysarte has given Alan a tape recorder so that he can anonymously speak of what is on his mind. From the tape, Dysarte learns that Alan talks with the horses.

Alan's father tells Dysarte that Alan has long, Old Testament-like genealogies made up for his mythical horses, and that the genealogies end with, "I give you Equus, my only begotten son." Mr. Strang also says that, on the night of the crime, Alan was out with a girl—but refuses to reveal how he knows.

Dysarte has hypnotised Alan, and now he discovers the truth of his midnight rides. Alan acts out the secrecy and excitement of the experience. The rides are a mixture of religious and sexual ecstasy in which Alan communes with the spirit of all horses: Equus. In a riveting scene, Alan mounts Nugget and "rides" furiously, declaiming his biblical texts, as the turntable revolves.

In the second act, Dysarte reveals to the audience that he knows what will "cure" Alan, but that he has severe doubts about what a "cure" would mean. It would mean removing from the boy all the things that give his life meaning, severing all the rich, mythic filaments which sustain Alan in his punishing and otherwise meaningless world. Dysarte confesses that he envies the very connectedness which he will destroy in Alan.

But do it he must. He tells Alan that he is giving him a "truth drug"—really only a placebo—and Alan begins to enact the whole story of the night in question. Jill had coaxed Alan into taking her out. They had gone to a movie in a neighboring village—a pornographic film. And there Alan meets his father. His vision of his demanding and perfectionist father is totally destroyed. Later that night, Jill takes him to the stables and invites him to make love to her. In the stable—which she cannot know is the Temple of Equus!—Alan is confused and unable to complete the sex act. Jill tries to reassure him, but he becomes more and more upset. He believes he has betrayed Equus, and the eyes of the horses looking out of their box stalls reproach him. They have become the eyes of an implacable, avenging god. And the desperate Alan feels he can only slash at them and all they represent. At the end of the scene, he is lying on the floor screaming, "Find me. Kill me!" and stabbing at his own eyes with the invisible hoof pick.

But the final image of the play is not Alan. It is Dysarte. Alone in his light, he says, ". . . I cannot know what I do—yet I do essential things. Irreversible, terminal things. I stand in the dark with the pick in my hand, striking at heads!" And then he adds: "I need—more desperately than my children need me—a way of seeing in the dark."

wright! These people, these characters, begin intruding into his or her life, taking on a life of their own. Some playwrights have even gone so far as to confess that they first sat down at the typewriter to exorcise those characters!

But back to our original question: what starts off this whole train of events? There is no rule. Shaffer found his in a story told by a traveling companion: other playwrights report sources as divergent as childhood memories, chance encounters on planes, jokes, historical records, or existing sources such as novels, poems, and songs. The start can be less than inspirational: excellent work has been done by writers commissioned to do a piece on a given topic; beginning the task as drudgery, they soon found themselves fired up by the project and becoming personally involved.

Ultimately, that may be the secret: personal involvement. If the topic is one which, for whatever reason, captures the attention of the playwright in some personal way, there is a good chance it will do the same for an audience—if it is cast into a theatrically satisfying form.

Getting Underway.   How a playwright begins to transform a dramatic idea into a potential theatre piece is highly personal. At the very least it depends upon the form of play the playwright has adopted as a possible model. (See chapter 11, "The Form of the Experience.") For example, a highly structured, linear play such as a murder mystery is dependent upon plot; in such a case, the playwright would probably begin by roughing out the plot, turning to other elements only later. If the finished play aims to be a penetrating portrait of a personality, character elements might come first. A topically organized play might start with a series of striking, but disconnected, images. Each writer probably employs a different method of getting started.

Plot. The incidents that link together to make up the plot of a play can usually be organized in a number of alternative ways. Some playwrights jot all the "incidents" appropriate to the basic dramatic action on three-by-five-inch cards. These cards are then fastened to a wall or other surface in such a way as to provide visual continuity. (In films and television, the finished display is called a storyboard, and usually contains quick sketches of the action as it would be seen by a camera.) The value of a storyboard of this kind is that it allows incidents to be moved about quickly and easily. It is the work of only seconds to move a key piece of dramatic action from an early scene to a later one or to introduce a clue early in such a way that a character can recall it later. A storyboard also allows the playwright to consider such devices as flashbacks or fantasy sequences. With work, the plot eventually begins

Storyboards, widely used in films, are taken into the field to aid with shooting. Here we see such a storyboard at work during the shooting of *Jaws*.

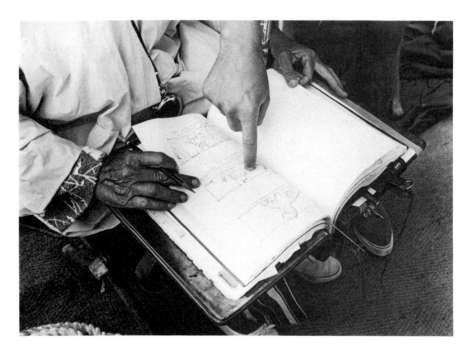

to break down into individual scenes and acts. This last is important; not only does it give the playwright a chance to see what the "shape" of the finished play might be, but it gives him or her some reasonable estimate of the work which lies ahead. The prospect of writing a 2½-hour play is intimidating in any case, but it somehow becomes less formidable if you can see the smaller segments which make it up.

Character. Some playwrights would not dream of beginning the actual writing of a play until they had the characters clearly in mind. To do this the playwright may start collecting information about his or her characters, essentially creating bulging dossiers on each fictional character as might a detective who was searching for a missing person. Elaborate descriptions may be composed; biographical or autobiographical statements are written; composite portraits of the characters are assembled. Shaffer visited a child psychiatrist to learn more about deeply disturbed young people. Some playwrights go so far as to write letters to and from their characters describing their dreams, exploring their motivations, and of course establishing the kind of dialogue they will use. Not all of this information will appear in the play, of course. But the expectation is that once the characters have the same richness and detail as very close friends they will assume a life of their own. Playwrights frequently report this phenomenon: fictional characters begin to act in unanticipated (but coherent) ways, and the playwright is left with the task of simply "recording" what they say and do.

Note how close this approach is to one which might be used by an actor playing a role. It is entirely possible that a playwright could come to empathize as completely as an actor with a character but, lacking the expressive skills of the actor, is forced to describe the character in a script rather than perform it. Without such empathic understanding of their characters, it is difficult to explain how Shakespeare could have written the character Juliet, and Ibsen, Hedda Gabler Tesman.

Theatrical Image. The writer of a play with topical organization may be close to a poet in his or her use of imagery. Therefore, careful plotting may be of no interest and detailed and consistent characterization of less importance than a striking image. Such a playwright may wish to work at a more intuitive level. Accordingly, he or she will probably stay carefully attuned to even the most fleeting and apparently extraneous images. Dreams, the playwright's or someone else's, are a possible source. Free association becomes important. Jokes, puns, and unintended verbal errors may be avidly collected. Infrequently, automatic writing and drug-induced hallucinations are employed. It is as if such a playwright were collecting bits of information from seemingly unrelated sources with the expectation that a central image will emerge. If and when such an image does appear, it becomes a conceptual pivot around which the finished play will move, a tether that ties together seemingly unrelated dramatic images.

Shaffer begins his play with a very theatrical image: a young boy standing motionless, his cheek pressed against the neck of a "horse." Dysarte sees the image, too, and it haunts him. In fact, the image forces him to turn to the audience to confess his doubts about his life and his work.

Point of View.   Throughout dramatic history there have been playwrights—some very good ones—who maintained that they had no point of view, that they were absolutely neutral observers describing the world with scientific detachment. They have tried to adopt the theoretical stance of social scientists, detached from the behaviors they describe in such a way that their reports are without bias, judgment, or point of view. Such a purist notion was, and is, preposterous. It has been abandoned by scientists, and few artists would dare to propose it today. A more reasonable position has come to predominate: Be clear about your point of view, then the audience can take it into account when making up its mind.

As a result, the modern theatre is characterized by playwrights of every persuasion: Marxist, nihilist, Christian, feminist, black, Chicano, gay, etc. In addition, each point of view can usually be expressed in any number of theatrical styles (absurdist, expressionist, realistic, etc.) and genres (tragedy, comedy, farce, etc.). The result is a dizzying number of combinations in which any guidelines are deeply appreciated.

The beginning playwright who is just discovering her theatrical "voice" may have real difficulty deciding which point of view best suits her needs. The search is a lonely one because only one person can make such fundamental decisions—the playwright. In the course of this self-discovery, one victim may be consistency; frequently a first play begins as a Marxist indictment of commercial values but halfway through turns into a light-hearted, absurdist farce.

Shaping the Material.   There are no general rules of playwriting (though there may be some fairly rigid expectations about certain kinds of plays). There are, however, some important questions the playwright must ask in the course of shaping a basic dramatic idea.

Where is the conflict? Everyday action that flows smoothly and without interruption from start to finish is usually boring. Dramatic interactions, on the contrary, are filled with obstacles which must be overcome. If the original idea does not have a conflict between opposing forces, the playwright had better introduce one.

Playwright Shaffer introduced conflict at several levels in *Equus*. The psychiatrist wants to know why the young man has done this awful thing, but the patient will not tell him. (So far, the conflict is person against person.) But does the boy himself know why? Part of the boy does not want to reveal his secret; thus, the boy is in conflict with himself (person against oneself). Then, once the psychiatrist knows the reason and has a chance to cure his patient, he hesitates: does the doctor wish to remove something which, however bizarre, has given wonder and meaning to the boy? Thus Shaffer finds still another way to introduce an internal conflict.

Is there action? Theatre is about people doing things with and to one another. It is not merely descriptive; it is not about situations which remain static. The action can be internal or external, but things must contend and change. Characters are dissatisfied with the way things are; they seek to achieve objectives; obstacles arise; they either overcome those obstacles or are frustrated by them. But always there is change or the impulse toward change. The successful playwright is sensitive to this pattern of action and finds ways to exploit it.

In *Equus*, there is both external and internal action. Externally, Dr. Dysarte has been given a job to do by the judicial system; will he succeed? But the *internal* action is far more interesting; it is fully exploited by using two dependable theatrical devices. The psychiatrist is given long, wrenching soliloquies in which he makes clear to the audience the direction and force of his internal action. The problem is more difficult for the boy since, presumably, he does not know what is going on inside himself. Here Shaffer introduces the device of hypnotism; in a trance the boy relives important moments in his life, building up to the key scene in which he blinds the horses.

Is the action in the present tense? Just as all theatre is played in the present tense, all scripts are written in the present tense. This means that audiences are always living through the moment with the character. Of course, historical incidents are often portrayed on stage; but when they are, they are portrayed as taking place "now." Characters frequently remember past experiences or anticipate future events. In such cases, however, it is the act of remembrance or anticipation which is the portrayed action. Novelists, who are used to creating entire works in the past tense, sometimes find this requirement very frustrating.

In writing *Equus*, Shaffer had a number of alternatives. He could have told the story of the hapless boy chronologically, starting in his youth and following him until the fateful day when the horses are disfigured. Instead, he chose to set the play sometime after the event, thereby focusing attention on the act of recollection. In doing so, Shaffer effectively moved the center of his play from the boy to the psychiatrist. When the play opens, things are at an impasse. There is no reason for anything to change until, in the continuous present of the play, the psychiatrist begins to probe.

Are the characters interesting? Good stage characters are larger than life—there is no other way to put it. However ordinary they may seem at first glance, they tend to be less easily satisfied, less compromising, more persevering, and generally quicker to action than the rest of us. If theatre is "virtual autobiography," we must want to see ourselves drawn more clearly and more forcefully than the people with whom we deal each day.

Dr. Dysarte and Alan Strang in *Equus* are such characters. (As an exercise, consider what the playwright might be telling us about these two characters through their names.) Dr. Dysarte is a highly competent and successful psychiatrist, but his life has lost all meaning and, by the end of the play, one would not be surprised to hear that he had killed himself. Alan is a confused, psychotic teenager—but a young person with an extraordinary ritual life that reaches back to the roots of religion. Both characters are revealed as complex, even contradictory, characters. Their presence on stage together almost guarantees the conflict which makes exciting theatre.

Does the action employ nonverbal communication? Particularly when a would-be playwright has experienced success in some other literary form, it is sometimes difficult for him or her to imagine how important information can be communicated by anything other than words. As a result, beginning playwrights frequently produce scripts in which people talk about everything. Not only is this totally unrealistic (people seldom verbalize everything they do or mean) but it is redundant. An actor can provide with a single, skillful vocal inflection, a point of view that would take the character a paragraph of dialogue to express. The inexperienced playwright includes the paragraph *anyway*. The result is a duplication of effort that leaves the audience feeling patronized. In short, a playwright must be able to imagine a complex interaction between characters, describe it in sufficient detail to give the actors and directors something to work with, and provide only the dialogue required by the scene.

Is there an interesting and appropriate dramatic structure? When Shaffer decided not to tell his story chronologically, he had begun to give it dramatic structure. In *Equus* he uses late point of attack: he begins the plot late in the story, providing exposition as needed. Furthermore, he withholds important information until late in the work in order to build suspense: We find out *why* Alan blinded the horses only when it is the last major piece of the puzzle still missing.

Good dramatic structure is provided by a playwright who understands the subtle play of emotions in an audience as they receive first one piece of information and then another, as they grow to empathize with important characters, as they anticipate certain incidents (thus making them open to surprise), and as their sense of completion and unity is fed by being provided a coherent set of events.

Production Values. A good playwright can imagine how certain events might be staged. Therefore, a playwright can ask for certain elements of production which capture the audience's imagination, clarify the play's intention, and increase its effectiveness.

Peter Shaffer worked with John Dexter, director of the premier production of *Equus*, to create a perfectly stunning production concept. The bare acting space, ostensibly the office of Dr. Dysarte, is, in fact, a kind of operating amphitheatre in which the play is laid out as if it were a demonstration. To capture this sense, the acting area was thrust into the audience and bleachers built on stage, bringing the actor/audience configuration into full arena. In addition, the production is assisted by a corps of stage managers who help in staging important scenes. Gradually, ritually, these stage managers are converted into horses by the addition of symbolic wire masks and hooves. Their participation in the scenes requiring horses is absolutely riveting; but even the scenes in the doctor's office are given enormous power by the brooding presence of the half-seen, occasionally stamping or snorting "horses" who, like the audience, are witnesses to the ritual demonstration. By working closely together, the playwright and the director have created original production devices which capture the sense of the play in ways which are totally theatrical.

THE PLAYWRIGHT AT WORK

Playwrights have special personal characteristics. On the one hand, because they may spend weeks or months working in isolation, they need great personal discipline. They also need a capacity for "delayed gratification," psychological lingo for having to wait a long time until seeing the outcome of the original idea and receiving positive feedback.

So, except for those playwrights who are commissioned to write works, or who work in the special circumstances of a television series, playwrights begin in isolation. It is not at all unusual for a playwright to produce a complete first draft of a script before showing it to anyone—except, perhaps, for a few friends and family.

The first professional colleague to read the script is often the playwright's literary agent. Circulating and promoting scripts is such a time-consuming job that most professional playwrights retain an agent whose job it is to bring scripts to the attention of potential producers. This an agent does for a contracted percentage of the playwright's fee for any script placed. Artists often complain—often in the form of unflattering jokes—about their agents; they never seem to feel that their agents do enough to advance the artist's career, and the healthy percentage they collect seems—usually after the fact—to be excessive. Many playwrights, however, form close friendships with their agents, frequently benefiting from the advice of an experienced and perceptive representative.

The agent will circulate scripts to potential producers, pointing out the good points of the work and soliciting useful ideas even from groups or individuals who reject the work. The good agent, then, creates a useful channel of communication between the playwright and the producing theatre companies.

In the professional legitimate theatre the competition for scripts does not favor the inexperienced or little-known playwright. Numbers tell the story: in any given year the 70 or so regional theatres in the United States produce, say, 400 plays; Broadway, off-Broadway, and off-off-Broadway produce roughly 200 more. Of this total of some 600 plays in a given year, much fewer than one-half are original scripts; the majority are revivals of relatively new scripts or classics. In fact, in only an average year the total number of premier productions is probably not much more than 100.

The number of new scripts looking for production is very large. For example, the Actors Theatre of Louisville, a highly respected theatre with a traditional commitment to new plays, receives about 5,000 scripts a year—from which they may choose 10 full-length plays and 20 one-act plays.

Even those playwrights who are lucky enough to receive a production are not guaranteed continued support. A single production earns a playwright very little money and not much more attention. Every playwright hopes that a successful production in a regional theatre will result in favorable attention leading to subsequent productions, perhaps on Broadway—and television and film offers. As a result, that first production is extremely important.

The playwright usually works closely with the producing company to improve the script. This usually means rewriting of some kind. Rewriting can be very extensive; sometimes the script which is played on opening night is hardly recognizable as the one submitted months earlier. If all goes as planned, the playwright learns a great deal from rehearsals. Accordingly, while the actors and director are rehearsing, the playwright may be rewriting scenes or whole acts. One of the challenges for the company is the flexibility needed to change scenes which have already been rehearsed. This process may continue into preview performances; it is not unusual for actors to be asked to integrate new lines—even whole new scenes—into a piece within a single day. The pace is hectic and the pressure intense. However, if all goes well, the production is a success and the script is optioned by other theatre companies.

This usually happens indirectly. A play brokerage company buys the rights to the script and thereafter represents the playwright in negotiations with other companies. For a percentage of the royalties charged and all of the profits from sale of acting copies of the script, the brokerage company enters into contracts with production companies, sells them the scripts which they need, collects the royalties, and monitors the field for unauthorized productions. This last is especially important: the playwright has made an enormous investment of time and creative energy in his or her script and deserves the reward of royalties. The production company which attempts to produce a play without paying royalties is cheating the author and cheating the art form. They should remember that theatre needs the best minds of the age putting their very best work into new scripts. The rewards are slim enough as it is, and anything theatre people do that discourages good playwrights is self-defeating.

The absolute importance of fine writing to our theatre is underscored by efforts to encourage it. Each year there are dozens of playwriting contests with substantial cash rewards—and production—for

The Actors Theatre of Louisville, home of the Humana Festival of New American
Plays, operates from two historic buildings in downtown Louisville, one of them
a 19th century bank.

new scripts. Some of these are solicited on subjects important to the
producing organization in question; some are open as to subject matter,
style, and tone. The American Theatre Association, through its American College Theatre Festival, annually offers valuable and prestigious
awards in several classifications of student playwriting.

Another development is the promotion of programs in playwriting
at American universities. Many institutions now offer programs in playwriting—usually defined so as to include writing for television and
screen. The best of these programs provide ample opportunity for new
playwrights to see their work produced and to grow as a result.

One point is certain: Skilled playwrights are needed to provide the
live theatre with the provocative ideas which the art needs if it is to
flourish. The function of the theatre is to provide a vision which extends our collective imagination, and to convey new information to us
through theatrical means. The playwright's vision is the first and most
important step in the crucial process of self-discovery and growth. Par-

ticularly in the Western tradition, the whole process cannot achieve its potential without the contribution of skilled playwrights.

Discussion Questions

1. Give some possible reasons why writers who have proven their excellence in other areas—as journalists, novelists, poets, etc.—sometimes have difficulty as playwrights.

2. How is the role of the theatre company altered if the playwright is seen as being the sole creative artist—and having the final word in all respects?

3. Why is it necessary for a playwright to have a solid grasp of theatre as an art?

4. Why do so many modern playwrights despair of achieving a point of view which is totally "objective"? Is there a danger in the bias of a playwright?

5. Why is it important to theatre and to society that the best people are attracted to playwrighting? Define "best" in this case.

7

The Director

Of the major artistic, specialties in theatre, only one—directing—developed recently enough for us to be able to document the event. The actor? There has been at least one since the beginning. The playwright has been providing dramatic ideas since the invention of writing—perhaps even *before* the invention of writing. The origins of the scenic and costume designers predate history; we can only speculate about the circumstances under which these specialties arose.

But the stage director? The role arose in the 19th century. We have a great deal of information about the historical circumstances which made the director a necessity back then—and which continue to make him or her one of the most important people in Western theatre today. The director remains a facilitator in the complex interaction between audience and performer.

THE EMERGENCE OF THE DIRECTOR

Some of the director's contributions have always been needed. Tradition tells us that the early Greek playwrights were responsible for tasks which would never fall to the modern playwright. They coached the actors, choreographed the dance sequences, and oversaw the scenic and costume designs.

Since the Renaissance, there has always been someone in the theatre company who accepted responsibility for overseeing the effect of the production. Sometimes it was a playwright, sometimes a manager; most often, however, the person who made major artistic decisions was the most prestigious member of the company—the star actor. By the 18th and 19th centuries, the major figures in this regard had become the great actor-manager. These heroic figures—people like Henry Irving, Edwin Booth, Edmund Kean, Sarah Bernhardt—accepted personal responsibility for all aspects of the production. They commissioned plays to be written to their specifications; scenery and costumes were designed to complement their acting in the major roles; company members were hired to enhance the stature of the star—and fired when they did not. Even when the star traveled without a supporting company, a production could be mounted by a hosting repertory company with a speed which astounds modern theatre artists. These stars were ready to perform a number of major roles at any time. The major plays (a *Hamlet*, a *King Lear*, a *Richelieu*, for example) could be presented with very little rehearsal because everyone in the profession was familiar with the conventions of their staging. It is only a slight exaggeration to say that the blocking of any of these plays consisted of placing the star downstage center—facing the audience, of course—with a semicircle of supporting characters surrounding him or her at a respectful distance. These secondary actors would advance a step or two to deliver an appropriate line, then retreat to allow the star to declaim the major speeches. Scenery was conventionalized: a standard "room in the palace" would suffice for any classical play; a "city street" worked for nearly all comedies; ballets and rustic pieces played in front of a painted scene of generic woods and fields. As a result, little was needed in the way of coordination.

But dissatisfaction with these familiar modes of production created a vacuum, or niche, into which new forces were moving. Impatience with this dead conventionality led first playwrights and later actor-managers to explore dramas which displayed some singularity. If a play took place in a particular period, nation, or district, they argued, it made no sense to have a generalized setting or costume or stage dialect or style of acting. *Julius Caesar* should not be acted in a scene depicting a 19th-century London street, the critics complained. Gradually individuals began to specialize in making these and other elements conform to the special demands of each script. Increasingly, audiences came to expect that each production would be different from all others.

The same forces were at work demanding unity within each production. The early realistic drama, especially, forbade the "star" performance; ensemble acting became favored. Overt theatricality also fell out of favor; audiences came to expect a more natural, more honest style of acting. Finally, playwrights with a particular philosophical bent came to expect that someone in the company would champion their point of view. All of this meant that someone other than a performer would have to accept responsibility for shaping, molding, unifying, encouraging—in short, directing—the production.

THE MODERN DIRECTOR

Today's stage director still serves many of the functions of the 19th-century forebears. New tasks have been added, some have been refined. Some have even been abandoned; many of the management tasks such as raising money, promotion, and bookkeeping have been adopted by still another specialty, the producer. The artistic niche created well over a century ago continues to be a viable one. But, like its biological analogue, the newly emerged role of director is constantly redefining itself to meet changing conditions. It is wise, therefore, to focus on the major dimensions of the job before turning to a detailed description of the director at work.

Leadership and Managment.   The director is situated at the very center of the organization of the theatrical company. It is usually the director who gathers the major design leadership; it is the director who casts the play; it is the director who leads in the development of the "concept" which serves to unify the production. Finally, it is the director who accepts responsibility for all artistic decisions. With this level of authority and responsibility vested in a single person, it is not surprising that the success or failure of a production can rest on the ability of the director to attract fine artists, to demand and hold their loyalty, and to inspire the group to achieve its highest potential.

Some directors are particularly strong in this regard. Blessed with charismatic personalities, they seem always to be able to gather the best artists, energize them, and create a warm working environment.

Another aspect of the job, however, is equally important, and its lack can often be even more disastrous than poor leadership. A theatrical company is an organization created to accomplish a given task: the production of plays. It is a complex organization pulling together a large number of specialties—often represented by extremely volatile people. The organizational aspects of the job should not be minimized.

Because all the members of a professional company are on salary, the old stage adage that "time is money" is particularly true. The time available for rehearsal and production is seldom sufficient and, therefore, the need to move ahead with the task at hand is always paramount. Rehearsal schedules have to be made up, costumes and scenery have to arrive on time, theatre and rehearsal hall availabilities sometimes shift, and the slightest delay or false start can create an emergency. In the professional theatre there are also union rules to abide by; while the rules themselves aim to make life bearable for the people in the company, they can introduce another level of challenge in the already demanding task of a director. Helped by his or her stage manager and a corps of assistant stage managers, the director brings various management skills to his or her complex task.

Interpretation. Between any script and any production of that script lies a maze composed of interpretative paths; to move from the script to production, the company must move through that maze. As they do so, they must make a multitude of decisions concerning the intention of the playwright or the special nature of the production at hand. Some are small; some are large; all are significant. And all are interrelated. The principles by which these interpretative decisions are guided gives the production its special character; the consistency with which they are made provides the unity of the production.

In the chapter on the company we saw some different ways in which these decisions are reached, and suggested that the process of decision making is one of the hallmarks of any company. The role of the director in this process is crucial. Whether the director is trying to faithfully reproduce a recent Broadway production, or mounting an ex-

perimental treatment of a classic, or helping a company create a piece
through improvisation, it is his or her interpretative skills that are being
tested. The questions, large and small, crowd in. If we set the play in a
different historical period, what changes? What does a different vocal
inflection do to this line? Is it better? Would this character carry a
personal prop of this kind? Is this the costume that this character
would wear at an occasion of this kind? Is this interpretation of the
third act consistent with what we decided for the first act? Is it clear?
Is it audible? Is is working? Why isn't it working?

This last question gets asked a lot. "Why isn't it working?" (*Working* is jargon for "succeeding.") A good director is a good diagnostician;
he or she can watch a scene in rehearsal and tell the actor whether it is
working, what isn't working, and, hopefully, what needs to be done. Of
course, to do so, a director needs a clear sense of what the play is
about, what the playwright's intention might be, and how an audience
would respond. All of these are developed skills.

Directors become adept at reading scripts. At their best they have
a highly developed sense of what is happening in a scene, and what the
"action" is. Remember, the script usually contains little more than the
dialogue between the characters. This is important evidence, of course,
but it is hardly the whole story: plays are seldom *about* people talking
to one another. So the director can help actors decide what is really
happening in the scene. What does this character want? What stands in
the way of him or her getting it? Will he or she succeed? But the director
also learns to take a broader view than the actor: The actor has to
live the life of the character second-by-second in the scenes in which
that character appears; the director, on the other hand, has to focus on
the play as a total experience. What is the climax and where should it
fall? Will this piece of apparently random information become meaningful
in the next act? Is this character fully developed? Is this subplot
interesting? Is this laugh inappropriate given the tone of the piece? Are
there enough laughs? The questions are endless.

A frequently asked question is, what is the playwright driving at?
The director who can answer this question with some authority has
done considerable research into other plays by the same author, into
critical comments about the playwright and his work, and into the
period in which the play takes place. In short, the director has become
something of an expert on the sources and intentions of the playwright
and, to some degree at least, is able to represent the writer in his or her
absence.

Surrogate Audience.   Whatever else a director does, he or she watches rehearsals. This sounds simple. At one time or another, nearly everyone in the company watches rehearsals—but the director does it *all the time.* The director never appears on stage; the director is always in the audience—standing in for the audience.

Actors are notoriously unable to judge themselves. They need a steady, trained, supportive presence in the auditorium to feed back the information they need. Can I be heard? Seen? Understood? Was the character's motivation clear? Was it funny? Rehearsal hour after rehearsal hour the director watches and takes notes and answers questions and makes suggestions.

To a certain degree the director takes on a role. Just as the actor pretends to be a character, the director pretends to be an audience member. It can be a demanding role. The director knows a great deal about this play, much more than the average audience member, yet he or she has to assume the role of someone encountering it for the first time. For such a person, will this particular plot twist be clear? Will these familiar words be understood? Will this joke (long ago grown stale through repetition) prove funny? Successful directors have an almost uncanny ability to think as an audience member would—or will, come opening night.

Expressive Skills.   The modern director is an expressive artist in his or her own right. Theatre lore is loaded with stories of creative directors who took an otherwise undistinguished script and made it part of a memorable evening. Playwrights sometimes flinch at the bitter truth that a good director can understand what the playwright is trying to say better than the playwright can. In such cases the director becomes something akin to a collaborator—certainly more than just an interpreter.

For the director, the expressive materials become the script, to be sure, but also include the bodies and voices of the actors, the setting, the costumes, the volume of stage space, and, some would maintain, the memories and imaginations of the audience. All of these the director uses to create corporeal events from the written suggestions of the playwright. A few key terms will illustrate.

Blocking and Composition. Blocking is the gross movement of actors in the stage space. *Composition* refers to the "frame-by-frame" placement of the characters in the same space. How the characters move in physical relation to one another can say volumes about their psychological relationship. Indeed, a well-directed play would communicate a great deal even with the sound "turned off." Good staging is like choreography in this respect—probably because choreographers and directors are both students of the physical behavior of humans.

Tempo. The speed at which people speak is a characteristic we all recognize. It is less common for us to think of all human behaviors as having different tempos in different circumstances. And yet they do. And it is these changes which provide significant variety in a play. One scene starts slowly and accelerates; another does the reverse. Slower scenes may alternate with faster ones. Different characters move at different tempos. Like a good piece of music, the well-directed play has its fast movements and its slow ones.

Energy. Although scientifically elusive, the concept of energy is well understood by theatre artists. Partly it is related to the "size" of stage characters: they are larger than life in their conception and actors must work hard to expand into and fill every crevice the character provides. In addition, the performers must exert energy to fill the theatre with the sound and action demanded by performance in a large room. Finally, there is that ineffable something which a true artist brings to the context of performance. He or she "takes stage." With a physical presence reminiscent of a circus performer or a bullfighter, the actor seizes and holds the attention of the audience with a force for which the term *energy* is entirely appropriate.

But energy is a variable and more is not always better. Some scenes need to crackle with energy—but others need a more relaxed, mellow approach. The audience needs the contrast as much as the players: unrelieved high energy is emotionally draining on both.

Patterns. Plays are about human experience; and human experience is filled with patterns, luckily. We would be driven mad if everything which happened to us were for the first time and all connections were random. In theatre, the patterns of life are exaggerated and the audience's capacity to detect those patterns becomes crucial. If the audience sees an ominous pattern developing, they are filled with dread for the hero; feelings of wellbeing are reinforced when patterns of justice are discovered; even the delight of humor arises out of patterns— the audience (and the characters) expect one thing and get another.

The director has the power to detect, emphasize, and even create those patterns. For example, a character who betrays another may be blocked into the exact position he occupied when, in an earlier scene, he pledged undying loyalty. Or a vocal inflection can be repeated in such a way that the audience detects a comic pattern which would otherwise be lost.

Concept. The director's concept is a means of unifying a production by providing a central image to which all the parts may relate. The concept also provides an important way for the director to contribute to the creative process. If all goes well, the director's concept informs and enriches the ideas provided by the playwright; in a few cases, the director's concept may be at odds with the playwright's intention—or even contradict it altogether. In this last case, the director is treading perilous ethical ground and should make it clear to everyone—especially audiences—that he or she is making a conceptual leap which is not necessarily sanctioned by the playwright.

But what *is* a concept? Definitions vary, but in practice a concept is an image which captures the central image of the play—at least as it will be seen in this production.*

The best concepts are usually somewhat poetic and engage more than one of the senses of sight, hearing, feel, taste and smell. In this way, the concept is useful to the costume and scenic designers as well as the actors. A provocative concept can even help the promotions staff come up with a fruitful sales campaign.

Here are some possible production concepts for some familiar plays:

Richard III: A deformed spider crawling across a white rose.

Twelfth Night: A dusty, nostaligic memory of an old clown (Feste) yearning for a simpler time.

Equus: A medical experiment takes place in an operating amphitheatre while both human beings and gods look on.

The Glass Menagerie: The faint sound of a wind chime nearly drowned out by a jazz band.

The Taming of the Shrew: A group improvisation by a group of travelers spending the night in a country inn.

Notice how brief these are: they are not intended to explain everything that happens in the play—in practice they may only provide a

---

*Do not confuse a director's concept with the theme of the play. The theme is a verbalized (or verbalizable) statement about the world or human experience which is proved true by the play. For example, the theme of *Macbeth* may be that "overweening ambition will destroy a potentially decent person." A concept for a production of *Macbeth* might be, "War is a disease; when the war is complete, the fever persists unto madness. Macbeth is a victim of a plague."

starting point for the ongoing discussion called rehearsal. It is even possible that an audience would not be able to identify the specific concept which had shaped the play they had just witnessed. Still, if the concept provides unity and inspiration, it has done its job.

The modern director is expected to bring managerial, interpretative, and expressive skills as his or her contribution to a production. These skills show themselves in the course of the daily work of the stage director.

THE DIRECTOR AT WORK

In the professional theatre there are several employment contexts within which a director may work. The most common assignment is one in which a freelancing director is hired to direct a single play or a package of plays. Single assignments are the rule in commercial Broadway theatre or off-Broadway theatre; in regional theatres there is a chance that a director will be assigned two or more productions in a single season. There are advantages to each: a Broadway hit will run for a long time and swell the director's reputation and pocketbook; an assignment with a regional theatre provides professional stability and the opportunity to work with a single company on several productions, and this is usually the more artistically rewarding situation.

A director has much artistic influence when assigned to a production, but he or she seldom has absolute freedom in selecting the play. Commonly, a producer will decide which play to introduce into a season and contract a director accordingly. Of course, the director can refuse the assignment; he or she may even be asked to suggest titles to the producer. But the possibility remains that a director may end up directing a play for which he or she has less than total enthusiasm. The remedy is for the director to concentrate on the positive aspects of the assignment and put any reservations aside.

Professional directors in the United States are represented by unions: Directors in the legitimate theatre belong to the Society of Stage Directors and Choreographers; film and television directors are affiliated with the Director's Guild of America. Some directors move freely from film and television to the stage, and therefore belong to both unions. These unions represent the directors in contract negotiations, enforce minimum conditions of employment, and help theatre companies contact directors.

The first task of a director is to surround herself with a core group to provide artistic leadership. This process varies: if the director is hired by a regional company, the scenic designers, costume designers, and stage manager are probably already in place. A commercial producer may have some firm ideas about design staff—in such a case the director provides appropriate advice and counsel.

With the artistic leadership in place, the director sets out to cast the play. Again, the producer may have some input: for example, a Broadway producer may have already committed a star to a major role; in fact, the play and the star may have been part of the "package" offered to the director originally. In any case, one of the primary skills of any director is casting. First of all, he or she must be able to recognize generalized acting talent. Then comes the almost mystic ability to recognize the potential for a fine character in an actor who may not be an obvious choice. First-rate directors have an uncanny knack for discovering the kernel of a great performance in unlikely actors.

Finally, the director must come up with a *balanced* cast. It is not enough to cast a fine actor in each role. Attention must be paid to such mechanical elements of the cast as contrast: not everyone can be the same height, nor can they all have the same vocal quality. On the other hand, it might simplify things if the actors all had roughly the same training and way of working. Is the company compatible? Some excellent actors do not get along very well with other excellent actors. On the contrary, some actors spark others into doing their very best work. All of these issues, and more, must be kept in mind as the director casts the play.

There are as many ways of beginning rehearsals as there are directors. Some prefer to work with the leads in isolation during the early days of rehearsal, calling the other characters as needed. The majority of directors gather the company for a series of readings of the play. This tends to remind each person that they are a company and give everyone a chance to discuss the script, the concept, and any special problems presented by the production. With some directors this period of reading and discussion is quite lengthy; many, however, prefer to move directly into staging.

All directors worthy of the title have done a great deal of research and planning before rehearsals begin; however, there are differences as to how this preparatory work appears in the company production. One school of directing recommends that the director arrive at the first rehearsal with a prompt script already prepared. A prompt script is a copy of the script laid out with copious notes and stage directions filling the margins. In the course of rehearsal the stage manager will make up a prompt script with all blocking and cues clearly shown. This script will be the record of this production; if an actor forgets blocking or has a question about some technical aspect of the production, the prompt script will be the source which everyone will consult. This is standard procedure.

What is *not* standard is the idea of beginning rehearsals with the prompt script already prepared. This suggests that the director has already blocked the show (in his or her head, with coins on a floor plan, with models, etc.) and that the actors will now simply convert that plan into stage action. Presumably this principle also applies to all other aspects of the production. This pattern is a characteristic of an authoritarian director. It has the virtue of maximizing the influence of the director; by the same token, however, it tends to minimize the contribution of the other members of the company. It is fair to say that some actors deeply resent this approach.

Another approach, admittedly extreme, is to just let things emerge. For example, the task of blocking was reportedly handled in the following way by one professional director: the first two days of readings were held in a large room around a table; on the third day the company arrived to find the chairs in position—but the table gone. Gradually the actors were invited to get out of their chairs to relate to one another, forming appropriate groupings for each scene. By the end of the week, the chairs were discovered standing around the perimeter of the room, actors moved them into scenes where they were needed. All this time, the director had given no stage directions at all; when queried, he had only asked, "What would feel right to your character?"

At the same time the director, knowing that actors would treat him as surrogate audience, systematically moved about the room, first sitting on one side, then on the other. As a result, no side of the room became downstage; emphasis was kept entirely upon the interaction between the characters.

Gradually it became clear that a door would be needed in such-and-such a scene and, through repetition, it became clear that it should be in a particular place. Just as gradually, the design staff would provide what was needed (refining the floor plan as required). Only very near the end of the rehearsal period did the director add some finishing touches to the composition. The critics praised his "carefully conceived" blocking!

Between these extremes, most directors find a compromise: they may begin a rehearsal with a clear idea of what *could* be done—but stay open to ideas from actors. To facilitate this flow of ideas the director and the actors keep the channels of communication open. Questions are more numerous than any other form of address. What is your (your character's) objective? What do you need here? How does this feel? What if we tried it a different way? Through this interaction, the character of the production emerges.

When the actors are secure in their lines and clear about what they are trying to achieve, the director may have to become a diagnostician. Problems develop: a scene loses its freshness; an actor cannot find a full, genuine emotional response; a piece of comic business is not working. The director may employ a different technique for each problem.

Let's say that a scene has become stale because the characters are not listening, watching, interacting with the urgency that would be natural were they experiencing this moment for the first time. The actors, of course, are *not* experiencing the event for the first time; they have rehearsed the scene repeatedly and have long since ceased to be surprised. One way of recapturing a sense of spontaneity is to improvise the scene; actors make up their own lines in a rehearsal in which they are given the freedom to explore the dramatic action—even if it moves substantially away from the author's intention. This forces the actors to listen more carefully than ever before and deal with totally unexpected twists in the scene; they may find themselves saying and doing things which had lain dormant in the action before. As a result, the sense of sameness can be overcome and a refreshing spontaneity reestablished.

If an actor cannot capture the emotional state of a character in a demanding scene, the director may be able to help. Intense private discussion, perhaps combined with improvisation, may allow the actor to recall a parallel situation in his or her own life. The actor's memory of his or her emotional response to that situation could trigger a deeper and more affecting response to the stage situation.

Mechanical problems, such as those which come up in comedy, present special challenges for a director. Because they can be so technical (while appearing spontaneous, of course), the instincts of the actor may not be very helpful. The cool, experienced eye of a director may be just what is needed as the business is rehearsed over and over until the perfect comic pattern is achieved.

As rehearsals move toward opening night, the director's attention is more and more absorbed by the total pattern of production. Properties, scenery, lights, sound, are all gradually integrated into the production and the chief concern of the director becomes "orchestration." Just as the conductor works to coordinate the various sections of a symphony orchestra, the director does the same with all the elements of a production. And, again, the endless multitude of questions arise. Should the music which ends a scene begin during the final speech or in the blackout? Is the wallpaper too fussy and distracting for a scene of this power? Are the colors of the lights correct for the mood? Is the train on her gown too much for the leading lady to handle? (And, if so, how do you tell both the actress and the costume designer?) Is the energy of the first scene too much to sustain? If so, what do we do? Are the actors feeling abandoned? Given only two more rehearsals before opening, what needs work the most?

Even after a production opens, the director is responsible for staying close by and giving "notes" for a specified period of time. Ultimately, however, the director must relinquish control to a stage manager. It is the stage manager who "calls" the show (cues the lights, sound, and scenic changes) and accepts responsibility for maintaining the character of the production through the weeks, months, or even years of the run of the show.

Long after opening night the director should be able to attend a production he or she has directed and find it as it was originally conceived. Then the director will have the unique pleasure of watching his or her dramatic vision worked out on stage by an exceedingly complex art organization. With luck, the director will then be able to experience the production as an audience member does, as a shared adventure created between the performers and the audience. The difference will be that for one audience member—the director, sitting unrecognized in the theatre—the experience is not entirely new. Instead it has the special power that comes from seeing one's own fantasies made manifest on the living stage.

Discussion Questions

1. The description of the historical reasons for the development of the director's role mentioned two concepts: uniqueness and unity. How do these two concepts assert themselves in a single modern production?

2. Describe in your own words what the director's "concept" is. How is that different from the theme of a play? (For a more complete discussion of theme, see chapter 11.)

3. How does the director "stand in" for the audience? Is there a sense in which he or she "stands in" for society?

4. Who can fire a director?

5. Is it necessary for an effective director to be well liked by the company? Is it important for the director to know a great deal about the private lives of the actors?

6. How is it possible that a director can accept responsibility for *all* artistic aspects of a production?

7. Discuss the ethics of a director taking liberties with a script. At what point does the director's contribution become a violation of the playwright's rights? Give examples, hypothetical if necessary.

8

The Designers

INTRODUCTION

All human life takes place in an environment. Indeed, it is the constant interaction with the environment which serves to define life: A comatose patient in an intensive care unit is pronounced dead if, among other things, he or she is not interacting with the environment. Since environment plays such an important part in human interactions, it is not surprising that the modern theatre has developed specialists in creating meaningful environments. Actually, the modern theatre has created four specialists: one, the *theatre architect*, creates the environment in which the actor/audience interactions take place; the second, the *scenic designer*, is responsible for the physical environment in which the actor/actor and character/character interactions take place. Because these roles are so intertwined, the term *scenic designer* will here include much of what a theatre designer might do in actuality. A *lighting designer* shapes the parts of the environment defined by light. In years past—and in some theatres today—lighting was designed by the scenic designer. Increasingly, however, the lighting designer is becoming accepted as an independent theatre specialist. The last specialist, the *costume designer*, enriches the character/character interactions by shaping those aspects of character expressed in clothing.

As we might have inferred from other cases, very traditional theatre forms seldom have specialized individuals who accept responsibility for designing the environment. In those theatre traditions which use a formal stage and conventional props and elements of setting, it would be superfluous to assign a new person to decide issues which have been common practice for centuries. The carefully ritualized Japanese *no* theatre, for example, does not need a scenic or costume designer on a daily basis—because the physical aspects of the productions do not change in any important way over the years. But this does not mean that they do not have an effective environment. Hundreds of years ago the collective wisdom of an early *no* company decided how the space would be used and decorated, how the few props would be constructed and placed in that space, and how both the actors and the audience would be placed in relationship to one another. The result is an effective environment that has remained largely unchanged for centuries.

THE AUDIENCE'S ENVIRONMENT

Whether planned from scratch by a single individual or developed collectively over long periods of time, the design of the audience space has much to contribute to the theatre event. Consider, for example, the various demands placed upon that space.

It must be separate from the rest of the world. Theatres, even if they are simply a cleared area, nearly always have a sense of isolation from the world; the most important theatres have a special feeling about them that borders on the mysterious. The oldest theatres in the Western world, those of ancient Greece, were frequently placed in physically isolated surroundings of breathtaking natural beauty. Theatre was a religious exercise and the "seeing place" was planned to evoke religious awe. But even a poverty-stricken touring company playing at a village fair tries to create something akin to this special feeling, perhaps by nothing more than encircling the audience space with a shabby screen of canvas panels. And, surprisingly, it works! Stepping into this area, the audience member and the actor are symbolically separated from the outside world.

It must be secure, if needed. If a theatre is dependent upon paid admissions, there must be some way to control access. Usually this is done by walling in the audience space and collecting admission from anyone who wishes to enter. However, there have been some interesting variations on this: for example, in Restoration and 18th-century England, audience members were allowed to witness a number of preshow entertainments and the first act of a five-act play for free; *then* they were charged admission if they wished to stay for the whole evening.

Obviously, a theatre which does not charge admission does not need to secure the audience area—unless it is also concerned about excluding rowdy or disruptive elements.

It should be free from distractions. The space shared by audience and actor is designed to maximize the intensity of the interaction. Therefore, it should exclude distractions—for example, noise. In many American cities, outdoor theatre is made all but impossible by the sound of jet aircraft overhead. Even New York theatres are notorious in this regard; traffic and construction noise from the street outside—including the everpresent police and fire sirens—make it difficult to experience serious, quiet drama in the very heart of America's theatre center. By the same token, those theatres which depend on carefully controlled stage lighting must be able to exclude daylight, moonlight, or automobile headlights.

It should allow the audience to see and hear the actor. In small theatres, this problem seldom arises. But, as economic pressures require that larger and larger numbers of people attend each performance, the problems of sight and hearing become extreme. Large indoor theatres present serious architectural problems because, in order to support the roof, pillars usually must be used. However, pillars obstruct the view of the audience—and an audience member who cannot see all or part of the playing area can be expected to become cranky. In addition, wonderful as the human eye may be, it has limits. Beyond a certain distance—especially under artificial lighting conditions—the eye simply cannot detect small movements and other details. Hence the inventory of techniques available to the actor is reduced. Sometimes, in very large auditoria, the actor is reduced to using gross movements and vocal extremes if he or she wishes to communicate to the audience members farthest from the stage. In such a situation, even a good actor may give a performance lacking in subtlety—when only the theatre is to blame.

The same principle applies to sound: sound diminishes as the square of the distance from the source. Hence, an audience member seated in row 10 is receiving four times the sound of his friend in row 20. A person in row 30 receives only one-ninth the sound, and so on. This "ideal" situation is complicated when the design of the auditorium walls allows too much reverberation of sound coming from the stage, or when sound-absorbing materials dampen any natural amplification which the walls of the setting might provide. Poor acoustics are the bane of any actor's existence since they prevent vocal communication.

Another aspect of theatre design which applies here is not widely understood. Seeing and hearing are closely related. For example, when audience members can *see* the actor's mouth, they report that they hear better. Some of this is purely psychological; but it is true we all read lips a great deal in ordinary life—and we bring that skill to the theatre with us.

Of course, in some kinds of theatre the physical relationship of the audience and actor may reduce certain aspects of seeing and hearing. These choices are usually conscious ones; the director and the scenic designer have decided to sacrifice some aspects of seeing and hearing in favor of what they feel are compensating benefits. We will return to this question when discussing arena and thrust staging.

It must combine comfort and attention. An uncomfortable audience is not free to give its full attention to the theatre event at hand. At the other extreme, however, an audience that is *too* physically comfortable tends to doze or daydream. Since some dissatisfied audience member or actor first identified the problem, theatre architects have been trying to find a satisfying balance of these forces.

Part of the problem is that audience comfort and attention are anything but universal conditions. They have varied from culture to culture, period to period. For example, daybreak in March is usually quite cold in Athens. Yet 5th-century B.C. Athenians were happy to bundle up in the predawn dark and stumble to their places in the Theatre of Dionysus. It is highly unlikely that modern American audiences would do the same—or if they did, could give the play their full attention. Some scholars believe that Shakespeare's Globe Theatre held over 1,000 persons. Since we have some general idea of the size of the Globe, we may conclude that those people were jammed together "so close as to form adhesions." Modern American audiences would not tolerate public crowding of that density and, if forced to endure it, would hardly be receptive to a demanding play.

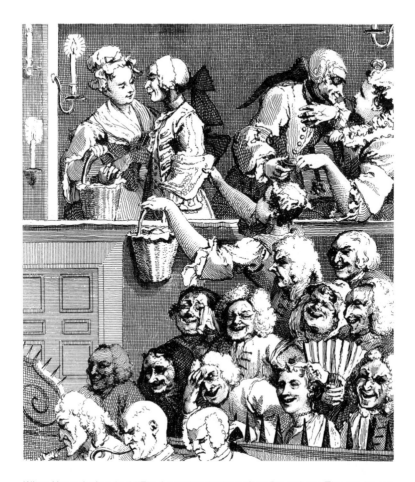

When Hogarth sketched "The Laughing Audience" at Drury Lane Theatre, he captured the conditions which were an expected part of attending the theatre in the 18th Century. Modern audiences would not tolerate such crowding.

Yet, when a modern audience is given all the physical comfort imaginable—soft, wide seats which recline, wide aisles, arm rests, numerous intermissions, and the like—something seems to happen to reduce the intensity of the experience.

It must develop a sense of community. As we have often noted, the human being is an intensely social animal. And theatre is one of the species' most intensely social activities. It is an event associated with crowds. Dilute the crowd too much and the occasion seems to be diminished.

Those who believe in the existence of auras have an explanation:

at moments of peak public experience—at a political rally, at a concert, during a church service—the auras of the individuals in the audience fuse to become a single, all-encompassing, and very powerful aura emanating from the entire group as if it were a single organism. Whether this explanation is literally true or not, the idea of a unified audience makes a great deal of sense to theatre artists. If an audience is too widely scattered—as they may be during a performance playing to a less than capacity audience—there is this fundamental barrier to overcome. Theatres have even been designed to physically close off parts of the auditorium to force a small audience into closer proximity with the stage and each other.

The best theatres in the world have a special character to them. They have a combination of mystery and psychological comfort; they have good acoustics and fine sight lines; they have an arrangement of spaces which weld a group of strangers into a single audience.

Finally, excellent theatres have a physical relationship of actor and audience which helps create the event that culture needs.

THE SHAPE OF THE ACTOR/AUDIENCE INTERACTION

Imagine you are walking in a busy public space. Suddenly you notice that two people are engaged in a violent argument. Having nothing more important to do, you drift toward the two who are arguing; so do dozens of others. Gradually, the crowd forms a circle around the combatants. Notice how close the nearest come to the action; it is probable that the closest spectators move close enough to hear and see everything but remain distant enough for safety and to hold both of the arguers in the visual field without moving the head.

As the number of spectators grows, the late arrivals have trouble seeing; shorter people may squeeze to the front of the crowd; thoughtful members of the front rank may squat, kneel, or even sit. Those at the rear of the crowd may stand on benches and walls or even climb light poles or trees to see and hear more closely.

In this simple example we see the major elements present in the physical aspects of any actor/audience interaction.

Arena Theatre. Without question the first actor/audience interactions took place in what we now choose to call an *arena* configuration, that is with the audience completely surrounding the performers. It may have been in a circle which also shared a campfire; it may have

Early man must have gathered to see and hear impromptu performances in a con-figuration like arena theatre.

been an impromptu recreation of the day's hunt for the benefit of those who remained behind; it could have been a harvest ritual acted out on the surface of a threshing floor. Whatever the location, there can be no doubt that the first audience crowded in on all sides, like spectators at a schoolyard fist fight.

There is a certain immediate logic to such a grouping: the largest number of spectators possible is brought into the closest proximity to the actors. If distance alone is the object—as it is when people crowd around a religious relic carried through the streets—this is unquestion-ably the best configuration. But other aspects of the performance expe-rience are lost. For one thing, not everyone can see clearly; for another, the actors have no way to get "offstage."

Thrust Theatre. A suitable compromise was developed by the an-cient Greeks. They found a way to *almost* surround a dancing circle, whose sanctity kept the audience from crowding into it. At the open part of the circle a small hut or enclosure (*skene*) was built; this became

The Theatre at Epidaurus, though built in the 4th Century B.C., displays the characteristics of Greek theatres of the Classic Period. The most striking element is that the 14,000 seats wrap around more than 180 degrees of the circular dancing space or *orkastra*. In addition, the acoustics are outstanding.

a place for the actors to change costumes and prepare themselves, an unseen realm from which a previously familiar person could emerge changed in some inexplicable way. By placing the dancing circle (*orkastra*) at the base of a hillside, the more distant members of the audience had a chance to see if they perched on the slope. Finally, increasingly elaborate construction was added until the raised seating for the audience all but enclosed the dancing circle.

A key point about this *thrust* form of staging in that the *audience is oriented toward the center of the projecting acting area, not toward the stage area* which was slowly emerging in front of the *skene*. In a thrust configuration, the audience is constantly reminded that they are part of the action: as in arena theatre a large portion of the audience sees, when it looks past the actors, more audience on the far side.

Modern theatre artists have so valued this combination of intimacy and shared experience that they have constructed ingenious thrust theatres which combine these ancient principles with the impressive capacities of modern stagecraft. A good example is the Tyrone Guthrie Theatre in Minneapolis, Minnesota.

Two innovations which were first tested in the Guthrie Theatre are an asymmetrical acting area and auditorium design, and entrances called *vomitoria*. Seen in plan, this remarkable theatre has an irregular stage and an auditorium which uses balconies and sweeping arrays of seats in a combination which is aesthetically satisfying but gives the space an energy which an audience feels as soon as it enters. The *vomitoria* (or "voms" in theatre slang) are two tunnels which emerge from beneath the audience and which, when combined with the usual upstage exits, give a director the opportunity to flood the stage with action—and clear it just as quickly. Guthrie planned his theatre to complement the very physical and flamboyant productions of Shakespeare and the classics for which he was famous; however, the thrust design of the Guthrie Theatre and others modeled after it has proven very effective for a very wide range of periods and styles, including realistic modern drama.

The interior of The Tyrone Guthrie Theatre in Minneapolis attempts to capture some of the same characteristics of a classic Greek theatre. The seated audience surrounds the thrust stage in a 200 degree arc. None of the 1,441 audience members is more than 52 feet from the center of the stage.

Proscenium Theatre. Because it constantly reminds an audience that they *are* an audience, a thrust theatre is not particularly good for illusionistic productions which feature magical changes of elaborate scenery. In the Italian Renaissance a type of theatre began to develop which was ideally suited to productions requiring much movable scenery.

Renaissance thinkers were compulsively eager to recreate what they understood to be the glory of ancient Greece and Rome. Unfortunately, their sources of information were limited and many of their efforts are now seen to be fanciful reconstructions of what they thought a golden age *should* be, not what it was. In stagecraft and theatre design, this led to an increasing dependency on stage machinery which

The Teatro Olympico shows how the proscenium arch theatre began to develop during the Italian Renaissance. Its architects tried to combine a Roman stage with their newly discovered use of perspective. Gradually, the street scenes, observable in very forced perspective through each of the arches, became more important than the acting areas downstage. One can easily imagine the central arch in this theatre simply growing and growing until it becomes a huge peephole through which all the action is viewed. When it does, the proscenium arch theatre has arrived.

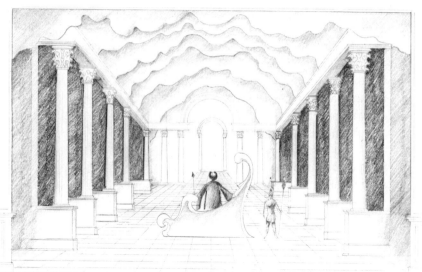

Notice that the forced perspective of this setting looks convincing if seen from the point of view of a nobleman seated exactly in front of the proscenium arch. However, a tradesman seated or standing to one side of the center line sees quite a different version.

moved scenery; the whole set was hidden from sight in "another room." The audience could view the events in this "other room" through a large hole in the wall which is now called a *proscenium arch*. To do this, the audience had to be placed at a point as directly opposite the scenic display as possible. A clear physical separation of actor and audience became necessary and inevitable.

The fascination of the Renaissance mind with the newly discovered rules of perspective drawing accelerated this reorientation. Scenic artists attempted to recreate on stage what they had done on the easel, using the tricks of perspective to devise huge vistas within the limits of the proscenium arch. The problem was that these tricks only work when the eye of the viewer is presumed to be at a single, fixed point. Hence, only one seat in the auditorium had a perfect perspective view of the scenic wonders being performed on stage; all other seats were nothing more than a close approximation of what the designer had in mind—and the effect deteriorated even more catastrophically the farther the viewer moved from the centerline of the theatre.

Today, proscenium theatres are the most common, though scenic designers seldom attempt the tricks of their Renaissance forebears. The major advantage of a proscenium theatre today is the ready accessibility of modern stage machinery, including ease of lighting.

The proscenium theatre has strong implications for the kind of actor/audience interactions created in it. All, or most, of the audience are facing the proscenium arch; the aim is to have each audience member's vision move in parallel and unobstructed lines of sight—as if each one were alone in the theatre. Seated in a darkened auditorium, each audience member is invited to enter into an individual performance contract with the actors; and to ignore the fact that the event is being shared with many others. This is the condition to which many film-makers aspire, but modern theatre artists are questioning whether it is appropriate to live theatre.

Environmental Theatre. Arena and thrust productions have strong historical roots; it is those roots to which modern directors often return when they seek alternatives to the familiar proscenium theatre. However, another possible relationship, environmental theatre, has emerged in recent years. Environmental staging has, in fact, historical precedents; but it seems far more radical because it calls into question a premise which underlies all of the forms we have discussed: that the actor has his or her space, the audience has its space, and the two are different. The important feature of environmental staging is that the acting space and the audience space interpenetrate or are shared. There are many ways to do this:

When the Free Theatre of Rome set out to stage Ariosto's sprawl-ing epic poem *Orlando Furioso*, they sought a way to capture the huge number of settings, the vast size of the cast, and the whimsical nature of much of the action. Their solution was to stage the piece on a number of small, rolling platforms which could be used as individual stages; these movable stages and the audience shared the same open area. Since the audience stood for the entire production, they were free to follow and surround the individual stages as those platforms were pushed by stagehands into their predetermined positions. In fact, at some points in the play, scenes were being played in as many as three locations simultaneously; audience members had to choose which scene they wished to see and move to that stage. The overall effect for an audience member was that they had been part of a complicated and exciting event—but no single audience member experienced everything. In fact, the audience was left with a feeling analogous to having participated in an extraordinarily successful county fair.

Another example was rather less complicated—but did force the actor/audience interaction to take on a very special character. A pro-duction of Shakespeare's *As You Like It* at Oberlin College in 1972 re-quired the audience to participate rather like the gallery at a golf match. The opening scenes, those set in and around the court of Duke Frederick, were staged outdoors near some abandoned stone buildings left over from the city of Oberlin's 19th-century waterworks. The audience sim-ply stood or sat on the grass as the action swept around them. When Rosaline, Celia, and Touchstone flee the estate of Duke Frederick to seek out Duke Senior in the forest, the three actors made their way to the edge of an adjacent pond. There they boarded a raft and paddled themselves across to the far side—Touchstone serenading them on his banjo! The audience had no choice but to follow them by walking around the pond on a path provided and, taking their lead, move into a clearing in the city arboretum which lay a short distance beyond. There, the audience followed the adventures of the young people after they reached the forest. Audiences quickly learn the special conventions em-ployed in such a production and delight in the unfamiliar challenge. Most do, that is.

The popularity in recent years of productions which use environ-mental staging has raised an interesting and recurring question: is there something intrinsic in the performance contract which requires that audience and performer spaces be separate and inviolate? Some audience members are made profoundly uncomfortable at the idea that actors will move into "their" space. Of course, this may in part be a concern with what the actor might do once he or she gets there: in the sixties and early seventies, there were a number of productions which took delight in discomforting the audience. Audiences were verbally abused, hugged, kissed, threatened, sprayed with water, and generally attacked for being "complacent." It may be the memory of those practices—or the possibility that they might happen again—which causes some contemporary audience members to flinch when an actor hops off the stage and starts into the audience. Still, the question of the privacy of space is an interesting one.

Flexible Theatre. The great variety of possible actor/audience configurations in modern theatre give the director, the playwright, or the scenic designer a great many options. Clearly some will work better for some plays than for others. But the theatre company with only a single fixed theatre in which to perform is going to be frustrated occasionally: either it selects only plays which work well in their theatre—be it arena, thrust, or proscenium—or it foregoes attractive production options. The "flexible" theatre is a popular compromise.

Since the 1950s, especially in America, there have been a number of theatres built or remodeled to provide flexibility: that is, through the use of hydraulic lifts, wheeled wagons, and electric winches, the interior of the theatre can be significantly changed in a relatively short period of time, moving from proscenium, to thrust, to full arena—often in less than an hour. Some of these designs are truly ingenious and, provided the equipment does not break down, come very close to meeting their designed goals.

However, some theatre artists have, after several decades of experience, grown skeptical of such all-purpose designs. They argue that a theatre which attempts to do all these things, does none of them very well. A theatre, they point out, is like a person: It has its own integrity, and it is better to have a solid theatre with its own character, however limited, than one riddled with compromise.

SHAPING OF THE PERFORMERS' INTERACTION

A theatre is perhaps the most complicated artistic tool ever devised. Seen from the perspective of function, a physical theatre is a machine built to achieve specific goals. Some of those we have already touched upon. For example, we noted that in every permanent theatre, there must be a place offstage, a place to which an actor retires and from which he or she emerges transformed. What we have not mentioned are those spaces which are necessary or useful for the support of the performer—but which are never seen by the audience.

In a well-designed theatre, the audience spaces (auditorium, foyer, lobby, restrooms, ticket offices, etc.) occupy less than one-half of the total space. The remainder is used by the company and is, therefore, an extension of the actor/actor interaction. This space may not be under the personal control of the scenic designer, but it exists, and it becomes part of the environment created to support the interactions that make theatre such a dynamic art form.

For example, most theatres have shops associated with them: a scene shop for creating the scenic elements needed by the company, a costume shop for costumes. In addition, however, a modern theatre may also have prop shops, electric shops, wig shops, armories, poster shops, and photographic darkrooms. Design studios are kept busy by designers creating upcoming productions. Storage areas hold costumes, props, and scenic elements from previous productions until they are needed again. Actors and directors work in rehearsal rooms preparing the performers for future productions (a busy theatre can seldom provide the stage for early rehearsals, so a rehearsal room of the same dimension as the stage is home for a company of performers until shortly before opening).

During performance, the offstage areas are especially designed to support performers. Comfortable dressing and makeup rooms are provided in which the actor has peace and quiet to compose herself before the performance. In the *kabuki* theatre, each major character is also provided with a small meditation room in which the fully costumed and made-up actor comtemplates this reflected image in a full-length mirror—and thereby gets into character. Even Western actors frequently treasure that time spent gazing into the makeup room mirror as their character emerges.

Finally, those spaces offstage and in the wings are important to the performer. From a comfortable *greenroom*—the traditional name of the room in which actors wait to make an entrance—to safe stairs and passages behind the set, great thought is given to the psychological and physical support needed to assure a good performance. Indeed, a visitor backstage during a performance might be surprised to see that the activity there is as carefully planned and executed as what is happening onstage. Careful advance planning can make the offstage blocking of actors—as they race to change costumes, pick up props, and ready themselves to reenter—as effective as the blocking onstage.

CHARACTER/CHARACTER ENVIRONMENTS

The major task of the scenic designer is to create the environment in which character/character interactions take place; his or her function is to discover and express the powerful influence of environment in the world of the play. As a result, the scenic designer must be both an interpreter and a creator. On the one hand, he or she must be able to understand and interpret the ideas of the playwright and director, faithfully providing those scenic elements which both have decided must be present if the audience is to understand the play. But, in addition, the scenic designer is often asked to provide a visual image, a decorative touch, a sculpted space which extends and invigorates an idea in ways that the playwright never anticipated.

Read the stage directions provided by, say, George Bernard Shaw or Henrik Ibsen for one of their plays. They are crammed with detailed information about the setting. This is not just an expression of a playwright's obsessive ego. These two giants, like most modern playwrights, have a clear idea of the importance of environment in the lives of their characters—and they truly believe that unless we understand the environment in which those characters live, we can never fully understand them.

The Physical Environment. Certain physical demands of any script or dramatic idea must be captured by the scenic designer. A stage set must allow the actor to be seen and heard. These requirements may seem so obvious as to require no comment; but is surprisingly easy for a beginner to design a set with jutting walls which prevent significant portions of the audience from seeing key scenes, or with a floor plan which forces intimate scenes into inaudible upstage corners. A skillful designer also uses platforms, ramps, stairs, and traps to control the elevation of the actors so that, even in crowd scenes, every performer can be heard and seen.

Plans demand certain familiar elements—like doors and windows in useful and believable numbers and locations. (The author once received from a student designer a floor plan for a box setting in which there was no provision for doors or windows! He had forgotten to include any—thus effectively barricading the actors offstage.) Architecture has certain familiar rules and audiences tend to wonder about things like windows directly over a fireplace, or bathroom doors which connect with the kitchen, or garden doors which open onto brick walls. These and other distractions can be avoided by a scenic designer who reads a script intelligently and then carefully works out the physical demands of each scene.

Expression of Character.   As Sherlock Holmes was so fond of proving to Dr. Watson, every person leaves some special impact on the physical world around him or her—if we only knew where to look. So, too, with a good stage setting: every detail tells us something about the people who live in and use that space. Or it tells us how that space must influence anyone who moves into it. Successful and unsuccessful examples abound, especially in realistic plays: the scuff marks on a closet door

Realistic stage settings provide the opportunity to explore the interaction between character and environment. Innaurato's *Gemini*, seen here in a production at the University of New Mexico, lets us see how a group of eccentric characters in inner city Philadelphia celebrate with a background picnic. Scenic design by Roy Hogland.

tell us that the owner habitually kicks the door shut; the contents of a refrigerator say volumes about the eating habits of the owner; conversely, a picture of the Madonna hanging in the apartment of an orthodox Jew tells us that the prop room had only one painting and that the prop crew didn't bother to do its job correctly.

A recent production of Innaurato's *Gemini* portrayed a backyard of a Philadelphia row house in a working-class district. Among the details provided were a yard overgrown with weeds, rolls of sod that had never been laid, a rusty lawn mower covered with vines; together they told the perceptive audience member a great deal about the frustrated plans of the people who lived in that house—and that message was clear even before the actors made their first entrance.

Emotional Environment.   Plays are designed to evoke an emotional response from audiences. And scenic design has much to contribute in this regard. For example, a light-hearted farce may be enhanced by a bright, cheerful, perhaps even silly setting which reminds the audience that this evening nothing is to be taken seriously. On the other hand, a dark, brooding setting for a classic tragedy supports the tone of that work. First-rate scenic designers are famous for their ability to support the mood of the production through color, texture, lighting, and design elements. And directors have expressed grateful thanks to many a scenic designer whose set and lights *finally* conveyed to the actors the proper tone for a scene.

Unity.   With the possible exception of the director, the scenic designer has the greatest power to give each production a "look." Modern audiences especially expect a production to have a unity, a complementary and harmonious relationship of all parts. A good scenic designer finds ways to assure that, if a play has several scenes, each scene has contrast *and* unity; that the properties fit together; that the colors have an underlying harmony even in their diversity. The world created by each play should have its own rules—and those rules should be followed in every aspect of its environment.

Aesthetic Statement.   Finally, the most important contribution of the scenic designer is the most difficult to anticipate—because it is the most creative. Successful scenic designers have the capacity to create a visual metaphor for a play which captures and enhances the production without overwhelming it. The Czech designer Josef Svoboda's designs

At the conclusion of Bertolt Brecht's *The Caucasion Chalk Circle* two women, both claiming to be the real mother, try to pull a child out of a circle of chalk. The concept for the Minnesota Theatre company's 1966 production made extensive use of debris left in a mountain village after World War II, for the costumes and props.

for modern plays have mixed movies, slides, and painted graphics of the actors in a way that accurately captures the fractured personalities of the modern person. Tanya Moisewitsch's design for Brecht's *The Caucasian Chalk Circle* built on director Edward Payson Call's concept. Soviet peasants are presenting a play at the conclusion of the Second World War: all the costumes, props, and settings are created from scavenged, war-surplus equipment. Thus Brecht's point that property belongs to those who would use it most creatively is extended to the scenic elements of the play.

In the artistic give-and-take which marks a modern production company, it is often the scenic designer who finds the visual image which crystallizes the production concept.

Environment as Character.   Sometimes, though not frequently, a play is written in which the environment becomes one of the characters. In those situations, the scenic designer is called upon to create a setting which is truly interactive. *K-2*, a recent production by Washington,

D.C.'s Arena Theatre dealt with mountain climbers scaling an ice face; the setting, a breathtakingly beautiful design by Ming Cho Lee, took on a malevolent character all its own during the course of the evening. The interactive pattern is thus between the climbers and their environment. Jean-Claude Van Itallie's *America Hurrah!* has a sequence in which oversized puppet people gradually destroy a motel room—a case of an environment which does not prevail.

Cases of settings which take on the attributes of character are especially interesting to designers because they allow a major shift in their work: Instead of playing a supportive role, such a setting must become assertive and responsive.

THE SCENE DESIGNER AT WORK

Like a playwright, a novelist, or a painter, the scenic designer begins his or her work by developing a profound understanding of the imaginary world to be created. This means detailed research: repeated readings of the playscript, library research, perhaps a visit to the actual location of the play. Scenic designers have shown great ingenuity in this preparatory work; important ideas have come from reading biographies and histories, studying the arts of the period in question, visiting museums, poring over period mail-order catalogs, and referring to old diaries and photograph albums.

And always sketching! Good designers arrive at early production meetings with armloads of sketches, photocopies, resource books, and other visual material. An architectural detail here, a prop there, a period window, a carpet pattern, anything could be the stimulus for the discussion that will pull the disparate scenic elements into a coherent whole.

The director generally has ideas as well. He or she wants a door roughly here (the director is scratching some indecipherable floor plan on the back of an envelope) and wants to stage a key scene in this general area (more incoherent marking on scraps of something). This idea is all wrong; but this one is terrific. And so it goes.

After each meeting, the designer returns to the drawing board to try to incorporate all the new information, returning to subsequent meetings with more detailed and comprehensive designs. Gradually, complete plans (the stage design seen from directly above) and elevations (seen as the audience will see them) emerge. But always there are changes: because the director is increasing the size of a crowd, the room must be slightly larger; a window is now being used as an entrance, hence it must actually open and shut; the costume designer objects to the color of the set because it does not work with the emerging palette of the costumes, etc. The changes go on seemingly forever.

At some point, however, the process of change must halt. After all, ultimately these settings must be built in wood, canvas, steel, and plastic; after that, change is both difficult and expensive. So, at some point in the design process the director "signs off" or initials the design, formally indicating that he or she agrees to no further changes. At this point, detailed construction drawings are prepared and sent to the scene shop, where construction begins.

In regional and university theatres, the scene designer remains in close contact with the shop during construction. In New York, however, scenery construction is completed in specialized shops—frequently at some distance from the city—and the designer may not see the setting until it is trucked to the theatre. Even in New York, however, the designer is usually involved in supervision of the painting. This step of the work is so crucial that a designer seldom trusts it completely to others.

In the course of preparing a single production, a scenic designer will create sketches, elevations, working drawings, and models—all in preparation for the finished setting.

The completed set will not, of course, be ready for the actors until shortly before opening. But it is critical that the actors understand the environment in which their characters will be living. Because actors—and even some directors—do not read plans well, a convenient device has been developed to help everyone understand the set: a model. Professional designers often build highly detailed models of the settings to convey their ideas to people who might otherwise be caught totally by surprise later. These models are usually built to a scale of ¼ inch : 1 foot; but they may be as small as ⅛ inch scale since larger models are difficult to carry around in overcrowded New York.

Plans, elevations, construction drawings, and models also help to explain how scenery will shift. If a play has several scenes, or if a single-set play is performing in repertory, provision must be made for set changes. A fully equipped modern theatre gives the designer much to work with: revolving stages, hydraulic lifts, wagons, and a counterweighted fly system provide ways to move scenery quickly, quietly and safely. But it is the scenic designer, working with the technical director, who decides how each piece of scenery is moved and stored until needed. Again, a visitor backstage would often be amazed to see how cleverly bulky scenery has been flown, stacked, nested, and dismantled while not in use.

The scenic designer's hour of trial begins in technical rehearsals when the set is assembled in place on stage, dressed with properties, and actors begin to use it. If all the planning has gone well, there are no problems.

But there are *always* problems. Occasionally they are catastrophic. Theatre artists love to recount tales of those technical rehearsals when *nothing* worked, when someone forgot which way the turntable revolved and the elegant parlor set ended up with a bathtub in the corner, when a tree proved so large that it couldn't be gotten offstage, when a wagon stage rolled into the audience. But problems of this magnitude are rare. Usually the scenic designer's attention is absorbed by smaller problems: rehanging a door which swings the wrong way; repainting an element which visually stands out; and the continuous selection and arrangement of properties.

On opening night, nearly any scenic designer is pleased when, as the curtain rises, the audience gives a spontaneous round of applause to the setting. But on reflection, most would also agree that a good setting should not attract attention to itself. A good scenic designer, like any responsible member of the production company, receives his or her greatest satisfaction from the praise directed toward the entire production, when perceptive audience members and critics recognize the settings as only one part of a totally unified production.

THE LIGHTING DESIGNER

The lighting designer is really a 20th century specialist whose rise corresponds to the increasing artistic potential of lighting technology. Before the development of gaslight in the early 19th century, theatre artists had only limited control over light in the theatre; the productions were either played outdoors by daylight or indoors by candlelight or oil lamps. Indoors, both stage and auditorium were illuminated by chandeliers hung over the forestage or footlights across the front of the stage; these lights were lit just before the play began and extinguished as soon as it was concluded. In between, only minor lighting control was possible.

The introduction of gas, however, allowed remarkable control. A gas table—rather like a modern dimmer board—was installed where an operator could see the stage and operate an array of valves. Although this method may seem primitive to us, the effects achieved were astounding to audiences of the time, and its potential encouraged playwrights to include more elaborate lighting effects in their plays.

Probably the most severe problem with gas theatre lighting was the danger. The history of Western theatre after the introduction of gaslight is scarred by some of the worst theatre fires on record; the average life of theatre buildings plummeted.

The introduction of electric light toward the end of the 19th century provided a welcome alternative. Not only was electricity safer than gas, but it could be controlled in many different ways; electric light gave the modern lighting designer the materials of the art.

ELEMENTS OF LIGHTING DESIGN

The primary need in any indoor theatre is *illumination*. Modern theatres are designed to be absolutely light-tight; without some form of artificial illumination, nothing is possible. Of course, with the power to give light comes the power to withhold it; a modern lighting designer's first concern is to be able to provide light any place a director may require it, and not have light spilling into areas where the director does not want it. In this way, lighting can control the visual focus of the audience, moving it from area to area, actor to actor as the action of the play demands. A primary visual image for many theatre artists and audience members is a single pool of light on a single actor in an otherwise black space. Of course, some directors may not want this sharp contrast—they may prefer audiences to see other parts of the stage or the auditorium—but the lighting designer must have the capacity to illuminate one part of the acting area while keeping the rest in near-absolute darkness.

Once an object or person is illuminated, however, the task is far from complete. For example, there must be some modeling to the subject. A single light source can illuminate an object from only one side, a visual condition that may be appropriate in some cases but not in others. A light shown from exactly the same direction as the viewer will illuminate the object, but like an object seen in the beam of one's flashlight, it will not have much of a three-dimensional quality. So, the lighting designer tries to model the subject by providing lights from several sources in such a way as to give the subject a "roundness." For some kinds of theatre and dance, the silhouette of the performer is very important; to emphasize the silhouette the designer may hang lights in the wings, directly over the performer, or even upstage of the performer. This side- or back-lighting will give a very sharp edge to the performer, making him or her stand out from the background. Again, the director of the play may not require this kind of lighting, but if it is needed, the lighting designer must be able to provide it.

The quality of the light cast upon the subject is also important. The lenses and mirrors of some lighting instruments are so arranged that the light falls on the object either very strongly in focus or slightly fuzzy. The result is a light whose quality is hard in the first case and soft in the second; the first provides a sharply defined pool of the light, the second a pool which can be blended easily with the light from other sources. There are even some lighting instruments that provide light that flows in essentially parallel beams, casting shadows with the same sharp edges as sunlight.

The second major element of stage lighting is *mood*. This is normally provided by either color or intensity. Color is an inherent quality of any light, including the artificial illumination used in the theatre. While the manufacturers make every attempt to create lights that cast absolutely white light (light in which every part of the visible spectrum

A single figure, well-illuminated, is what many people consider a primary image in theatre or dance. Notice here how back lighting defines the silhouette of the dancer.

is equally represented), a naked stage lighting instrument throws light which has a distinctive color—even when that color is the wholly artificial white. However, modern stage lights are equipped with the means to change the color of the light; the usual method is by placing translucent, colored sheets of plastic material just in front of the lens. These are called gelatins (or "gels" for short). These gels are available in a remarkable range of colors, enough to meet the needs of even the most demanding lighting designer. As part of his or her design, the lighting designer decides on the color of light that will achieve the effect needed in a particular scene. An early morning scene may emphasize pinks; evening may demand blues; midday may mix the two. For special effects, magentas, chocolate browns, or grays may be called for.

The amount of light demanded by a particular scene is usually controlled by controlling the intensity of the light emitted from each source. Since each of these sources is controlled by a single electrical circuit, and each circuit is controlled by a dimmer, the lighting designer has control over the intensity of every light on the stage. He or she may decide that a scene needs strong light from stage left, medium light from the front, and low intensity on the upstage scenery. All that is needed is an accurate setting on the control board to achieve the desired effect.

The combined power of color and intensity to influence an audience's mood has to be experienced to be believed. In a production of Shakespeare's *Love's Labours Lost* at the Tyrone Guthrie Theatre, the lighting designer helped to underline and reinforce a very difficult mood change. Most of this play is a lighthearted romp exploring the irresistible power of love in overcoming the best intentions of young men and women. By Act V, the four major couples have been paired and the audience is ready for a conventional happy ending to a play which has had a warm summery quality throughout. However, a messenger then arrives with bad news: the King of the realm, father to the princess who had planned much of the previous shenanigans, has died. She is naturally depressed, and the play takes on a much darker quality at the conclusion. This was captured by the lighting designer who, as the black-clad messenger entered, subtly began to change the quality of the light. The colors moved from pink and amber to blues and grays; the light became softer, the sources became lower. Imperceptibly it has become autumn in the world of the play; summer is over, and the less-attractive aspects of reality have begun to assert themselves.

The seemingly endless magic of the lighting designer includes a collection of special effects that can be employed on demand. For example, the lighting designer is responsible for projections, which are realistic or abstract patterns projected by special equipment on screens placed anywhere in the stage space or on the stage floor itself. Some designers depend heavily on projected scenery intended to communicate the location of the action or to make some other comment on the environment. Or the effect may be much simpler: the pattern of a stained-glass window cast on the floor or the patterns of leaves dappling the floor of a forest.

For truly extravagant effects, the lighting designer has a full range of technologies that have been developed by the motion pictures, Las Vegas shows, and rock bands: lasers, color organ effects, stroboscopic lights, computer generated sequencing, and the like.

In short, the lighting designer is in the remarkable position of being the newest member of the theatre design team, and is the one with the most up-to-date technology. This technology is frequently so advanced, in fact, that we all need to be reminded that the greatest evocative power often resides in the simplest lighting effects: a pool of light that focuses our attention on the actor allows us to see and understand that actor, sets a mood which supports the action, and generally puts itself at the disposal of the production concept.

THE LIGHTING DESIGNER AT WORK

The lighting designer usually joins the company at the same time as the other members of the design team, and begins his or her work in much the same way. In the early conferences with the director, the lighting designer pays close attention to the concept of the production at hand: Each concept makes different demands on the lighting, and it is crucial that the lighting reinforce that concept. In addition, the lighting designer will listen closely to what scenic and costume designs seem to be emerging. The scenic design will govern much of what the lighting design can achieve. The placement of scenic elements will govern where and when lighting instruments can be hung; the colors of the set can be enhanced—or totally ruined—by the selection of gel colors; textures can be underscored or wiped out by lighting choices. The relationship between the costume designer and the lighting designer is especially important; the most careful and imaginative costume design and construction can be ruined by thoughtless lighting design. As a result, the lighting designer will visit the costume shop regularly to see what materials have been chosen and to confer about gel choices.

The lighting designer is also a frequent visitor to rehearsals. All the designers want to become familiar with the play as it develops; this is especially true for the lighting designer. He or she must know where actors will be placed in certain scenes, how long scenes are running so as to anticipate any recircuiting problems, and to gauge the tempo and mood of each scene. After all, the general pace of a play is often governed by the speed with which light cues are accomplished, and the lighting designer wants to make sure that his or her thinking is locked into the same rhythms as the director.

The lighting designer begins his or her work on paper. Like the other designers, the lighting designer reads the script again and again, always asking a series of questions: What time of day does this scene take place? What time of year? If the lighting is natural, what special qualities might it have? If artificial, what are the sources? Candles? Oil lamps? Is there a fireplace? What is the mood of this scene? What colors would capture that mood? Where should the audience's focus be? And many more.

A lighting plot is prepared. Using a scale plan of the setting, the location of each instrument is indicated and a line drawn from that point to the center of a circle drawn on the plan of the stage. This tells the light crew where to hang the light and where, generally, to focus the beam of the instrument. Next a lighting schedule is prepared; this shows the kind of instrument, the detailed location of each instrument, the gel for that instrument, the circuit into which it is plugged, and the dimmer into which that circuit is patched. This enables the lighting crew to begin hanging instruments as soon as both the theatre and the instruments are available.

As technical rehearsals approach the pressure on the lighting designer grows perhaps more quickly than on others: After all, the scenery and costumes are close to being finished; the other designers have had a chance to see their work in the shops; but the lighting designer will not know whether the design will really work until all the lights are hung, the scenery is in place, and the costumed actors have peopled the stage. Late in the rehearsal period, the lighting designer and the director have a session in the theatre with no one present except the light crew and the stage managers. This is the time they set the lighting levels for the individual scenes. Sometimes it is the first time the director has seen the lights in action, and the pressure on the designer can be intense. But together the director and the lighting designer look at the "pictures" the designer has composed for each scene, and the director gives tentative approval for each. If the levels are properly set in this rehearsal, there will only be minor changes during dress rehearsal; if the pictures are unacceptable, it is back to the drawing board for the lighting designer—and long nights for the light crew.

During dress rehearsals, the major problem of the lighting designer is to integrate the lights with the action of the performed play. Precise cues for each light setting must be established and rehearsed; not a small task when one considers that a complex production may have two hundred cues.

Gradually, as the opening date approaches, the lighting designer slowly disengages from the production. Once the play opens, all the cues are called by the stage manager and performed by the members of the light crew. It is also the responsibility of the light crew, led by the master electrician, to keep the lights and other equipment in working order. Each night the crew arrives early at the theatre to make sure that each one of perhaps several hundred lighting instruments is working properly, and to review the light cues that may not have been as exact as they should have been the night before.

The result of all this care is an aspect of modern theatre production that combines science and art to create a form of magic every night.

THE COSTUME DESIGNER

Another design specialist whose rewards come from audience response to the entire production is the costume designer. As much as any artist in the company, the costume designer is concerned about the character/character interaction—and specifically how that interaction is clarified and enriched through the clothing worn by those characters. Other issues may arise: a star may have a color which she thinks is flattering, physical difficulties may have to be disguised, technical problems will have to be overcome; but always the costume designer asks, what would this character, in this period, wear in a place like this, under these dramatic circumstances?

ELEMENTS OF COSTUME

Period. Only relatively recently in the history of theatre has there been much expectation that costumes would be historically accurate. In Shakespeare and Molière's companies actors wore contemporary clothes on stage—sometimes with only the merest suggestion of some other period. A drape might evoke a classic period; a turban might give a 17th-century Parisian courtier's elaborate outfit some hint that the character was, in fact, a sultan. Those days are long past, however. A modern costume designer is expected to be something of a costume historian.

The task can be a formidable one. Some periods of costume history are not well known, or else they are unevenly documented. There may be plenty of visual evidence describing the king's costume, but what of the servants, the peasants, the shopkeepers? And what of the small but important distinctions of rank and prestige which were as surely incorporated into historical costumes as in our own? What of the subtle marks of use which are unfamiliar to our society since we seldom, if ever, carry and use fans, ride horses, drive chariots, wear powdered wigs, sport beauty marks, carry swords, or engage in the thousands of activities which were second nature to our ancestors?

A director may devise a concept which does not work well in the period in which the play was originally set. In such a case, the costume designer may become a consultant as he or she searches for a more appropriate period.

Concept. A director's concept may ask for very imaginative solutions from the costume designer. For example, it may require that essentially historical costumes be exaggerated in such ways as to emphasize existing aspects of the characters. Several of the characters in Ben Jonson's famous satirical comedy *Volpone* (the fox) are named after animals: the director may ask that such characters as Mosca (the fly), Voltare (the vulture) and Corvino (the crow) be costumed in such a way as to reinforce their animal parallels. Other challenges might include a punk rock *Midsummer Night's Dream*, a production of *The Tempest* set on an asteroid a thousand years in the future, or *The Taming of the Shrew* set in the American Old West.

Character. The aspect of the costume designer's work which requires the greatest empathy is the creation of character. In effect, the costume designer must go with the character to his or her closet and pick out the clothes for the next scene. What would a person of this sex, this age, this education, this experience and sophistication, this wealth, these aspirations, etc., choose to wear to achieve these ends? Usually the costume designer can depend on the help of the director and the actor playing the role. Step by step, the picture emerges and the trained eye and instincts of the costume designer begin to create a costume which tells the audience volumes about the character even before he or she begins to speak. The overdressed fop whose self-love prevents him from seeing how ridiculous he is; the inept young lady with much to learn about high fashion; the relaxed elegance of a character who has always lived in the lap of luxury; the heedless desperation of a starving beggar; all of these and more can be communicated by clothes alone.

To this basic effect can be added individual touches which reveal important aspects of the character. One character may have a worn place on his vest from constantly referring to his pocket watch. A smoker may have burnt ash holes in his suit. A weepy matron may have mascara stains on her handkerchief. A worn-out shoe; a sagging hem; a torn pocket; a new collar on an old shirt. All tell us about the character.

Palette.   Color can contribute information as well. Upbeat, sunny characters—like their parallels in real life—frequently seek out clothes from the warmer end of the color spectrum; gloomy characters may do the reverse.

Just as importantly, characters appear on stage together and their colors make a collective statement. For example, certain dramatic forces may have costumes in roughly the same range. It is not as simple as "bad guys wear black hats"—but the same principles apply. Even subconsciously, the audience comes to sort out the groups, or forces, or family affiliations by color. Indeed, in some plays the sensitive audience member can probably anticipate which suitor will "get the girl" by anticipating which costume goes best with hers.

THE COSTUME DESIGNER AT WORK

The costume designer participates in all those conferences which develop and expand the play's concept. And, like the scenic designer, the costume designer's visual sense can help unify all aspects of the production. It is not unusual for a costume designer to remind the director of the *sounds* which costumes will contribute to a production: the clump of boots, the rustle of silk petticoats, the clink of armor, the swish of trains across the floor. The costume designer also provides an especially detailed sense of each period and, as a result, may be able to suggest properties, aspects of movement, and general attitudes which will help everyone in the company—especially the actors. The costume designer's relationship with the actor is often very special. The aspect of the actors' environment which is closest to them is their clothing; if the actors feel uncomfortable with their costumes, not much else can rescue the situation.

Usually, the costume designs (or *plates*) have been worked out well in advance of the beginning of rehearsals. The first company reading may even include a presentation of those plates by the designer.

The plates themselves are large color renderings of each character in the proposed costume. In plays with several scenes, each new costume has its own plate. Costume plates serve a number of purposes: First of all, they give the director a clear idea of what a proposed cos-

A good costume plate becomes part of the creative interaction, which leads to successful productions. Here a costume plate can be compared to the garment as it was eventually worn by the actress. Costume designer: Gwendolyn Nagle.

tume will actually look like once it is constructed and placed on the body of the actor. In addition, the plates are valuable resources for the costume construction staff as they construct the garments. Finally, the actors need a good strong visual sense of what they will ultimately look like; to this end, a costume designer is seldom above illustrating for the actor how the character might stand, what postural alignment the character might adopt—even what facial expressions might be employed.

As rehearsals start, the period of costume production begins. A well-equipped theatre will have a fully staffed costume shop including pattern drafters, cutters, stitchers, tailors, wigmakers, and other craftspersons. A shop supervisor distributes the work assignments and assures that work proceeds smoothly and on schedule. The diversity of skills demanded by a full season of plays can be staggering: the shop may have to provide suits and dresses for several periods, wigs and hair pieces, shoes, hats, armor, masks, plus an endless list of such novelty pieces as puppets, breakaway costumes, special padding and the like. In addition, the costume department usually accepts responsibility for personal props—properties which an actor carries—such as eyeglasses, snuffboxes, purses, wallets, canes, and some weapons.

Some directors schedule a dress parade early in technical rehearsals. This is when each actor wears his or her costume for the first time on-stage. One by one the costumes are scrutinized by the director and notes are given.

A costume designer is ethically and contractually obliged to provide costumes which look like the plates which the director approved.

A good costume design anticipates the contribution of the other elements of production. At the same time, the designer is required to provide a costume that bears a close resemblance to the approved plate. Costume designer: Gwendolyn Nagle.

Fairly ugly scenes have resulted from a costume designer having made unauthorized changes in costume designs; or from a careless director suddenly realizing that the design approved was not what he or she thought it would be. And, of course, there is always a chance that an unprofessional actor—at this juncture stressed to the breaking point anyway—will begin to complain that the costume "isn't right." (Dress parades can be very exciting!)

Unless the production has a specifically assigned makeup designer, the costume designer usually accepts responsibility for makeup design. This includes hairstyle and any facial hair for the men.

The best costume designers understand from the outset that costumes are to be *used* by the actors; the actor is not a living clotheshorse to display the lovely garments. This means that the designer is willing to accommodate the needs of the role, adding a pocket if necessary, adjusting a hem, letting out a seam, finding a different hat—until the

Sumptuous costumes can become a major element in an otherwise rather spartan production. Here, elaborate costumes mark a production of Mark Rozovsky's *Strider: The Story of a Horse* at the Chelsea Theatre Center.

needs of the actor and character are reconciled. Only then is the costume designer satisfied.

Theatre patrons seldom recognize scenic and costume designers on the street; their names are familiar only to the most avid fans. In many way, however, they are the unsung heroes of the modern theatre since their contributions within the company are often credited to the people who receive more public acclaim. Good design is much more than pleasing ornamentation applied to the surface of an otherwise intact production. It is, on the contrary, an integral part of the entire creative process. The designers should participate early and continuously in the production process, and their work is subject to the same forces as any other aspect of modern theatre. Their rewards come from the knowledge that they have created an environment which supports and enriches the interaction between audience and performer in such a way that both can better understand the interaction between character and character.

Discussion Questions

1. Is there an ideal theatre building somewhere? Could there be? Speaking only for yourself, what would the best theatre for you as an audience member be like?

2. Discuss *all* aspects of the unwillingness of most legitimate theatres to sell refreshments—or if they do, their rules against taking food into the auditorium.

3. Aren't all the questions about the relationship of audience members to performers made pointless by the development of film and television cameras? After all, everyone has a front row seat in film, so why worry about seating at all?

4. How do *you* feel about the idea that actors have *their* space and audiences have *theirs*? Does it bother you to think that you, an audience member, may become part of the action?

5. Why is it that legitimate theatre is less interested in flamboyant scenic effects today than, say, a century ago? Few playwrights write plays—and fewer producers mount plays—which call for chariot races on stage, or floods, or earthquakes. Why?

6. Consider one of your personal spaces—say, your bedroom—as an expression of your personality. What would a stranger know about you from studying that space?

7. Come up with another source to which a designer might turn for information on a particular period, a source which is not mentioned in the text.

8. Actors frequently report that they understand their characters much better after the first dress rehearsal. Give some reasons why this might be the case.

9

Critic

> Critics are to theatre what ornithologists are to flying.
> —A disgruntled director

This unhappy director is only saying what many working theatre artists believe: that the critic has little or nothing positive to do with the creative process of theatre. They argue further that the modern theatre critic, given the enormous power of the press and television, has influence far beyond any human's ability to use with discretion. Then these angry artists may go on to give examples of the destructive power of inexperienced, stupid, prejudiced, or thoroughly unscrupulous critics who have closed productions, blighted careers, and extinguished important movements in theatre history. All of it is true—in part.

But the history of theatre is also filled with critics who used their influence to champion causes, encourage promising performers, and shape public perceptions of whole areas of the discipline. On balance, the newcomer is often left not knowing *what* to believe. The only certainty is that the critic does have influence and that the force and direction of his or her contribution must be included if we are to understand the dynamics of theatre.

WHAT IS A CRITIC?

Some definitions are in order. Let us begin by distinguishing between *drama* criticism and *theatre* criticism. A drama critic is concerned with the evaluation of dramatic literature, playscripts in short. The theatrical critic aims to understand and evaluate the *performed* work; he or she deals with the theatrical experience as we have described it.

Some people choose to make a distinction between *reviewers* and *critics*. Reviewers, they argue, are journalists—sometimes with limited experience of the art of theatre—who report on the experience as if it were any other kind of public event, an inauguration, for example, or an airline disaster. Because a reviewer usually has to formulate opinions in a very short period of time, some people think there is a strong possibility that a reviewer's comments will be ill-considered snap judgments. And some reviewers even argue that their function is to help theatre consumers find good "buys" for their entertainment dollar.

For those who relegate reviewers to a secondary position, a true theatre critic is someone who has the background and leisure to analyze the theatre experience from the broadest perspective using the most demanding standards.

Such a distinction between a reviewer and a critic may be theoretically useful, but in practice the differences disappear. Some very fine criticism has been pecked out in a white-hot frenzy between final curtain and a 1:00 A.M. deadline. Conversely, months of reflection can culminate in drivel. In some cases, the honest response of a working journalist is preferable to the self-conscious jargon of the insider. In short, the process of criticism seems to be the same whatever the person is called—so long as the critic is genuinely trying to understand the theatre experience and enrich it through analysis and evaluation.

In fact, roughly one-third of the critic's role is precisely the same as that of the good audience member. He or she experiences the event as completely as possible, trying to become involved as an active participant. A second part of the critic's role, however, involves commitment to a full understanding of the experience; the critic is always asking *why* the experience took place as it did. Finally, the remaining part of the critic's job is to communicate his or her insights to others.

Critical Trap #1: The Critic as Censor. "My mission is to stamp out offensive characters, ideas, and language!"

The overall function of the critic, then, is to enrich the audience's experience of theatre. How can this be done?

THE CRITIC AND THE FEEDBACK LOOP

At one level, the critic becomes part of the feedback loop we spoke of in chapter 1. You will remember that we discussed the ways that the actor knows he or she has communicated: applause, laughter, sobbing, and so on. We even mentioned such things as reviews as a means—delayed in time, of course, and very complicated—for the performer to receive the necessary feedback.

However, it is this kind of feedback which can so enrage a performer. One critic put it gently: "Actors don't want criticism, they want praise." We can hardly blame them; theatre is an insecure profession and theatre artists are demonstrably human. And few of us like rejection—especially when it is read by thousands of people who are not at the performance in question and, hence, cannot have an independent opinion.

Then why do we continue the practice? Why do newspapers and television commit valuable space and time to opinions of such dubious merit? For the same reason that audience members nudge each other during key moments of a play—to remind each other that they are sharing the experience. At intermission one can hear fiercely disputed opinions in the lobby, and after the final curtain audience members will assure one another, "It was wonderful, wasn't it!" They will reflect on the experience for days afterward—and continue to share opinions. The audience is developing a consensus, testing its opinions, and generally extending its own communication net in such a way as to define its relationship to the play and to the theatre. The critic can be an important part of this process.

The balance is a delicate one. Critics are both like and unlike the audience. They are capable of following the action, of becoming involved, of being deeply moved. In theory, anyone in the audience can do this. But in addition, critics should understand *why* they are involved or moved; whether this performance was more or less effective than others like it; whether the experience was ultimately worth anything.

Critical Trap #2: The Critic as Fan. "Theatre is so wonderful! And it always needs paying audiences. So I'll emphasize only the best things about each production—and audiences will come flocking."

Finally, critics have the skills necessary to share these insights with others. Some of these others will have already experienced the production; their experience will be enriched after the fact. For the rest, the critic will influence *how* they experience the production the first time. This last is what some theatre artists find so offensive. They believe that an audience member ought to be—like a courtroom jury—naive and unprejudiced. These artists forget that no audience is *really* free of bias. Indeed, a review is only doing for large numbers of people what word-of-mouth does for a smaller group. And theatre people usually do not complain about word-of-mouth.

The critic is one of the prime means by which the institution of theatre is shaped by society. The theatre artist who rages against a successful critic should bear in mind that—to some degree, at least—that critic is saying what the audience wants to read or hear. Furthermore, to the degree that the critic does represent society, the whole future of the art is at stake.

THE CRITICAL PROCESS

Early in the 19th century, the thinker and artist Johann Wolfgang Goethe (1749–1832) suggested that serious criticism responded to three basic questions:

1. What was the artist attempting?
2. Did he or she succeed?
3. Was the enterprise worth the effort?

Goethe himself was a major artist of extraordinary breadth and productivity; it was typical of him to propose three questions which could apply, with little modification, to *any* art experience. Still, the questions need some modification when they are applied to something as immediate, sensory, and complex as a performed play. So let us examine them one at a time.

What was the artist attempting?   Who is the artist here? The playwright, the director, the designer, the actor? You will have to clear up this issue before proceeding. If everyone had exactly the same intention, fine; but what if one participant goes in a completely different direction? For example, you may believe that the playwright had one goal in mind—

but that the director and actor took an entirely different tack altogether. What do you do then? Well, a good critic will probably want to note the discrepancy in his or her comments; a critic who chooses not to notice a misdirection of this kind is not worth much.

But how does a critic (or anyone, for that matter) determine what a playwright's intention is? Especially a playwright who is dead? First, by knowing a great deal about the history of theatre, the other arts, and the culture of the period. However unique an individual artist may be, he or she is subject to the influences associated with a particular period. Shakespeare was an extremely intelligent and sensitive person with a wide-ranging curiosity—but he could only know what he had experienced directly or indirectly. He shares his view of the world with his fellow Elizabethans; he displays the same values, superstitions, scientific knowledge, curiosity, and zest for life. Therefore it is possible to infer a great deal about his intentions in his plays by reference to his fellow Elizabethans—not everything, to be sure, but a great deal.

And if this is true for historical figures, how much more must it be true of contemporary ones, including directors and actors?

In fairness, it should be noted that there is a school of criticism which believes that Goethe's first question is pointless—because the "intention" of the artist is immaterial. These critics argue that a work of art is only what is experienced, and that any effort to see "through" the work to the mind of the artist is futile and unnecessary. In some works of art this may be true, but in the huge majority of theatre experiences it is not. In fact, for a critic who is attempting to understand the dynamics of success or failure in the theatre, the intention of the playwright, director, actor, or any other member of the production company, should be a crucial clue.

Critical Trap #3: The Critic as Exterminator. "There are only two kinds of productions: good ones and bad ones. My job is to close the bad ones."

What happens, for example, when a director knows perfectly well what the playwright intended—but decides to do something else with the script? An example might be a 19th-century melodrama, originally written as a very serious moral lesson, which a modern director chooses to parody. This director chooses to exaggerate the already farfetched plot, hams up the acting style, mocks the conventions of 19th-century theatre, and even goes so far as to rehearse into the production mistakes which would have been considered calamities even by the relaxed standards of the worst theatre of the time. The effect may be well received by modern audiences. They may laugh, hoot, shout out encouragement to the hero and boo the villain. But what of the playwright's intention?

Forget it. The director's intention is so clearly divergent from the author's that there is no fear of confusion. (Though even a favorably disposed critic may regret that the production so grossly misrepresents the theatre of a previous age, complaining that modern audiences could be misled into thinking anyone who enjoyed *that* kind of theatre must have been a fool.)

There are other clues to such discrepancies. A good example was the wonderful production of Shakespeare's *A Midsummer Night's Dream* which received such a unique staging by the British director Peter Brook. Shakespeare would have recognized nothing but the language. But Brook's massive and intentional change in Shakespeare's intention was signaled to audiences on the posters advertising the play. "Peter Brook's production of Shakespeare's *A Midsummer Night's Dream*." The fact that Brook's name came first on the posters signaled that *he* was the star of this production. Although all the critics noticed this key change, none objected. Several suggested Shakespeare himself would have agreed to the changes.

This step requires that the critic be a very knowledgeable audience member. To understand the intention of the artist, a critic must be open to the experience, familiar with the cues provided by the actor, director, costume designer, and so on, capable of responding both intellectually and emotionally, and alert to the responses of the audience. Sometimes the best service a critic can provide is the faithful reporting of what actually happened.

One final point here. This question does not require any judgments; it asks only that the critic understand what is happening. In fact, it demands that the responsible critic reach out to the production *before* making judgments. True evaluation begins as we turn to the next question.

Critical Trap #4: The Critic as Teacher. "No one can possibly understand this production without my help. So I'll tell them all about the period of the play, the life of the playwright, all previous productions, and . . . ."

Did he or she succeed? Theatre people frequently speak of a scene as "working" or "not working." The meaning is purposely vague, but the sense is well understood: is the scene, the play, the design, or any other aspect achieving what it set out to do? Of course, this assumes that everyone is clear as to what was intended—sometimes a director will announce with delight that a scene "works" when the only honest comment that can be made is that it seems to be having *some* effect on an audience.

This second question, then, must be gauged in terms of the *audience*. Put another way, the most marvelous idea in the world means nothing in theatrical terms unless an audience is moved, touched, affected—in short, *changed*. But how does a conscientious critic determine the effect of a play on an audience?

The critic can start with the person he or she knows best: himself. A critic does not relinquish rights as an audience member when becoming a critic; and the critic's own responses become a good starting point for evaluation. Were *you* touched? Did *you* laugh? Did the ideas in the play disturb and intrigue *you* afterward? And so on. Of course, the critic is not the *only* audience member. Other members of the audience may have been emotionally involved when the critic was not. It would be grossly unfair for an adult critic to report that a children's theatre play was "juvenile and silly" when child audiences had been thoroughly entertained. (Reviewers of children's theatre productions frequently take a child along in order to judge the success of the play.)

Again, the elements of success or failure are relative and separable. Seldom is a play an unqualified success; usually some parts are more successful than others—and notice should be taken. For example, a good script remains a good script even in a thoroughly incompetent production. Good acting can sometimes surface despite bad lines and poor direction. A single bad costume will seldom destroy a whole production—though it might be noted. In short, a good critic is able to sort out the successful elements from the unsuccessful ones—and place responsibility where it belongs.

Was the task worth the effort? Of all the questions asked by the critic, none evokes a response more deeply rooted in his or her values. Hence many reviews, objective and responsible up to this point, burst into fiery rhetoric on this question of value, and the whole piece ultimately turns to ashes. Part of the problem may lie in a critic's uncertainty about the possible functions of theatre as an art form; or it may be simply that the critic does not agree with the goals set by a particular production. For example, when the plays of Beckett, Ionesco, and Genet first appeared in the 1950s, many critics were totally unprepared. Used to judging the value of strictly logical, well-made plays, contemporary critics sometimes dismissed the work of the absurdists as completely inept and unworthy of serious attention. Or worse, they accused the writers of intentional fraud! In such cases, it would have been more appropriate if those critics had discussed the production's clarity of intention and successful achievement—*then* they might have dismissed the whole effort as pointless. As it was, critics with a strong religious bias attacked even the best productions of those plays as misleading and dangerous—just as so many of their religious forebears had attacked the work of playwrights such as Molière and Ibsen.

Critical Trap #5: The Critic as Consumer Reporter. "Your best entertainment buy is. . . ."

Since the critic's own value system *is* so much a part of this final evaluative step, it might be the best policy for the critic to openly acknowledge his or her biases in advance—even while attempting objectivity. A strongly Marxist, or Christian, or feminist critic can register objections to or support for a particular kind of theatre while, at the same time, acknowledging the production's quality, or lack of it. A reviewer who tends to emphasize the "consumer report" aspect of his or her role may especially want to identify the kinds of theatregoers who would like this production and those who should stay away. Of course, if talent, energy and expense have been squandered on a production with no redeeming value to anyone, the critic has a moral obligation to point that out.

This third and final question can lead to much more than a final judgment on a single play, a performance, or a production. The best critics have sometimes taken the opportunity presented by even a poor production to raise issues about the art of theatre, art in general, aesthetic values, or even the place and function of humankind. Some of the very best have served as theatre critics and philosophers at the same time. In the hands of a novice, these larger issues can be immaterial and tiresome; but when treated by the experienced and profound critic, such responses can remind us of the potential importance of an art which is too often dismissed as a fleeting diversion.

THE CRITIC IN ACTION

Although many modern critics work for television, the majority still write for the print media. And even those who appear to be speaking to a camera are, in fact, reading what they have written. Therefore, we may assume that a critic is writing a review, and give some attention to this very demanding literary form.

Who is the critic writing for? Every writer must have some idea of who will be reading his or her work. The critic is no exception. Newspaper editors make clear to their writers the reading ability, interests, and attention span of their "average" reader. This, in turn, governs the vocabulary, slant, and length of the piece they should write. If the editor believes that the paper's readers are most interested in the gown worn by the major's wife on opening night, a penetrating discussion of the playwright's philosophy may not be in order. (Actually, a major

Critical Trap #6: The Critic as Entertainer. "My job is to sell newspapers! So, I'll be funny, or indignant, or moralistic. Anything to make my readers buy newspapers!"

opening of a play could be covered in two different articles: a review in the arts section and a piece on the audience in the society pages.) A serious review of a production of *Hamlet* in a scholarly journal would not spend much time recounting the plot; the writer could assume that his readers are very familiar with the play. However, a review in a school paper of a new play might spend considerable time explaining the plot—in order to give the reader a chance to learn something about the play in advance.

The potential reader will also influence the vocabulary the writer uses, the references he or she uses, the detail provided, and the overall tone. For example, reviews in *Variety*, a journal written for the show business professional, are famous for their slangy, breezy, and opinionated style. In fact, they are often so full of abbreviations and jargon that a layperson can hardly follow the gist of the article.

What does the critic choose to write about? A play can last well over two hours and may be full of interesting characters, plot twists, dialogue, scenic effects, and costumes. Not all of this can be conveyed to a reader, and most of it doesn't deserve individual comment. To be sure, a critic will want to mention the playscript, the performances of the actors, the scenic design and execution, the costumes, the direction, and the audience response. Furthermore, some space must be left for an overall evaluation.

So the good critic will limit his or her main points to just a few; but these few will be explored in considerable detail. Ideally, the points selected by the critic for close examination will be those which have implications beyond themselves. For example, if the critic notes that an actor missed an entrance in the second act, it is not just to record the fact or embarrass the actor; it is to indicate that carelessness and inattention were evident throughout the production. Conversely, if an actor in a minor role is given special praise, it might be as an example of first-rate casting—or to illustrate what the *major* characters *neglected* to do. Some of the best reviews, in fact, are those which focus on some apparently trivial fact and show how it is not really trivial at all, but symbolizes a very important fact about the production.

How important is style? Put the question another way: How important is it that someone *reads* the review? A review without a reader is like a play without an audience: nothing. So, whatever else the critic is, he or she must be interesting. Of course, some critics are splendid stylists—amusing, bright, irreverent—but essentially empty. These people will slip into disregard. But unfortunately, so will the profound critic who is unreadable.

Journalists give us good examples of the importance of style. A newspaper writer knows that the first paragraph must involve the reader, and lead him or her to the second; the second must lead to the third; and so on. Furthermore, a journalist knows that news stories are cut from the bottom; that is, if the editor does not have enough room for the article, the story will be shortened by omitting the final paragraphs. With this in mind, a good journalist does not save the most important points for the end of the article—they may never appear. The result is a fast-moving style, usually in the present tense, which intrigues the reader early and leads from one paragraph (i.e., major idea) to the next.

Critical Trap #7: The Critic as Theatre Artist. "This is how *I* would have performed that role. . . ."

A unified feeling emerges when the critic repeatedly refers back to a central idea or image—especially in the concluding paragraph.

A successful review combines perceptive observations about the production with an evaluation of the success of each part, and does so in a readable, interesting form. By doing this, the critic enters powerfully into the interactive pattern which influences both the individual production and the future of the art itself.

Discussion Questions

1. Are Goethe's three questions for critics still suitable for the performing arts? Do they work for film and television? Painting? Rock video?

2. Suggest some ways in which the time pressure faced by reviewers (i.e., having to write a coherent theatre review in time for the next edition of the paper) is a disadvantage. Are there any advantages? Are there disadvantages to having leisure to reflect and write?

3. What should a critic do when a performance which he or she thinks is inferior bowls an audience over? Or when an audience does not respond to a performance the critic feels was first-rate?

4. We are used to the idea of a single critical voice, a qualified individual whose opinions appear in the media. But what about a critical board or committee, a *group* of people who meet to establish an "official" critical position on art works? In 17th-century France, powerful cardinals attempted to do that for much of the performing arts. Is there any virtue in the idea?

10

The Audience

No discussion of the partners who make up the creative interaction called theatre is complete without a description of the audience. And yet the audience is seldom considered a participant; no one ever includes the audience as part of the production company, feeling, no doubt, that the audience has no influence on the character of the play which ultimately opens. The audience has not decided on the concept, has not designed the costumes or scenery, has not helped the actors hit upon a striking character. Or has it?

Not all influences are direct and immediate. There can be no doubt that the audience has been *indirectly* involved from the very beginning. When the playwright's first ideas began to take shape, it was with an audience in mind; he or she had something to communicate and, without question, it was to an audience. The director developed a concept for an audience. The designers, the actors, the technicians, the publicists, all went about their work with at least some dim idea of—an audience. In every person's imagination there were, from the very outset, ghostly people sitting in the vacant seats of that empty theatre. Always, the question was—how will this read to an audience?

But what audience?

DEFINING THE GHOSTS

Every person in theatre has a mental image evoked by the word *audience*. Sometimes it is singular: a drama teacher will summon up some mythical older woman who, though hard of hearing, chooses to sit in the last row anyway and for whom every word spoken from the stage had better be crystal clear. Professional actors may fantasize the image of a hated critic who will, *this time*, be so taken with their performance that they will rhapsodize in print. Or the audience may be plural: the director has an idea of a composite "New York audience." There may even be subcategories: "preview audiences," "Friday-night audiences," "theatre-party audiences." The list is endless.

And yet, when a play does open, the seats are filled not with myths, fantasies, or composites, but with real breathing people, with all the complicated experience, unpredictable emotional potential, and tricky perceptions of any actor or stage character. In her absorbing play *Talking With*, American playwright Jane Martin sees the problem through the mind of an actress putting on her makeup before a performance.

> O.K., O.K., O.K., O.K., . . . so it's fifteen and I am in here getting ready for an evening of "lacerating self-exposure" and there are people out there reading the program, reading my bio, you know getting a little personal insight, getting to know me. And what I want to know is who are they? Fair's fair, right? What I would like is a program delivered to me every night with bio's of the audience, you know, so we'd start out even, where they live, last play they saw, favorite color, sexual preference, last relationship they screwed up, you know just basic stuff. Because then we'd be in this together, right? I do a little lacerating self-exposure, they do a little lacerating self-exposure and afterwards who knows maybe we get together for a drink, . . . because then there would be an exchange, an exchange and not this unilateral crap, this "I'm in the light, you're in the dark" stuff, which truth to tell is beginning to wear on me.*

*Jane Martin, *Talking With* . . . Reprinted by permission of Alexander Speer, trustee. Copyright 1983 by Jane Martin.

But the actress overlooks an important fact: individual personal histories of individual audience members cannot predict group behavior. Even if you had thumbnail biographies of each audience member, it would not help predict the "group personality" which emerges when individuals become an audience.

What are the many variables operating in any audience? It is worth taking a few minutes to review even a partial list.

Age. The life experiences of audience members—individually and collectively—shape their response. Certain human dilemmas are unfamiliar to younger audience members, and older people can be short on the idealism of youth.

Sex. The ratio of men to women in the audience can have an influence on how certain material will "play."

Time of day. Matinee audiences frequently have a very different composition from evening audiences. Even if they didn't, however, the time of day influences audience response. Actors who have played two evening performances a day report significant differences between, say, a 7:00 P.M. audience and a 10 P.M. audience. (And we are not even ready to discuss here the actor's attitude toward a 9:00 A.M. school performance!)

Are the audience members strangers? In small towns or at performances bought out by single organizations, audiences frequently have so much in common that they do not need "warming up." They bring to the opening curtain a similarity of point of view which it may take an audience of strangers hours to achieve.

Does the audience have leadership? An audience can develop a communication net among itself during the course of a performance. This is particularly true with laughs and applause. One quick, hearty laugher in an audience can frequently help the rest of the audience learn where and when to laugh; one responsive audience member who is not afraid to start applause can lead an audience toward appropriate and satisfying ways to show its pleasure. When this leadership arises naturally and is unforced, the audience can benefit from the ease of response—and from the better performance which good response elicits from performers.

This last comment does *not* apply to the practice—still present in opera today—of hiring individuals (called *claques*) whose sole task it is to start and extend applause for the performers who employ them.

News of the day.   However much they may wish to do so, audiences are even less able than performers to leave their workaday lives outside the theatre. Bad news depresses audiences; good news elates them. Both influence how they respond to events on stage. Theatre companies can take advantage of this fact. For example, for years theatre companies in Eastern Europe have carried on private communication with their audiences despite the best efforts of the censors. Their audiences can be expected to see the parallels between what is happening on stage and what is happening in the repressive societies outside the theatre. Simple things (the choice of a particular play, a humorous situation, a striking piece of dialogue) have special meaning to audiences who are used to implied criticism of the conditions of their lives.

Theatregoing experience.   Naive theatregoers can be interesting to play for, but the members of a theatrical company save their respect for knowledgeable audiences. The word spreads quickly backstage: "This audience gets everything!" They catch references to other plays; experience helps them anticipate where the playwright is heading; they quickly pick up and delight in the traditional conventions—and enjoy the new ones—built into the production.

Demands made upon the audience.   Some plays ask an audience to reach farther than others; that is, they require rather more active participation. Such plays may force an audience to listen very hard, to grasp the significance of relatively minor pieces of information, to make some strenuous leaps of imagination. For example, a play may stay entirely within the *representational* mode, that is, it adopts a set of conventions which presume that the audience is not present in the action of the play and that the audience members are like peeping Toms, peering out of the dark through a hole in the wall, and into the next room. Other plays are *presentational:* they assume the presence of the audience and build it into the action of the play. In a presentational play the actors may talk to the audience—for example, by taking a vote or asking for discussion of important points. In either mode, however, the conventions—once established—are maintained throughout the play. But some playwrights choose to move back and forth between the two modes; in short, they establish a set of conventions which say that the audience is present in some cases—but not in others. This means that the audience must remain very attentive in order to know which conventions are in force at the present moment. Such a play is making special demands upon the audience and expects that the audience will be able—and willing—to meet those demands.

These are just a few of the considerations which must be kept in mind as the indistinct, generalized idea of an audience in our minds becomes a specific group of people filling a given theatre on a specific night for a specific play. Their reactions each night are a mix of the attributes of the individual people—plus a composite personality all its own.

The living presence of the audience directly shapes the theatre event in ways which are only somewhat predictable. But one thing is certain: good audiences make better theatre.

Now, what makes a good audience?

AUDIENCE SKILLS

Once we have agreed that audiences differ from one another, and that some audience responses are more desirable than others, we are ready to discuss the special skills which good audiences display. The very idea of "audience skills" may be offensive to some people: they may prefer to think of audiences as undifferentiated consumers, a faceless, passive, mass of slackjawed recipients. Bertolt Brecht described them as "people who look as if something were being done to them."

But, as we have seen, even the most compliant audience imaginable must be actively engaged in the audience/actor interaction for theatre to work at all. The higher the level of that involvement, the better the experience usually is. The quality of involvement increases as audience members brings skills to the task.

Concentration.   An audience member must be prepared to focus all of his or her attention on the theatre experience. It is a common complaint that modern audiences—especially young people—have been so conditioned by television that they have only a limited capacity for concentrating. Most television assumes a maturity level of eleven to thirteen years of age; the capacity for sustained concentration for most people in that age range is severely limited. That is why a television situation comedy format lasts much less than 30 minutes—about 26½ minutes to be exact. Even then, the commercial interruptions guarantee that an audience member will not have to endure more than about 8 minutes of sustained concentration. There are seldom subplots to be kept in mind, character development is minimized, and physical action is favored above everything else. Is it, then, any wonder that audiences for whom this has been the whole diet can have difficulty sitting through a play in which the exposition alone may take longer than their favorite television program?

Television-trained audiences also may have trouble simply sitting through a play. They are used to being able to go to the bathroom every half-hour, to stretch during the inevitable commercials, and to talk out loud any time during the broadcast. No wonder they can feel restricted when attending a live play. However, good audiences have the capacity to concentrate on extended and subtle stage action.

Perception. It is not simply enough to pay attention; good audiences must be able to make sense out of the information coming from the stage. Take the simple act of listening.

Many people today are not ready for the subtlety demanded by live theatre. They're used to movies and television in which the sound is electronically doctored—no matter how loudly or softly the character is speaking, the sound is always the same. Some sound engineer is paid to assure that every word is audible to even the hard-of-hearing. Moreover, even such ambient noise as might normally be present in a scene is made palatable: sounds of crowds, background table conversations, furniture moving, foot shuffling, even the gunfire from adjacent wars is first removed and later mixed back in at acceptable levels. The same thing is impossible in live theatre. The audience has to listen carefully, selectively, actively if they are to receive the maximum benefit from the aural aspects of a production.

This is also true of the visual aspects. For example, if a key incident in a television drama involves a major character leaving an incriminating letter open on the desk, the television director knows exactly what to do: he or she zooms in on the letter, drawing the total visual attention of every viewer to the important oversight. The stage director has nothing to match that option. He or she must trust that members of the audience will remember that the letter is important, that the character placed it on the desk—open—and that another character now has the opportunity to read it. Of course, there are some staging devices which a director might use to emphasize the letter—he or she might even focus a small spotlight on the letter so as to highlight its presence. But, in doing that, the director might risk offending the audience; their unspoken response might be, "All right, I see the letter. What do you think I am? Stupid?" The irony is that the same audience would hardly notice the close-up shot in the television drama. In the television drama the conventions are aimed at so low a denominator that audience members have ceased to realize how completely they are being patronized.

Good theatre audiences pride themselves on seeing and hearing "everything." The barely averted eyes of the character trying to disguise her villainy; the slightly seedy costume of a character trying to pretend he is more than he is; the scenic detail which tells us more about the owner than he would like to have known. The game can become even more complicated: a playwright or director may appear to have let more slip through than was intended. The audience, thinking that it has caught unintended information, is skillfully led astray.

But all of this depends upon the ability of the audience to perceive accurately all of the information coming from the stage. The audience member who cannot perceive—due to inexperience, physical disability, bias, or some other interference—is truly handicapped.

Openmindedness.   A good audience member is prepared to meet the production halfway—or go even further. The enemy here is bias: against Shakespeare, against absurdist theatre, against plays written by socialists, against—well, the list seems endless. This does not mean that a good audience checks its opinions at the cloakroom. But it does mean that a good audience sets aside those opinions which would prevent it from dealing freely with the production at hand. Part of the problem is the connection in the biased audience member's mind between theatrical reality and the outside world. At a philosophical level, the fact that a work of art portrays an injustice does not increase the amount of injustice in the world; nor will a beautiful work of art immediately increase the beauty of the world outside the theatre. By the same token, attending a play does not imply support for any or all ideas in that play. An ardent feminist may safely attend a production of *The Taming of the Shrew* without even appearing to support its sexist view of women, and could even enjoy the play. In the same way, a Jew can experience *The Merchant of Venice* without supporting anti-Semitism. A capitalist can attend Brecht's *The Caucasian Chalk Circle* without fear of encouraging revolution. In fact, the reverse is often the case: By experiencing and fully understanding an opposing argument one can counter it more effectively.

More difficult to deal with are artistic biases, especially when they prevent people from exploring new works. What is an artistic bias? Let's examine a few examples:

"Opera sung in English is inappropriate."

"Plots must always be logical."

"Injustice must be punished."

"Actors shouldn't speak directly to the audience."

"Poetic language is just an affectation."

A person who firmly holds these views will have some difficulty with specific kinds of theatre experiences. He or she may avoid those kinds of plays, of course—or attend the production and be miserable on principle. In either case, the audience member will be denying himself or herself through a process of self-censorship the possibility of a rich experience.

Imagination. Of all the subtle skills an audience member brings to the theatre, imagination is surely one of the critical ones. Without the capacity to make the imaginative leap required of the audience by the performance contract, everything in theatre collapses. In the 19th century, the poet Coleridge called this basic step a "willing suspension of disbelief." In saying this, he was highlighting the fact that the normal mode of human operation is skepticism, the constant suspicion that others will try to mislead you, and the effort to maintain an appropriate level of doubt about the motives of others. A more recent commentator, the psychotherapist Paul Kris, recognizing the childlike quality of this imaginative leap, refers to the act as "regression at the service of the ego."

Whatever the terminology, an audience without an imagination is forever locked out of the theatre experience. And, within the limits of mental health, the deeper the imaginative involvement, the richer the experience. This is why some of the most sophisticated theatre conventions require the greatest imaginative leaps. If a scene requires a character to be discovered sculling a boat on a stream, it requires nothing except hard work and money to flood the stage, bring in a real boat, and teach an actor to scull. It requires much more from everybody to create that scene on a bare stage, with only a shimmer of light and an oar for support. That much more is imagination.

The subcategory of imagination which applies most powerfully in the theatre is empathy, the capacity to reach out and into someone else's experience, to get inside their skin. The inability to empathize is one symptom of psychopathology; the absence of empathy is common among professional killers and other sociopaths. One may safely assume that the theatre has little appeal for them.

Emotional Responsiveness. When all is said and done, the power of theatre appeals less to the intellectual realm than the emotional. It works best when the audience's emotions are captured, held, manipulated, and—ultimately—enriched. A good audience member is one who has the ability to respond emotionally to imaginary experiences. The last observation invites some discussion: certain writers have expressed concern over this fact. Bertolt Brecht, for example, saw a great danger in the ease with which audiences became emotionally involved with live theatre. He advocated a detached, intellectual posture for audiences; emotional involvement led, he felt, to an uncritical acceptance of intellectual nonsense. However, he did allow room for a few selected emotions—such as anger at a world which contains injustice, and the desire to change it. But Brecht's position is extreme. By far the more popular approach is to see the special power of theatre as empathic involvement. Such involvement might, in fact, lead to more fundamental change; when audience members have experienced the world through the senses of another they may be prepared to change their world accordingly.

Demonstrativeness. We have spent considerable time elsewhere describing the communication loop established between the actor and the audience. Clearly, this loop cannot be closed unless the audience members are willing to demonstrate their responses. In some societies this is no problem; audiences are very demonstrative. If they like something, the actors know it immediately; if they do not, their disfavor is just as apparent. In American society the reverse seems to be the problem. Our main tradition seems to be one of attentive listening, polite applause, and restrained laughter. This is partly due to our interest in realistic drama—the convention of audience silence in realistic drama seems to have spilled over into other forms. Or it may be a misplaced reverence. At a recent student performance of a Shakespeare comedy, the teachers were busily engaged in "shushing" the schoolchildren whose proper impulse was to laugh uproariously at the comic business. Whatever the reasons, many modern American audiences are often disappointingly restrained from the actor's point of view.

It's worth noting, too, that cultural differences can lead to real misunderstanding. Some years ago, the New York Shakespeare Festival toured the plays of Shakespeare to the boroughs of the city. These free, outdoor productions were attended by a great many people who had never seen live theatre before. The huge majority reported that they loved the experience. In black and Hispanic neighborhoods, however, the actors described the audiences as "rude" and "unruly": they talked back to the actors, shouted encouragement to the characters, talked to each other, and walked about during the performance. When audience members were questioned by researchers, however, they gave a very different account. They reported that they had never seen their neighbors so quiet and attentive!

THE AUDIENCE AS SOCIETY

One of the patterns of interaction which has always fascinated the serious student of the arts is the interaction between the institution of theatre and the society which supports and sustains it. To some degree, the audience which attends a given performance is a surrogate for all of society—just as the performance at hand "stands in" for all of contemporary theatre. The analogy is worth pursuing.

We began this chapter by calling into serious question the idea that the audience is a passive consumer of a fully prepared experience. Instead, we are suggesting that the indirect presence of the audience shapes the production during rehearsals; and that the active direct presence of the audience actually creates the performance. This makes the audience a full collaborator in the experience. If the audience is unwilling, or unable, to participate, the experience does not take place and the creative effort fails.

This process illustrates by extension the degree to which society is a collaborator in the larger context of theatre as a performing art. So long as theatre as a discipline meets the needs of society, it will survive;

when it ceases to meet them, it will either die out completely—or evolve into something which will. In his famous couplet, Samuel Johnson captured the issue in both its superficial and profound senses:

The Drama's Laws the Drama's Patrons give,
For we that live to please must please to live.

If *pleasure* is defined as the feeling which arises when a need is met, we can see that Johnson could as easily be speaking for all of theatre as for the playwright. It is important that the anxiety-ridden, frequently isolated and seldom rewarded theatre artist see himself or herself in this context: as part of a larger, dynamic, and more important interaction between theatre as an art and human culture.

Discussion Questions

1. Explain the difference between the *direct* and *indirect* influences of the audience on the theatre performance.
2. Discuss the concept of *audience skills* in terms of special audiences (e.g., children, the deaf, the blind). How do the special conditions of these audiences shape the experience?
3. Can you imagine some other biases (other than those listed in the text) which audiences might bring to a performance and which might adversely affect the experience?
4. Describe in your own words the meaning of the term *empathy*. How is this skill used in everyday life?

11

The Form of the Experience

WHAT IS A PLAY?

In this book we have described a play as an interactive experience shared and created by two groups: the theatrical company and the audience. It should not be confused with the literary document called a *playscript*, or script, for short. Neither should it ever be thought to have a fixed identity; like any other human experience, it exists only as it is taking place. A play is created anew during each performance and has no immediate reality at any other time. The experience of a play is only anticipated in the imagination of the playwright and the company, and after the fact it is preserved only in the memory of the audience and the company. An audio and visual transcript of the performance, a videotape for example, can be an interesting record of a performance. However, it cannot be a theatre performance because it lacks the interaction between performer and audience which defines theatre.

A certain degree of confusion is inevitable here. There is a tradition in Western culture of considering the "idea" of any play as having a fixed reality somewhere (an *ideal*, to use the philosophical term) which every production only approximates. Not many people nowadays take this extreme position.* However, some would argue that the continuing reality of a play lives either in the playwright's mind (at least while he or she lives) or in the playscript. If all productions of a playscript were exactly the same, there might be some validity in this last point of view; but they are most assuredly not all the same. In fact, we have already seen that each performance of the same production is at least slightly different from every other performance. We are left with the inescapable conclusion that each performance is unique—and that the "play" exists *only* during that performance.

A final source of confusion results from the habit of theatre people (audiences, critics, performers) who speak of productions and the qualities of performances in the abstract. Through a trick of language and popular usage, we speak of *Hamlet* as having suspense or Shaw's *Heartbreak House* as containing ideas about human violence—in the same way that Mount Everest "has" altitude and water "contains" oxygen and hydrogen. If driven to levels of unaccustomed accuracy, most people would probably be forced to agree that they mean only that a production of *Hamlet* can evoke feelings of suspense in an audience and a production of *Heartbreak House* can communicate Shaw's views on the subject of human violence.

Before this line of reasoning becomes too precious, however, we should remind ourselves that even a unique and transient experience has certain identifiable characteristics. In the theatre, these characteristics have names and can be identified. In fact, it is the skillful manipulation of these characteristics of the interactive experience of theatre which makes plays different from one another.

THREE MAJOR CONCERNS: DURATION, COMPLEXITY, AND INTENSITY

How long a play lasts is a crucial issue with implications for nearly every other characteristic. Over two thousand years ago Aristotle, while comparing playwriting to the writing of history, noted that the subject of drama should be a topic of manageable size. History can deal with events of great size and duration; drama needs to be more selective.

*The opinions of two who do are given in the quotation on p. 115.

Comprehending a dramatic subject of too great a magnitude, says Aristotle, a writer not given to flights of whimsy, is like trying to understand a single animal a thousand miles long. He could as easily have been talking about the duration of the dramatic experience: outside certain limits the event begins to diminish in effectiveness. However, the existing range is fairly impressive: The short piece *Breath* by Samuel Beckett lasts only two or three minutes (no actors appear on stage); the epic work of the American Robert Wilson (*The Death and Life of Josef Stalin* and *Einstein on the Beach*) can last for up to 18 unbroken hours. And there are cycles of plays which last several days—though never without breaks. But the usual length of a play is between 20 minutes and four hours.

The length of any play is obviously governed by more than the attention span, resistance to hunger pangs, and bladder size of audience members. Complex material takes more time to explore, it is true; but intense emotional involvement on the part of the audience can only be sustained for a limited period. Somehow these two constraints must be balanced. One solution is common among the traditional theatres of Asia. Many of these plays are extremely long and complex by Western standards, but the conventions allow audience members to move about at will, to leave the auditorium and return only for a favorite passage or scene. These key scenes may be very intense, but they do not last long. And if a scene is well received it may even be repeated immediately— just as arias in Western opera used to be given regular encores. Asian audiences familiar with this kind of theatre experience would probably be dismayed and alarmed by the idea of filing into an auditorium, having the doors closed and the light turned off, and being forced to sit still and quiet for up to an hour-and-a-half.

Modern plays are categorized as either *one-act* or *full-length*. One-act plays usually run from 20 minutes to one hour in length and have no intermission; full-length works run from about one to four hours in duration and usually have at least one intermission. A single full-length play usually constitutes a full evening's experience, but one-act plays can be combined into *bills* to meet the expectations of audiences. Full-length plays range in structure from one to five acts. In certain historical periods a "complete" play was expected to have either five acts or three acts (regardless of how many scenes in each act) and provide for either four or two intermissions. These early rules are widely ignored today and the number of acts may have less to do with the number of intermissions than the director's expectations concerning the patience of the audience and such technical matters as scenery and costume changes.

The complexity of a production depends on the combination of a number of factors. For example, how many plots are there? Shakespeare and other Elizabethan and Restoration writers were fond of keeping two, three, or even four plots moving simultaneously. Regardless of how effectively these parallel plots are integrated, it will take time to develop each and bring each to a resolution. Accordingly, these plays can be rather long. By the same token, a play with a great many major characters—characters who need development—will take generally more time than one with a smaller number, unless there is a corresponding reduction in the number and complexity of the plots.

Even a single plot can be complex; a mystery, a complicated farce, even a portrayal of a twisted relationship can make time demands on an audience. So too can a play that takes time for lengthy philosophical arguments or song and dance numbers.

Finally, the degree of audience attention and involvement demanded has a great deal to do with its duration and complexity. An audience which must listen very carefully to complex dialogue may find itself worn out unless there is relief occasionally. Shakespeare frequently alternates scenes with demanding dialogue with low comic scenes which are so physical that one hardly needs to hear the language at all to follow the action. To create the same sense of relief and contrast, highly charged emotional scenes may alternate with light-hearted ones.

So we see that a playwright, when choosing a topic and setting to work, must consider the interrelationship of that topic and the length of the play he or she has in mind, the proposed complexity of the piece, and the intensity of the demands on the audience.

THE ELEMENTS OF DRAMATIC STRUCTURE

There is a familiar human need for rules, for structure; we can all be made uncomfortable by ambiguity. Hence even in the arts there are repeated attempts to find some formula which will produce predictable results. In the late 19th century, some European playwrights and critics thought they had found such a formula for dramatic structure. The design they proposed came to be called the *well-made play* and, in the hands of a few experts, it worked famously for a number of decades. Many elements of the well-made play can be found in playwriting today. But the formula is dead; and with it faded the age-old hope of a single, universal dramatic structure.

Today, most observers would agree that there are an infinite number of possible dramatic structures—just as many, in fact, as there are dramatic ideas to communicate. Some structures are more effective than others in a particular instance; the effectiveness of dramatic structure is governed by what it is that the playwright and the company want to achieve. A major aim of the playwright (and, to some degree, the company) is to find that structure which best matches the dramatic idea at hand. So, in theatre as in architecture, form has come to follow function.

Fortunately for students of both theatre and architecture, while the possible structures seem infinite, the materials involved are not. The elements by which dramatic structure is created are known and can be described. Furthermore, the outcomes of certain combinations of those elements can be predicted—or at least described.

It was that ubiquitous fellow Aristotle who first described the elements of theatre as falling into six categories: plot, character, idea, language, music, and spectacle. Those categories still provide a good starting point for us today.

Plot. *Plot* is the succession of incidents which go together to make up a play. When a friend asks, "What happened in the play?" you will usually repeat the plot. Plot and *story* are not the same thing. The story of a play—or the story on which a play may be based—can be quite different from the plot. It usually is.

Plot and story. The plot is the way the playwright chooses to tell the story. It is the order in which we, the audience, encounter the facts; it may also be the order in which certain key characters experience the facts. Few skillful storytellers—and a playwright is, along with everything else, a storyteller—would simply tell the facts in the order in which they occurred (i.e., chronologically). A good storyteller feeds them to us in a carefully selected order: withholding key facts to be discovered later, leaving mystifying gaps, allowing us to misunderstand early so that we may reassess later, frequently letting us think that we know more than we do and yet never baffling us to the point that we quit the game. It is this translation of a straightforward story into an intriguing plot which makes the game so interesting.

Point of attack. When someone decides to make a plot out of a story, the first question must be where in the story to begin. This is another way of dealing with the issue of *point of attack.* Playwrights, because they are pressed for time and impatient to get to the most dramatic material, usually employ *late point of attack;* in other words, they begin the plot late in the story. Since most good stories culminate in exciting action, this decision all but guarantees that it is the most interesting part of the larger story which will be enacted on the stage.

Exposition. Let us stay with the question of how the audience learns about the characters and their predicament. The curtain rises on a group of people who, one presumes, know something about their world. That puts them light years ahead of the audience who have just arrived in this world and who will need all the help they can get if they are to catch up with the characters. Some of this help comes from the scenic design and costumes ("Aha!" we say. "This looks like a late-19th-century British drawing room!"). This is just as well, because otherwise the characters would have to say things like, "I say, I don't think I've ever told you how much I admire your late-19th-century drawing room." At which point, the knowledgeable half of the audience would arise en masse, march out to the box office, and demand their money back.

But there are other bits of information which the characters know and which the audience must find out before the play can get interesting. This kind of information is called *retrospective exposition* or *exposition* for short. There are some straightforward ways of communicating exposition; one age-old method is to employ a narrator, someone (not a main character in the play, usually) who simply steps downstage and tells the audience what happened before the curtain rose. This device is fairly widely discredited; the argument is that a person standing downstage telling a story to an audience is not theatre. Maybe storytelling, but not theatre.

Other, more interesting, methods are usually used to convey exposition. The traditional device is to introduce into the play at an early point a character who does not know what has happened and has to be brought up-to-date—while we listen in. In the work of hacks, this person was always a new servant whom an older, wiser servant had to fill in on the family history. Better playwrights found better ways of providing exposition. In *A Doll's House,* Henrik Ibsen has Nora's girlhood friend return after a long absence. In her excitement Nora not only brings her friend up-to-date but reveals secrets that now only she and her trusted friend—and an audience of several hundred people—share. Described this way, exposition sounds silly and obvious—but in the hands of a good playwright, the necessary information is slipped in with the skill of a pickpocket. For examples of truly obvious exposition one has only to watch daytime soap operas. The writers know that their loyal audience is neither as regular or attentive as they might wish; therefore, they have characters repeat exposition to each other—including repetition of the characters' names!—over and over again. It is possible to return to a soap plot after a week's absence and be brought up to date in the first ten minutes.

Stasis. Usually, the situation just preceding the start of a play is one of relative harmony, balance, or *stasis*; the world is, as it were, at some point of balance and could continue in that state for some time. Then, early in the play, something happens: there is an *inciting incident*. A stranger gets off the stagecoach, a letter arrives, a chance remark brings a peculiar response—and the play is off and running. The balance has been disturbed and the action of the play will consume enormous energy before some new balance is reestablished.

Inciting incident. The playwright wants to establish this inciting incident very early in the play. The reason for this is the fact that balance, peace, harmony, and serenity, however laudable as life goals, make for boring theatre; the sooner you can get the characters into a mess, the better.

Dramatic question. Once the audience has become at least partly familiar with the characters and the inciting incident has taken place, we find ourselves asking *the dramatic question*, which is usually some specific version of the all-purpose "How will this all turn out?" In fact, in thoroughly formularized plays, the playwright actually says the words: at the conclusion of an action-packed first act, one observant character—perhaps that wise old servant—looks out over the audience and mutters to himself, "Ach, things look bad for young Master James. I wonder how this will all turn out!" Curtain.

The precise nature of *the dramatic question* has a great deal to do with the overall experience of the play since the major portion of the action is devoted to answering that question. For example, note how different versions of the dramatic question can influence the interpretation of famous plays.

Hamlet: Will Prince Hamlet be able to rouse himself to revenge his father's murder?

or

Should Prince Hamlet believe and act upon the unsupported testimony of a ghost?

A Doll's House: Will Nora's secret be revealed?

or

Will Nora continue to be forced to feel and act like a guilty child in her own home?

Equus: Can Dr. Dysarte cure Alan Strang?

or

Should Dr. Dysarte cure Alan Strang?

Suspense. Plot is normally built around a conflict between at least two opposing forces; the dramatic question takes those forces into account and asks the audience to speculate about the outcome. Of course, the dramatic question assumes a couple of things: for one thing it assumes that we find the characters interesting enough to be curious about the future; it also assumes that we do not see exactly how everything will work out. This balance of concern for the characters and uncertainty as to their future creates the tension in the audience called *suspense*. Suspense is an especially powerful emotional response precisely because the audience is not passive. We in the audience begin to leap ahead of the present action on stage to imagine possibilities which have not yet occurred to the characters. Some are small and immediate ("What if the murderer is hiding in the closet?!"); others are long-term ("What if she is only agreeing to marry him to help him face his terminal illness?"). Then, like gamblers who have made our private bets, we stick around to see if our number comes up.

Rising action. Gradually, the involvement grows in what is called *rising action*. Again like gamblers in a heated poker game, the pot grows larger and the involvement becomes more and more intense. The answer to the dramatic question is imaginatively deferred; as one obstacle is overcome, another one—probably more formidable—is introduced. Indeed, the structure of dramatic action is first to ask a good dramatic question—and then delay the answering of the question for as long as audiences will stand for it. Of course, the dramatic question becomes more complicated as new aspects of the problem are revealed. Toward the conclusion of *A Doll's House*, Nora is reduced to hoping that when her minor forgery is discovered, her husband will accept personal responsibility and stand loyally by her. At each step of this rising action the audience becomes more and more involved because—again, like gamblers—they have an emotional investment riding on the outcome, an investment which becomes heavier as the play continues.

Climax. At some point the rising action has progressed as far as it can. Every twist which can appropriately be introduced has been introduced; every dilemma has been explored; the characters are at the point of desperation; the audience's suspense has been heightened as far as possible. The *climax* has arrived. This is the point at which the dramatic question must be answered. In a murder mystery, this is the point at which the inspector calls everyone together in the library. It is showdown time!

Frequently, at the climax, the playwright introduces one last key piece of information—one which changes everything and resolves the dramatic question. In parodies of climactic scenes, it is usually the arrival of a messenger from the king with a pardon for the otherwise doomed hero; or the hero and villain recognize each other as twin brothers separated at birth—and fall into each other's arms. In good playcrafting, however, the new information does not arrive out of the blue; it has been there all along. The last twist may be one which is based on information that has been ignored by characters and audience alike for several acts. Perhaps it was embedded in the personality of a character and only now reveals itself. Whatever happens, audiences expect it to be related to the rest of the play and plausible under the ground rules observed to that point.

Dénouement. The French describe the climax as being the point in the play at which the strands of the plot are all "knotted up." Therefore, they called the period immediately following the climax as the *dénouement* ("untying"). The word is used in English for the same process, though we tend to muddle the metaphor by referring to the *dénouement* as the point in the play at which "all the loose ends are tied up." The idea is the same, however: once the major dramatic question has been settled, what of the secondary questions? (Example: Okay, the hero and heroine are getting married; what about their best friends—will they be married too? Will the villain go to jail? Will Uncle Waldo make friends with Clyde the Wonder Duck? etc.) When the *dénouement* is complete, presumably there is no outstanding business remaining; a new stasis has been created and the curtain can fall.

Multiple plots. The elements mentioned above may all relate to a single plot; but they may also be present in each of *multiple plots.* Classical as well as modern playwrights have been intrigued by the challenge of keeping several plots going simultaneously. Chiefly they are attracted by the levels of meaning which can develop when audiences are forced to keep two or more story lines in their minds at the same time. Traditionally this means that several *simultaneous* plots are developing in such a way as to converge at roughly the same climax. But another possibilty is for *serial plots* to be employed. The resulting structure in this second case is rather like a series of one-act plays placed in the same environment, thematically related, and—sometimes—employing the same characters.

Time in plots. The manipulation of time in plots is crucial. The traditional method has always been to move *chronologically* through time. Two alternatives may be employed: the playwright could use a late point of attack and show every second of the action that transpired after that point; or he or she can use an earlier point of attack and show, in chronological order, *only* those incidents (or *episodes*) which are germane to the play, sometimes skipping years between each unit. This last kind of structure is called episodic and, while deplored by Aristotle and the neoclassic writers, was a favorite of such giants as Shakespeare.

One potential use of episodic structure which Shakespeare seems not to have employed is the modern device of the *flashback* or the *flashforward*; in this technique episodes are portrayed out of chronological sequence. Flashback and flashforward techniques are especially popular with filmmakers, partly at least because of the great ease with which these time shifts can be made in the media.

Some contemporary playwrights have attempted to dispense with time altogether; instead, they have tried to create a world in which all parts of the plot are occurring simultaneously, and in which there is no sequence among the events presented. The difficulty with this approach is that there obviously *is* a sequence to the theatre experience of the average audience member—and, lacking any other directions, it is that sequence which an audience member will inevitably detect in or impose upon the plot of the play. Until such time as we can communicate knowledge in some absolutely simultaneous method, all communications will be sequential. It is, then, the sequential ordering of theatrical experiences in time which makes up plot.

Character.   Aristotle's second most important category is *character*. In general, it refers to the whole range of actions which distinguish the characters in a play from one another: their physical, mental, and emotional characteristics, their different responses to similar circumstances, their motivation and goal structure, and, ultimately, the entire variety and complexity of their interaction with the world around them.

The boundary between plot and character is, of course, an artificial one, and is often blurred. How does one discover anything substantial about character except through how people act? Yet these actions are precisely what go to make up plot. So we see that plot and character always interpenetrate. Still, a discussion of character as if it existed as a separate entity can be useful.

The playwrights of antiquity were often concerned with the issue of justice and questions of right and wrong behavior. Hence they tended to describe and categorize characters according to their moral status. Aristotle, for example, describes a suitable tragic hero as being an essentially good man who suffers mightily for a lapse of judgment, not as the result of a major character flaw. He goes on to imply moral standards when he says that tragedy portrays men as better than they are; comedy portrays them as worse. Much of our current theatrical language has such a moral cast to it: the words *hero* and *heroine* were once applied to morally upstanding characters; those who opposed them were called *villains* and could be so reprehensible as to be beyond redemption.

Protagonist and Antagonist. The more useful terms, however, are more or less free of moral judgment and have an even longer history. The Greeks referred to the major character as the *protagonist*—literally the first person to join a violent struggle or contest. Since there cannot be a conflict without resistance, they also coined the word *antagonist* to describe the force which opposes the protagonist. It is out of these two figures or forces that the conflict of the play develops. The other characters in the play usually ally themselves to one or another of these forces; or they may choose to remain aloof from the action, assuming the role of spectators and even—as with the Greek chorus—commenting on the action as the play proceeds.

This grouping of characters—especially as regards a particular moral stance—is typical of traditional plays around the world. The dance dramas of India and southeast Asia see the world as engaged in an ongoing war between the forces of good and evil. In these plays, the major figures fall clearly into one of the two camps, and their costume and makeup identify their allegiance in the cosmic struggle. This view of characters in drama would have been entirely acceptable to medieval European playgoers. To a very large degree it was present in 19th-century melodrama; there the obviously virtuous hero and heroine confront an easily identified villain. The tendency to group characters around moral positions is detectable today in film and television programs in which the ancient forces of evil are represented by "the mob," motorcycle gangs, corrupt politicians, J. R. Ewing and his friends, or "Eastern block interests."

Lines of work. The categorization of characters need not only be along moral lines. Some characters are identified according to the structural role they play. Consider some words which may be familiar to you in other contexts: *prima donna, ingenue, leading man, confidante.* These are but a few of the categories which have been employed by theatre companies for centuries—and the categories were developed in response to certain predictable roles in the plays they produced. For example, if there was sure to be a strong, attractive, mature male at the center of the action, a *leading man* in the company would inevitably be cast in the role; his female counterpart would be played by a leading lady (or *prima donna* in Italian). The *ingénue* was a younger, pretty, and more innocent girl, and so on. In the 19th-century stock company, these categories were so rigidly fixed that a play was frequently cast from a list of the characters only, without any reference to the script. In fact, actors were contracted for what were called *lines of work*; a leading man, for example, would contract to play those kinds of roles exclusively. *Male juveniles* or *character men* moved from company to company just as quarterbacks or wide receivers move between teams in the National Football League.

Today, we would call this practice *casting to type*; it corresponds to the playwright's tendency to "write to type." The practice has a long history in the theatre and casts useful light on how the element of character figures in the experience of a play.

Stereotyping. A *stereotyped* character is one which presents a simplified picture of an entire group by portraying a character who displays the major characteristics of that group. Sometimes the concept in question is drawn from a social stereotype; at other times it may have its origin mainly from the stage itself. An example of a social stereotype is the cowboy; the portrayal of a cowboy on the stage might be shaped by a popular conception (itself shaped by dime novels, cartoons, and an oral tradition) of a laconic, lean, naturally shrewd loner. The fact that there is no one real cowboy in the world which matches that picture is immaterial to the playwright, the actor, or the audience.

When the stereotype is drawn from the stage itself, we call it a *stock character*. The heyday of stock characters was probably the *Commedia dell' Arte*, which is peopled by special characters such as Arlecchino (Harlequin), Dottore, Pantalone, the braggart soldier, and others whose essential character changed little from play to play and only slightly more over about 150 years of history.

Even when a stock character is not employed and social stereotyping is minimized, playwrights are tempted to employ some stereotyping in their character development. For one thing, audiences grasp some stereotypes quickly and easily; the theatre experience has serious time constraints and anything which allows an audience to understand important information about a character quickly is attractive. This is especially true of minor characters in a single play. The playwright is prepared to invest a lot of time developing the major characters; the minor role of the New York cab driver may fall into a stereotype to save time. An exception is the television series: The long run of a series such as "M*A*S*H" allowed even minor characters to be developed with considerable depth.

Another advantage of some stereotyped characterization is that audiences quickly develop expectations concerning such characters and—as we have seen—these expectations allow the company to shape the experience in certain ways. For example, in comedy the secret of a big laugh lies in the fact that the audience expects one thing—and gets another. They know that Jack Benny is a penny-pincher; therefore, when a thief threatens him with the line, "Your money or your life!" Benny's long pause gets a laugh. His next line ("I'm thinking, I'm thinking!") is hardly necessary.

The danger in stereotyped characters is that the formula becomes so obvious and undemanding that neither the performer's nor the audience's imaginations are fully engaged. As a result, an experience which should expand the options open to the audience serves to reduce them; unchallenged, the audience leaves the theatre confirmed in the status quo.

Unique characterizations. Most modern playwrights, directors, and actors tend to reject stereotyped portrayals; they work hard to develop *unique characterizations*. The ultimate in a unique characterization would be a character who bore absolutely no resemblance to any other person—not only onstage but in the world. The futility of such an attempt is, of course, obvious, but still the goal serves to inspire all those concerned to avoid stereotyping. Many modern playwrights are deeply involved with the psychological life of their characters—always emphasizing the individuality of their creations as those characters interact with their worlds. Actors go to great lengths in their training and rehearsal to discover the spontaneous response which would be unique to this character, in this situation, at this particular moment. Both the playwright and the actor are seeking the universal truth in the unique human being.

Conflicts are inevitable. Sometimes a role is written with certain stereotyped behaviors inherent in it. Some of the most demanding roles in literature are, quite frankly, stereotypical. Take Shylock in Shakespeare's *The Merchant of Venice*. As great a humanist as Shakespeare may have been, there is little likelihood that Shakespeare ever met a Jew, and the role he wrote is largely an elaboration of the "stage Jew" tradition. Shylock is richer in detail than his predecessors, more fully human, and infinitely more interesting—but he remains largely a stereotyped character. Modern actors and directors have made Herculean efforts to circumvent the more unsavory aspects of Shylock—but the task remains vexing.

At some point, a stereotyped character either must be played with the stereotype intact, or abandoned altogether. The latter is the fate of Marc Connelly's *The Green Pastures*. This otherwise charming and well-intentioned play portrays a stereotype of the rural, southern black which some people find unacceptable. In the political climate of America in the sixties, seventies, and eighties, the play remains unproduced.

We have already seen that one of the strengths of a stereotyped character can be its accessiblity to the audience; following the same line of reasoning, a unique characterization may be inaccessible. If a character is too strange, too eccentric, too twisted in his or her psychological structure, an audience may have difficulty understanding and caring about the character. If so, the special theatrical power of empathy is lost. On the other hand, a skillfully developed, unique character may involve and affect an audience more completely than the more predictable stereotype. True, the audience may have to work harder to reach this special person, but once there, they may discover more than they bargained for. Ironically, at the heart of a unique character the audiences may find conflicts, drives, experiences which they share—but never knew they shared. That point of discovery is the revelation which joins the universal and the particular in a single insight called the truth of the character.

Idea. For Aristotle, serious drama was expected to embody religious or philosophical ideas. Much of the conflict in Greek drama is the struggle between competing ideas; without those ideas, Greek audiences would have felt cheated. The question of how ideas are embodied in a play is intriguing.

At one level, ideas are embedded in the language of the characters. In their continuing interaction with others in the play, characters use ideas to make their points: a character who has decided to settle for what she has gained so far may say, "A bird in the hand is worth two in the bush." The ideas need not be profound. In fact, in certain periods English drama was so concerned with expressing morally upright ideas that characters threatened to become little more than tiresome moralists cluttering their speeches with greeting card sentiments.

When ideas are naturally and forcefully expressed by fully developed characters they can have great power. There is some danger, however, that ideas spoken by a character will be confused with the playwright's own view of the world. Actually, the playwright may be mocking the idea by placing it in the mouth of the wrong person, or in an ironic juxtaposition of events. Shakespeare is commonly quoted as having "said" things which are actually "said" by his characters—and may not be Shakespeare's own beliefs at all.

It is far more likely that the personal beliefs of the playwright are captured in a play's *theme*. The theme is an overall statement of truth which is embodied in and illustrated by the action of the play. The theme can usually be communicated in language with some precision. Some examples might be:

Play	Theme
Oedipus the King	Those who believe that they are especially favored by the gods may be singled out for less pleasant attention.
Macbeth	Unrestrained ambition leads to disaster.
Equus	The power to make life "normal" may be the power to make life pointless.

The final way in which ideas can be communicated by the theatre is through the assumptions embedded in the experience itself. Each play creates a unique world, each with its own rules of cause and effect, of morality, of psychological truth. These ideas, usually implied assertions about the world, embody the theatre artists' opinions of the world as clearly as any formal interview. For example, the presence of the tragic hero in classic drama implies that at least some individuals are important, that their actions—even if preordained—influence history, and that there is a kind of nobility in suffering. By contrast, some modern drama ridicules the very idea of heroism, undercuts the potency of any human action, and gives the dry mock to anyone who detects any advantage whatsoever in suffering. By the same token, the familiar "happy ending" to most Western drama implies that a benevolent force rewards the good and punishes the wrongdoer.

Less obvious are the ideas which are implied by the very *form* of the play. The message conveyed by the form is most easily seen when it contradicts the other content. For example, immediately following the Second World War, the existentialist playwrights wrote a number of plays that explicitly denied the existence of a God, minimized the impact of the individual on history, and called into question our familiar expectations concerning cause and effect. Ironically, however, they chose to make these assertions in plays which were "well-made," i.e., they followed so closely the laws of cause and effect and counted so heavily on coincidence that some "unseen hand" was clearly implied. In short, the ideas inherent in the form of these plays contradicted the ideas in the content. It was not until the development of the dramatic form which came to be called absurdism that the existentialists found a theatrical form which matched their vision of an uncaring, chaotic world.

Language. Besides telling us a great deal about the characters who use it, language sets the tone of a play, and conveys a great deal about a playwright's world view.

Poetry and prose. The classic playwrights wrote dialogue in verse chiefly because it was felt to be appropriate to the occasion. The Greek writers were, remember, writing for a religious occasion and only verse was felt to be elevated enough for what was really a religious offering. In addition, tragedy deals chiefly with noble figures at the highest pitch of emotional excitement. In such a situation, it was believed, an ideal king, queen, or prince would use the most elevated language. However, Greek and Roman comic writers also chose to use verse—though for somewhat different reasons. Verse encourages the elaborate wordplay and extravagant language which can add so much to comic situations; furthermore, comic dialogue in verse can parody the poetry of tragedy when the opportunity presents itself.

Shakespeare and his contemporaries preserved part of the tradition: major or prestigious characters in both comedy and tragedy continue to speak in verse even when the low comic characters speak in prose. But gradually the primacy of verse erodes. By the 19th century only major characters in serious drama still spoke in verse. Today, only a few Western playwrights compose dialogue in verse. The classical dramas of Asia are still played in their original verse forms, of course.

The movement from poetic dialogue to prose generally parallels the rise of realism as the dominant dramatic mode in Western theatre. It is reasonable to assume that as audiences came to prefer theatre which created a familiar world, those same audiences wanted the characters to sound like real people as well. In giving up verse, characters moved toward "talking like" their audiences. But at another level, the language of plays remains very special—even in the most realistic plays.

The language of characters in plays is usually far more colorful, direct, and interesting than the language of most of the audience. In most respects, for example, Neil Simon's plays are extremely realistic portrayals of modern American life. Yet the language of his characters is richer than that of any person one would meet on the street: The endless succession of comic one-liners, colorful turns of phrase, and revealing character elements make the language delightful for its own sake. Furthermore, as a new generation of British and American playwrights have amply demonstrated, languages does not have to be written in verse to be poetic. Standard American speech is used to create a striking poetic image in this quote from Sam Shepard's *Buried Child*.

VINCE: (pause, delivers speech front) I was gonna run last night. I was gonna run and keep right on running. I drove all night. Clear to the Iowa border. The old man's two bucks sitting right on the seat beside me. It never stopped raining the whole time. Never stopped once. I could see myself in the windshield. My face. My eyes. I studied my face. Studied everything about it. As though I was looking at another man. As though I could see his whole race behind him. Like a mummy's face. I saw him dead and alive at the same time. In the same breath. In the windshield, I watched him breathe as though he was frozen in time. And every breath marked him. Marked him forever without him knowing. And then his face changed. His face became his father's face. Same bones. Same eyes. Same nose. Same breath. And his father's face changed to his Grandfather's face. And it went on like that. Changing. Clear on back to faces I'd never seen before but still recognized. Still recognized the bones underneath. The eyes. The breath. The mouth. I followed my family clear into Iowa. Every last one. Straight into the Corn Belt and further. Straight back as far as they'd take me. Then it all dissolved. Everything dissolved.*

Ultimately, a playwright's world view is captured in every aspect of his or her work, and language is no exception. The Elizabethan playwright saw about him a world in which every part was interconnected. He created such a world on the stage. Neither Shakespeare nor his audience saw anything inappropriate in this opening line from *Richard the Third:*

Now is the winter of our discontent
Made glorious summer by this sun of York. . . .

The idea that a world-class villain would begin a very serious work with a pun is doubly acceptable; Gloucester is a double-speaking scoundrel, true, but there is another reason. Poetic language captures the layered quality of everything in life for the Elizabethan. A pun was but an illustration that in life a single thing can have many meanings.

By the same token, the often-stilted verse of French neoclassic drama reaffirms the conviction that life needs—indeed, must have—structure. The flowery, extravagant language of romantic drama captures the exuberant, defiant individualism of the heroes of those plays.

One cannot help but wonder what the language of our plays, the language which sounds so right and natural to us, will tell future critics about our culture.

Music and Dance. Music and dance, two elements which have been part of all world theatre from the beginning, are today only found in special contemporary Western theatre forms.

Music, of course, plays a major role in opera and musical comedy; it functions to convey feelings which could not be communicated by other means. In music theatre the major characters burst into song when the emotional pitch has reached a point at which words alone are inadequate. That is the point at which the soaring power of music takes over. The degree to which words are transcended is illustrated by the fact that the lyrics of famous arias are often discovered to be unin-

---

*Sam Shepard, *Buried Child*. Reprinted by permission of Dramatists Play Service, Inc.

The Broadway record for longest running musical is now held by *A Chorus Line*, a loosely woven collage of personal testimony from dancers who are auditioning for the chorus of a musical. Based on the tape-recorded stories of real dancers, this musical has won audiences with its clear message about the commitment demanded by a life in the arts.

spired—or even silly—when examined without the music. In fact, the song often communicates perfectly well in a foreign language. By the same token, the least effective moments in operas are often those *recitative* sections in which the conventions of the art form force the performers to sing exposition which is factual and lacks any important emotional content.

American musical comedy tries to combine the best of both these worlds by arranging for the characters to express themselves in song only when the dramatic action has reached an appropriate emotional level.

Song is not the only way in which music can figure in a play. The power of music to evoke mood is widely used. Live or recorded music may be used as an *overture* before the play begins or as *entr'acte* music between the scenes to put the audience into a receptive frame of mind. Music can even be integrated within the stage action during scenes; this use of mood music has become so much a feature of films and television productions that younger American audiences often expect it when they go to the theatre and can be made slightly uncomfortable by the "silence" of most dramatic scenes in live theatre.

Dance is to human movement what song is to speech and it functions much the same way in the theatre. The narrative dance of some ballet would be analogous to opera. These narrative ballets have plots and characters and most feature some interaction pattern within a performance contract. Far more familiar to the average theatregoer, however, is the use of dance in musical theatre to create moments of emotional excitement.

Spectacle. Aristotle rated spectacle as the least important of his six elements, a view which few contemporary theatre artists share. Part of the disagreement may arise from confusion about what Aristotle meant: if he considered spectacle to be flamboyant dramatic displays intended only to liven up an otherwise dull piece, he certainly has a point. That kind of spectacle depends on shock value and includes the portrayal of dead bodies, natural calamities such as floods and earthquakes, and stage magic intended to amaze the audience rather than advance the action of the play. Filmmakers today seem especially attracted to this kind of spectacle; they refer to them as *special effects*, the name signaling that they usually have little to do with the dramatic action of the play. (The shooting script carries the simple notation: "The planet explodes." From that a group of specialists create a visual symphony of destruction lasting several minutes which will later be edited into the film—alternating with shots of the principal characters watching in horror.) Such spectacle is usually avoided and held in low regard in live theatre.

The spectacle which is indispensable to the modern theatre is such "spectacle" as effective scenic design, costumes which contribute to character, good blocking—all the elements, in short, which make a produced play different from a staged reading of the script. One has only to reflect on the truly memorable moments in theatre to realize how often they were experiences which could not be communicated in the script alone: the look in an actor's eyes, a special vocal inflection, a pause that says volumes, the perfect prop, the deeply moving play of light and shadow in a well-designed stage set; these are what modern theatre artists consider important elements in the structure of a play.

Tone. One element Aristotle did not mention—and did not need to mention since he was speaking only of tragedy—is tone. Should this production elicit laughter or tears from its audience? Or a mixture of both?

One idea that can be discarded immediately is the notion that a play with a serious intention can be only serious in tone. It is surprising that such an idea should have surfaced at all. One of the earliest playwrights whose work we know—Aristophanes—wrote ribald comedies concerning the most serious topics: abuses in education, government corruption, women's rights, and war and peace. At the height of a protracted war with Sparta, a war which was destroying everything that was great about Athens, Aristophanes wrote *Lysistrata*. In it, the women of the world, tired of wars which only serve male vanity, decide to go on strike until peace is declared. Foremost among the services they withhold is sex. The dramatic situation is—in the spirit of Aristophanes—fertile; he sets up scene after scene in which every comic situation is fully exploited for laughs. And yet his intention is clear, and even modern audiences leave a lusty production of *Lysistrata* with a changed perception of the "glories" of war.

Modern theatre has gone out of its way to manipulate the tone of plays for particular effect. Sometimes contemporary plays portray horrible situations in such a detached and cynical way that audiences are later jolted to reflect on what they witnessed so dispassionately. Or they may find themselves laughing hysterically at situations which would normally be offensive. "I can't believe I'm laughing at this!" they mutter to themselves when they pause for breath. Or, particularly in the theatre of the absurd, essentially ridiculous situations are presented with such high seriousness that our poor spinning minds are led to question the very nature of experience itself.

SUMMARY

The experience of a play is a shared interaction between performer and audience. That experience has a certain duration, complexity, and intensity; all of these are related to the topic of the play. The elements of the experience which can be manipulated by the playwright and the production company include plot, character, idea, language, music and dance, spectacle, and tone. It is these elements which create the various worlds of the play.

Discussion Questions

1. Describe in your own words the difference between *story* and *plot*. Use a play with which you are familiar to provide examples.
2. If you were writing a play about your own life (an autobiographical play, in other words), where would you place your point-of-attack? How would you handle the other elements of plot?
3. Describe some clever ways in which you have seen exposition handled in the theatre, films, or television. Do you remember any clumsy exposition?
4. What are the ethical questions involved in introducing new information at the climax? Why must it be played "by the rules"?
5. Is it possible that our choices of stereotypes in the theatre tell us something about our world? (For example, in Chinese theatre there is a long history of stereotype; one of the most popular is the villainous bureaucrat—which reflects the traditional Chinese dependency on a monstrous bureaucracy.) Pick a popular stereotype from television and discuss that character's meaning.
6. What ideas are communicated by the *form* of a comedy series on television? An action-adventure series?

12

The World of the Play

THE REPEATABLE MIRACLE

It happens every time the curtain rises. Every time the stage lights come up. Every time that first actor strides onto the stage. A little miracle. The anxious actors call it "magic time." A world is created—from scratch!

In the imaginations of the performers and the audience there is a tiny Genesis, a little bang, and—where there was nothing—a cosmos appears.

Complete. With its own physical laws. Peopled by its own population. Each new person operating in accordance with his or her psychology.

These worlds arrive full blown. They have their own history, their own myths, their own rituals. And the people who inhabit these worlds are discovered in mid-stride. They keep appointments made weeks ago; they pursue goals adopted last year; they suffer from wounds received in distant youth. These people are at home in their worlds.

We, the audience, are strangers. Tourists. And, like tourists everywhere, we struggle to understand this foreign country. If it is similar to our own, we catch on quickly—like Americans in Canada. If the culture gap is more profound, it takes us longer and requires more effort. This makes some of us cross; like tourists everywhere we wonder aloud why this world is not like the one we left behind. Why, we ask, would these people choose to behave differently from my friends at home? Even as we ask such a question, we are learning.

We can take some consolation from a fact: nearly every world we visit is subject to consistent laws—even if each world is very different from every other one. And each of these different worlds is constructed of the same basic building blocks or elements. What varies is how each element is employed and how important it is.

Sometimes it pays to prepare for a trip to a foreign country. You can do some reading, get some perspective on the upcoming journey, begin to acquire the proper frame of mind. Some tourists, on the other hand, like to travel first, experiencing the foreign country with few pre-conceptions, and reflecting only after the experience. Whatever approach you decide upon, consider the remainder of this chapter as a brief tour guide to some of the worlds you might visit.

THE WORLD OF TRAGEDY

This world is a harsh and forbidding one, a world suitable for journeys into the darkest interiors of human experience. By the time we leave it we will have passed through a harrowing experience which should leave us both wiser and more humble than when we began.

At the center of this world stands a single figure, the tragic hero or heroine. At the beginning, the tragic hero is usually secure in a position of satisfaction and high prestige; the only plot of any consequence is the account of his or her descent into calamity. The conclusion of the play will find the hero dead or disgraced—or both. The slide is both slow and inevitable; therefore, plots in tragedy tend to be relatively simple and unified.

The most striking aspect of the plot in tragedy is its inevitability. The entire world—the cosmos, in fact—seems to be organized for the destruction of the tragic hero. That ruthless intention is captured well in the title of a play by Cocteau, *The Infernal Machine*. With the relent-lessness of a colossal machine, the world catches up the careless sleeve of our hero and, inexorably, drags him or her to destruction.

But tragedy is much more than an industrial accident. The fate of the hero works as much from inside its victim as outside. What makes the machine so infernal is its ability to apparently enlist the hero as an unknowing accomplice. "Character is destiny," the Greeks said—and tragedy illustrates the principle very well. Everything the tragic hero does—no matter how well-intentioned—leads toward doom. Even the confidence with which he or she views the world at the onset is demonstrated to be a kind of madness, a moral blindness brought on by overweening pride.

Oedipus confidently does everything he thinks is necessary to avoid fulfilling the prophecy that he will kill his father and marry his mother. He discovers in the end that everything he has done—every twist, every turn, every evasion—has sped the curse to its conclusion. Willy Loman in Arthur Miller's *Death of a Salesman* does his best to live up to his idea of the American Dream, only to discover that his vision is warped and has destroyed both his life and the lives of his beloved sons.

In neither of these cases did the hero simply make a mistake. If so, their stories would be nothing more than moral lessons warning us not to repeat that particular error. The special impact of tragedy is that we

Douglas Campbell plays King Oedipus in this famous scene from the Stratford (Ontario) Shakespeare Festival production of *Oedipus The King*. The production was directed by Tyrone Guthrie; the costumes and masks were by Tanya Moiseiwitsch.

see the tragic hero trapped in a system which is determined to destroy him. In fact, his or her own confidence about what is right or what is known is part of the problem—and the first step toward disaster. The lesson for the audience—especially a self-satisfied audience—is: "Don't be so sure; your life isn't over yet!"

OEDIPUS THE KING (c. 425 B.C.) BY SOPHOCLES

Even among the limited number of extant scripts of Greek tragedies, there is enough variety to prevent any one of them from laying claim to clear title of archetypal Greek tragedy. Still, when Aristotle, writing roughly one hundred years after the Golden Age of the tragedy, searched for a play which most exemplified his ideal, he usually turned to one play: *Oedipus The King* by Sophocles (496–406 B.C.). Subsequent critics have found in this play many of the most important features of the classic Greek tragedy: a clean-lined, simple plot, a memorable tragic hero, great ideas, noble poetry, and the severity of tone most people expect from tragedy. It may be grossly unfair to other successful Greek playwrights, and perhaps even to Sophocles himself, but *Oedipus The King* is the example of choice for most modern theatre people— not to mention psychiatrists, journalists, and politicians seeking a ready example of some destructive human frailty or habit.

The myth on which the play is based was familiar to Greek audiences, and it is a strength of the plot—not a weakness—that audiences know what will happen. The play is filled with ironies that would be lost on those who do not know the myth in advance. Indeed, the fact that we do not have (or even know of) the other two tragedies and the satyr play which rounded out the full day of drama at the world premiere puts us at something of a disadvantage. Does Sophocles intend that the final words of the chorus, to the effect that no man should be considered fortunate until his life is finished, should be considered his final thoughts on the subject? Or is he reminding us of the issues which he intends to raise in the next play? Sophocles returned to other parts of the Oedipus myth in other tragedies, *Antigone* (c. 442 B.C.) and *Oedipus at Colonus* (after 406 B.C.), but they are not part of the trilogy which contained *Oedipus*.

Perhaps the most vexing problem for a modern theatregoer is the problem of justice in this play. We are disturbed by the calamities which rain on Oedipus. To be sure, he has done some unacceptable things: it is never forgivable to kill, especially one's father, and a marriage with one's mother is bound to end up badly. But the extenuating circumstances are, after all, convincing. Oedipus has acted in ignorance at every step; indeed, when warned of his fate, he has tried in every way to escape it.

Modern audiences do not find convincing the argument that it is a tragic flaw in his character, his arrogance, which leads inevitably to his downfall. We are tempted to respond, impatiently, "Yes, yes. Of course he is arrogant and impetuous. But if it had not been that, it would have been something else." Oedipus' problems could not have been headed off by more sensitive toilet training or wider roads, or even a willingness to call off the search. And therein lies a clue. Difficult as it is for us to do so we must not share Oedipus' delusion that there is anything to be "done." Fate is there, waiting, inexorable—and hidden. There is nothing to be "done" except to live it through. As with all tragic heroes, the great question is not their morality, but their integrity.

The plot of *Oedipus The King* is a perfect example of late point of attack and subsequent use of exposition—indeed, the first two-thirds of the play is exposition in one sense: it is not until Oedipus has all the terrible facts before him that he can embark on truly independent action. And even then, as one interpretation of the final lines of the Chorus serves to remind us, his story is not over yet: Oedipus has not finished suffering yet; he has years of pain ahead before being raised to the position of demigod.

The play begins with the city of Thebes in crisis: the city is being ravaged by plague, infertility, and crop failures. People, the priests included, are at their wit's end. In desperation, they have come to the palace of Oedipus, a man renowned for his cleverness, hoping for some solution to their problems. Oedipus announces that he already knows of their problems, of course, and grieves with his city. In fact, he has directed his brother-in-law, Creon, to travel to the Temple of Delphi to ask the gods what the problem might be. No sooner does he finish speaking than Creon returns with a message: Thebes is suffering because of the pollution of the unsolved murder of King Laius, Oedipus' predecessor. Oedipus never knew the previous king, he says, because the murder had taken place on a deserted road shortly before Oedipus arrived. Oedipus had been the one to successfully answer the riddle of the Sphinx, causing her to self-destruct and free Thebes from her evil influence. It was for that act that the grateful city asked Oedipus to become their king. Now, though the crime took place before his reign began, Oedipus pledges to seek out the murderer and to punish any and all involved in the crime. The malefactor is to be shunned, prevented from participating in religious rites, and exiled.

The Chorus suggests that Oedipus begin his inquiry with Tiresias, the blind seer who has the power to know secrets hidden from others. Tiresias is brought before Oedipus. He reveals early in the conversation that he knows something, but refuses at first to tell, saying that the information will cause them both great pain. Oedipus, clearly unused to being crossed, grows angrier and more abusive as the scene continues. Finally, Tiresias blurts it out: Oedipus himself is the polluter of the city. Now Oedipus is truly enraged; he charges that there is a conspiracy against him of which Tiresias is only a part. He accuses Creon of being the leader of the plot.

In the next scene Creon, having heard the accusations, comes back to the palace to defend himself. He and Oedipus are in the midst of a terrible argument when Jocasta, Oedipus' wife, emerges from the palace to calm them. She tells Oedipus not to be concerned about prophecies of this kind since they are seldom true. She cites the example of a prophecy which once said that if she and Laius had a son he would grow up to kill his father. But that prophecy had been frustrated; they had pierced the child's ankles, bound his feet together, and had him left to die on the slopes of Mount Citheron. In the course of her story, however, she lets slip the fact that Laius was killed at a "place where three roads meet"—but by a group of bandits, according to the report of the sole survivor. Oedipus is suspicious and begins his story. He was raised in neighboring Corinth by the king and queen there. One day, however, he had asked the Oracle at Delphi about his future. When told that he was fated to kill his father and marry his mother, Oedipus was horrified and, in order to prevent that awful development, he left Corinth and wandered far from home. Later, at a place where three roads met, he had encountered an imperious old man who would not give him room on the road. In the fight which followed, Oedipus killed the old man and several of his retainers. To clarify the facts surrounding the murder, the surviving witness, an old shepherd, is sent for.

Just then, a messenger arrives from Corinth with news that the king of Corinth is dead. Oedipus' grief is mixed with relief; if the old man has died, it was not by Oedipus' hand, and the curse he fears cannot be true. On hearing what has been on Oedipus' mind, the old messenger nearly laughs; Oedipus should not worry, because the King and Queen of Corinth were not his parents. In fact, this very messenger, then a shepherd, was the one who brought the young infant down from Mount Citheron and presented him to the childless rulers of Corinth for adoption. To prove his point, the messenger points to the scars on Oedipus' ankles, made by the cords which bound his feet (the Greek word "Oedipus" means "swollen feet"). Jocasta is aghast at this news, and begs Oedipus not to search any further. Oedipus is determined to follow the trail to its conclusion.

The shepherd who was the witness to the murder also turns out to be the shepherd who had been given the responsibility for exposing Jocasta's child, so his arrival is doubly important. Under close questioning, he reveals that, yes, he did give the child to the shepherd from Corinth and, yes, it was Oedipus who killed Laius. The last pieces of the puzzle are in place. Oedipus goes into the palace in agony. A messenger then relates what has happened within the palace. Jocasta has hanged herself with her own sash. Oedipus has taken the brooches from her dress and torn his own eyes out. The mutilated Oedipus then reenters and laments both his fate and his unwillingness to see the truth. He says goodbye to his two daughters, Ismene and Antigone, and announces his intention to wander throughout Greece, a poverty-stricken exile from his family and city.

Classic and neoclassic tragedy tends to be "regular," that is, it conforms to certain rules. These rules, only inferred from the work of the ancients, were given ferocious power by some critics and playwrights in the 16th and 17th centuries. During this period European critics expected tragedy to exhibit the *three unities*: a *unity of action* (only one, simple plot), a *unity of time* (the action of the play should be encompassed within a single day), and a *unity of place* (all action should take place in the same location). Of course, all these rules were ignored by the Elizabethan writers—whose tragedies compete with the world's best. Still, the structural compression encouraged by these rules give some idea of the pressure-cooker atmosphere of tragedy.

The fact that the traditional tragic hero is a king, a prince, a thane, or a princess reminds us immediately that the destiny of the state is intertwined with that of the hero. In modern tragedy, in which the hero is an otherwise ordinary person, he or she embodies the values of the audience, thereby involving the larger society in a different way. In both cases, then, the health of society is threatened by the plight of the tragic hero. He or she serves as a kind of moral pathfinder for us all, heedlessly charting new directions and limits in human behavior—even as he or she is cut down in the attempt.

In others, this compulsive drive to assert themselves might be called stupid or foolhardy. But the tragic hero manages to win our grudging admiration. Partly this is the result of the suffering he or she endures: To the degree that the tragic hero is trapped by destiny, his or her suffering is undeserved; and undeserved suffering is ennobling. Beyond that, however, we are grateful to the tragic hero; because he or she has lived through a painful destiny, we understand the world more fully. We know the limits of human experience—even though gaining the knowledge has cost us one of our best.

The writers of classic and neoclassic tragedy believed strongly in a kind of stripped-down purity in their worlds: tragic language has the compression of poetry, and the ideas are the most profound; plots are relatively simple; there are no comic elements; and spectacle is kept to a minimum. Shakespeare and his contemporaries take some liberties with these general rules. Plays such as *Hamlet, Macbeth,* and *King Lear* have more elaborate plots, employ some prose, have comic elements, and involve spectacle—frequently violent. Still, even in Shakespeare there is a severity which leads us to many of the same places as his ancient predecessors.

A visit to the world of tragedy can leave the audience with a complex collection of feelings ranging from relief ("Thank heaven, it didn't

The Trojan Women by Euripides is a classic play made even more remarkable by the fact that the author, a Greek, arouses great sympathy for the victims of Greek atrocities. The play is frequently revived in an effort to remind audiences that there are innocent victims of war—even among the enemy.

happen to me!") through a version of survivor's guilt ("I made all those errors; why didn't it happen to me?"). Aristotle proposed that audiences are to be left purged of pity and terror through the evocation of those feelings. He called the process *catharsis*. More recently, commentators have suggested that rather than being cleansed of pity and terror, the experience of tragedy allows an audience to transcend those feelings by seeing them in a context which makes both emotions immaterial. Thus, the tragic vision of the human condition allows the audience to move beyond pity and terror—to move beyond moral considerations altogether—and grasp the implacable disinterest of the universe.

Whatever the mechanism by which it is achieved, the audience experiencing tragedy must be elevated—mere depression will not do. In short, a successful journey into the world of tragedy changes the way an audience member experiences life at the deepest level and, in doing so, sends the traveller home refreshed and enriched.

THE TRAGEDY OF HAMLET, PRINCE OF DENMARK
(1601) BY WILLIAM SHAKESPEARE

The Tragedy of Hamlet, Prince of Denmark is widely thought to be William Shakespeare's (1564-1616) most effective tragedy; some even consider it the best of all his plays. Certainly, it is one of the best plays ever written in English—and one of the most influential. The amount of criticism this one play has generated is astounding. The thematic material in *Hamlet*, the philosophical issues raised, and the title figure himself have intrigued readers and performers for nearly 400 years. So much of the play has entered the public consciousness, in fact, that people who have never read or seen it are familiar with famous lines, and the figure of Prince Hamlet as an indecisive individual is a familar social label.

The very fame of the play has proved something of a liability. The original conception has been so overgrown with critical embellishments that the modern reader or producing group can have difficulty discovering the wonderful dramatic ideas which lie at the core of the play.

The content interactions in *Hamlet* are of all three kinds. At one level there is a rattling good murder mystery: Hamlet has good reason to believe that his father has been murdered, and must devise a trap to prove his uncle the murderer; once that is established, he must create an opportunity to take revenge. This was the story Shakespeare lifted and adapted from earlier sources—perhaps even a play of the same name which some scholars attribute to Thomas Kyd. It was Shakespeare's special genius, however, to take mundane material and lift it to unimagined heights. One method was to introduce a second level of interaction or conflict in which Prince Hamlet finds himself pitted against the society in which he lives: "The time is out of joint," he says, and then goes on to complain, "O cursed spite that ever I was born to set it right!" Critics who find this level of interaction useful see the play as one in which an essentially modern sensibility is trapped in a feudal world. Finally, Hamlet is in conflict with himself. Part of him wants to take immediate revenge for his father's murder. Another part cannot help but consider the consequences of such an action—indeed of *any* action. It is this tendency to consider all things too closely which makes Hamlet such a provocative symbol of one of the primary modern dilemmas—and the first great psychological hero.

As the play begins, we discover that the soldiers guarding the Danish royal castle at Elsinore have twice seen what seems to them to be the ghost of the recently-dead king, Old Hamlet, stalking the battlements. On the theory that he will be interested, they arrange for young Prince Hamlet to join them on the third night. Together with his loyal friend Horatio, Hamlet sees the ghost and is struck by the resemblance to his father. It seems to want to talk with him, and he resolves to confront the Ghost the following night. In the meantime, we discover the difficult situation in which Hamlet finds himself: his father having died suddenly, Hamlet has returned from college at Wittenberg to discover that the crown—instead of going to him—has been taken by his uncle, Claudius. To reinforce his claim to the throne, Claudius has married Gertrude, the former queen and Hamlet's mother. The marriage is close enough to incest to be questionable; the speed with which they married has created a scandal and further upset the very sensitive and already depressed Hamlet.

Claudius is supported by the elderly counselor Polonius, whose son and daughter, Laertes and Ophelia, are close to Hamlet's age. As we meet them, Laertes is leaving for school in Paris; Ophelia is being kept in the castle where, her father hopes, she will attract the serious attention of Hamlet.

Finally, Hamlet meets with the Ghost alone. The Ghost tells him that he is, indeed, the spirit of Old Hamlet and that he is forced to walk the earth until his murder has been avenged. Furthermore, the murderer is Claudius who, having come upon Old Hamlet sleeping in his garden, had poured a strong poison in his ear. The Ghost demands that Hamlet undertake the revenge, and Hamlet pledges to do so. Hamlet then swears the soldiers and Horatio to silence, and warns them that in the future he may seem crazy—though it will be part of his plan.

Claudius has plans of his own. Concerned about Hamlet's behavior, he and Gertrude have prevailed upon two of Hamlet's boyhood friends, Rosencrantz and Guildenstern, to spy on Hamlet and find out what is causing his disturbing melancholy. Polonius thinks he has the solution: Hamlet must be mad with love for Ophelia. To test this theory, he arranges a meeting between Hamlet and Ophelia in a place where he and the King can overhear their conversation. Hamlet discovers both stratagems, and is further disgusted by these proofs of the hypocrisy he finds all around him.

Hamlet hits upon an inventive plan to test the truth of the Ghost's charges: a group of strolling players arrives at the castle. Hamlet persuades them to modify a play which they have in their repertory by inserting some lines and business of his devising. The modified play, renamed by Hamlet "The Mousetrap," is presented that night before the entire court. It contains scenes in which a king is murdered by a close relative in just the manner described by the Ghost. Claudius is greatly affected, and in a rage brings the play to a halt. Hamlet has his proof.

Hamlet is called to his mother's chambers. On the way he passes Claudius apparently praying. Although he has the chance to kill Claudius, he does not because to kill him at prayer would gain Claudius immediate admittance to heaven. Hamlet will wait for an opportunity which will send his soul elsewhere. Ironically, after Hamlet exits, Claudius reveals that his guilt has rendered him unable to pray.

Hamlet uses the meeting with his mother to berate her for the early and unseeming marriage. As they talk, Hamlet realizes that there is someone hiding behind the drapery on the wall and, stabbing through the fabric, kills—old Polonius. He had hoped it was Claudius.

Thoroughly distrustful of Hamlet, Claudius now plots to do away with him. On the pretense of letting the scandal over the murder of Polonius die down, he sends the young prince to England in the company of Rosencrantz and Guildenstern—who carry a sealed letter to the English king ordering him to immediately behead Hamlet. On board ship, however, the suspicious Hamlet steals the letter and forges a new one demanding that the English king kill Rosencrantz and Guildenstern instead. Soon after, the ship is attacked by pirates and, during the fight, Hamlet finds himself isolated on the pirate ship as Rosencrantz and Guildenstern sail blithely on to their deaths. The pirates kindly put Hamlet ashore, and he sets out back toward Elsinore.

Meanwhile, enraged at his father's death, Laertes returns from Paris and leads a mob to storm the palace demanding revenge. It takes all of Claudius' guile to reassure the impetuous young man that Hamlet will be punished. Ophelia deals with her father's death and Hamlet's disappearance in a different way: she goes mad and drowns in the river—though whether a suicide or not is uncertain. The clouded nature of her death, however, demands that she be buried in unsanctified ground. It is there, at her graveside, that Hamlet learns of her death and has a violent confrontation with Laertes. The latter's anger is brought under control only when Claudius plots a suitable revenge with Laertes as the major figure.

Hamlet is lured into a fencing exhibition with Laertes. However, Claudius has arranged for Laertes' foil to be unbated, that is, unprotected with the rubber button which would make the match safe sport. Next, he has arranged to smear the tip with poison in such a way that even a scratch will kill Hamlet. Finally, to make sure, Claudius poisons the wine which Hamlet will surely drink to refresh himself during the contest.

Hamlet turns out to be a better fencer than the conspirators expected. He wins the first two touches, leading his mother to drink to her health—with his poisoned wine. Desperate, Laertes nicks Hamlet when the prince's back is turned. Grasping immediately that part of the plot against him, Hamlet disarms Laertes, exchanges swords, and manages to wound Laertes with the poisoned sword. A repentant Laertes tells Hamlet the remainder of the plot as Gertrude, as if to prove his point, dies of the poison. Hamlet then stabs Claudius and forces the dying king to drink the remaining poisoned wine. Finally, surrounded by the bodies of Claudius, Gertrude, and Laertes, Hamlet dies in the arms of his loyal friend, Horatio.

MELODRAMA

If the world of tragedy is one in which the traveller is lifted above morality, the world of melodrama is one in which morality, and the forces which reward moral behavior, are everywhere present. Furthermore, the scenery is flamboyant, full of extreme and ornate vistas. Finally, it is a world free from troublesome ambiguities.

The plot of tragedy follows a basically good person from an elevated position to destruction. Melodrama takes an unquestionably good person—or group—to the edge of destruction—but snatches them back at the last second and rewards them fulsomely. We, the audience, may be surprised about *how* that rescue takes place—but we are never surprised *that* it happens. The reason is simple: the world of melodrama is a world of moral balance. Ultimately good people are always rewarded and evil ones are punished. In the end, it is that simple.

THE FORTY-SEVEN LOYAL RONIN *(1748)*
(KANADEHON CHUSHINGURA)
BY IZUMO, SOSEKE, AND SHORAKU

This famous Kabuki play is loosely based on historical incidents dating from 1710. However, the original story has been modified, new characters have been created, and often fanciful incidents have been introduced. To further confuse the literalminded, sections of the original eleven-act version have been lost through disuse. What remains is a series of related scenes which constitute one of the classics of the Kabuki stage—but which are seldom performed together. Instead, famous scenes from the *Forty-seven Loyal Ronin* are presented as parts of composite Kabuki programs, much as if they were one-act plays.

Besides serving as an excellent example of Kabuki drama, this play displays all the characteristics of melodrama.

The "ronin" (literally "wave men") of the title refers to those samurai who, having sworn eternal loyalty to a lord, found themselves without any role in society once that lord was dead or disgraced. A strict reading of the code of the warrior demanded that they should kill themselves, but—understandably—mitigating circumstances often intervened. As the consolidation of power in the hands of the *shogun* continued during the 16th, 17th, and 18th centuries, the resulting reduction in the number of warlords left a great number of the samurai class as rootless as the "waves." The dilemma of a highly trained, dedicated person left without a clear social role has always intrigued the Japanese. So has the question of the limits of loyalty. Both ideas recur in this play.

The major plotline, the conspiracy of loyal retainers to revenge their lord's death, is little more than a thread which links the personal experiences of the colorful group of people whose lives are caught up in this famous conspiracy. Repeatedly, characters from all walks of life are forced to choose between personal happiness and a rigid code of honorable behavior. The characters are memorable, the circumstances are highly theatrical, and the outcomes are loaded with suspense.

Lord Kira has attempted to seduce the wife of Asano, Lord of Akao. He is rejected by Lady Asano, but he is a man who does not take rebuffs well. Kira taunts Asano during an audience with the *shogun*. At first Asano controls his temper, but finally goaded beyond endurance, he draws his sword against Kira. In doing so, he breaks the rigid sanction against drawing a weapon in the presence of the shogun. The shogun has no choice but to sentence him to commit *seppuku*, ritual suicide. So, after a moving scene in which he says goodbye to his family and his retainers, he takes his own life. The retainers are furious at the injustice of his death and wish to take immediate revenge against Kira, but they are restrained by Oishi—the most respected counselor— who exhorts them to be calm and plan for the future.

In the next scene we pick up the adventures of some of the *ronin*, especially Sampei, a samurai who is married to Okuru. Okuru had been a lady-in-waiting to Lady Asano, but the fall of the lord has brought ruin to both. Although he yearns to revenge Asano, Sampei has become a hunter, leaving his wife to live with her parents. They, in turn, are in such desperate straits that Okuru's father, Oichibei, has arranged for her to work in a tea house, presumably as a courtesan. On this particular day, Oichibei is returning home

Contending retainers confront one another at the conclusion of the *Forty-Seven Loyal Ronin.*

In a deeply moving scene, Asano, Lord of Akao, prepares to commit ritual suicide on orders from the *shogun*.

from the negotiations with some of the money in its distinctive wrapper. He is passing through Sampei's part of the forest when he is surprised by a highwayman who kills him, takes the money, and rolls the body into a ravine. The murderer is smugly counting the money when he is almost run down by a wild boar; he steps aside to evade the boar but is accidentally shot in the back by the hunter pursuing the animal. The hunter proves to be Sampei! Sampei realizes that the money is ill-gotten but decides to contribute it to the coffers of the conspiracy to revenge the death of Asano. However, when his mother-in-law sees the money in its wrapper, she accuses Sampei of murdering Oichibei, his own father-in-law. Shamed Sampei stabs himself. As he lies dying, however, two of his fellow *ronin* arrive with the evidence that clears him and, in fact, proves that he has unknowingly revenged his father-in-law's death. As they praise him, they show him the covenant which all the *ronin* are to sign. Sampei signs in his own blood before dying.

The leader of the *ronin*, Oishi, is trying to outwit the opposition by frequenting a tea house where Kira's men hang out—especially Bannai, Kira's favorite. This proves to be the same tea house where Okuru, Sampei's widow, works. His ruse works a little too well; his fellow *ronin* are afraid that his resolve might be weakening. A delegation visits Oishi, and are so convinced by his apparent drunkenness and flippant attitude that they nearly kill him on the spot. However, Bannai is also convinced that Oishi means no harm. That night Oishi receives an important letter from Lady Asano and steps out onto the veranda to read it in private. Okuru thinks it is a love letter and reads it while languidly taking the air on a nearby balcony by using a handmirror. At the same time, a spy beneath the veranda reads the ends of the very long scroll which trail over the railing. Finally, Oishi becomes aware of both tricks and begins by confronting Okuru. She is distraught and offers to kill herself to prove her loyalty. At the last minute, however, Oishi has her thrust her sword down between the floor mats, stabbing the spy lurking beneath. The delegation of *ronin* have witnessed this scene and enthusiastically welcome Oishi back to the conspiracy.

The next act deals with Rehei, a successful merchant who has decided to help the ronin buy necessary weapons. In the greatest of secrecy he has just sent off the last of seven boxes of arms, when the ronin burst in disguised as detectives, carrying the incriminating box, and demanding to know the plot. Rehei denies all knowledge, even when the *ronin* threaten to kill his young son. He is so steadfast, in fact, that he offers to kill his son himself if that will convince them. At the last minute, a voice from inside the box tells him, "Stop!" Oishi climbs out of the box and assures Rehei that this test has removed any doubts which they might have had about his loyalty. Rehei has no regrets and repeats his pledge.

Finally, the *ronin* break into Kira's house at night and, after a hard fight, corner him in a fuel shed. He is brought before the group but, in a final spite-

Having taken revenge for his murder, the loyal *ronin* offer up the head of Kira to the spirit of their master.

ful act, tries to stab Oishi. In a flash, Oishi cuts off Kira's head. The group then offers the severed head to the spirit of their dead master. As they do, however, two more of Kira's supporters attack Oishi. He kills them both. Then word arrives that Kira's brother has mounted a force against them and is waiting in ambush at Asano's tomb.

The *ronin* arrive at the tomb and, in a pitched battle, destroy the last of Kira's forces.

Of course, getting to that end is often a tortuous journey. Melodramatic plots are often very complex: they may combine multiple plots with extraordinary twists and reversals. The plots of melodrama are also peppered with coincidences: Important people arrive at just the right time, a piece of information falls into exactly the wrong hands, a split second, once-in-a-million opportunity makes escape possible and virtue triumphant. In addition, one of the secondary plots may be comic.

Even the main plot can have comic elements—but when it does, the comic episodes are alternated with the serious ones in such a way that there is never any confusion as to what response is expected of the audience.

Nor is there ever any question about whom to root for. Characters in melodrama tend to be very clearly good or evil, and uncomplicated by any internal contradictions. At the most extreme—as in late-19th-century Western melodrama—the good and bad forces are easily identified. The evil characters absolutely delight in their dastardly deeds and the good ones are so pure, upright, and innocent as to be laughable to modern audiences. However, that sense of superiority may be premature: Modern melodrama preserves that same easy identification. After all, who would confuse the crew of the Enterprise with a Klingon, a Green Beret with the enemy, or Indiana Jones with the Nazis? There is never any question about which team we should be cheering for.

And cheer we do—and hiss—and gasp—and shiver—and laugh. For the world of melodrama is a world of emotional extremes. The characters feel things deeply—and the audience is invited to participate. In fact, melodrama tends to be *sentimental*, that is, the emotional response is in excess of the stimulus provided. As a result, melodrama's heroines are generally emotional young things—and the audience is invited to weep with despair at their predicaments—and then weep tears of joy at their last-minute reprieves! The hero puffs up with national pride—and the audience shares his patriotic fervor. In short, by the final curtain of

A climactic scene from a typical 19th Century English melodrama, *Hands Across the Sea*. The illustration is even labeled with the curtain line: "Safe in a Husband's Keeping!"

a melodrama, both the characters and the audience have been through an emotional wringer.

The language, keeping pace with the emotional involvement of the characters, can be quite flamboyant; but in modern melodramas—for example in soap operas—it can be deceptively realistic.

Because of the emotional response it strives for, melodrama can use music extensively. In fact, the very name *melodrama* refers to the distinctive 19th-century practice of underscoring nearly all scenes with music. Films and television continue the practice today in order to achieve the same level of emotional response.

Finally, the spectacle in melodrama can be spectacular indeed: The car chases and exploding volcanoes of television and film melodrama were anticipated by 19th-century stage effects which were absolutely extraordinary: Steamboats blew up, floods destroyed cities, chariot races thundered across the stage, and supernatural effects were introduced with very little provocation. Even the settings of melodramas can be spectacular. Audiences are often taken to exotic environments like ruined abbeys, Oriental temples, fantastic planets, and fanciful sci-

The modern audience's need for melodrama is met by films and television. The *Stars Wars* films offer a good example of how the formula of melodrama is put to good—and profitable—use by modern filmmakers.

entific laboratories. All can provide the dramatic settings guaranteed to set the audience's pulse to pounding.

And yet, underlying all the menace in melodrama lies a benevolent force. Clearly no matter how much danger the forces of good may face, no matter how certain victory seems for the forces of evil, all will be resolved in the end. A moral balance will be established; that is the basic law of the world of melodrama. We can return home having exercised all our emotions. We will have cried, and held our breath, and feared, and cheered. And finally, we will have had our sense of the essentially moral bias of the universe completely confirmed.

DRAMA

In the realm of serious theatre, drama* has more variety than any other. It is serious in its intention, but the variety of means used to convey that intention gives the spectator a wide selection of dramatic landscapes.

*The word *drama* comes from the French *drame*, a specific kind of play; it should not be confused with *drama* as it is used to denote all of dramatic literature.

Take tone, for example. A drama may have a happy ending or a sad one. Essentially good characters may come to grief or they may prosper. The negative forces are far less obvious—far more complicated—and they do not always suffer retribution. Comic elements may be present and they may be important. In fact, the comic elements may be present in the leading characters—not restricted to "comic sidekicks" as is frequently the case in melodrama. This mixture of comic and serious elements in leading figures grows naturally from drama's generally greater concern for well-rounded character: as character development becomes deeper and more probing, people become more complex. In this complexity we discover human frailties and contradictions which can serve to make characters funnier at the same time that they become more human.

The best examples of this richness of character are probably the dramatic worlds created by Anton Chekhov. His characters are famous for being silly and noble, trivial and important, funny and sad—all at the same time.

The psychological values of Chekhov's work are so profound that they survive transplanting. Here, under Andre Serban's direction for the New York Shakespeare Festival, they bloomed in a production quite different from the realistic one that the author envisioned.

Whereas in melodrama the comic and serious scenes *alternate*, in drama the elements frequently *coexist*. This simultaneous view of the world gives drama greater complexity than any other world—excepting, perhaps, comedy.

Psychological Drama. This complexity is echoed in the differing goals of drama. One popular modern goal is reflected in *psychological drama*. Psychological drama attempts to understand the characters in a play, even if plot suffers as a result. Great attention is given to the motivational structure of the characters, frequently following the antecedents of some present action back to its roots in much the same way as psychotherapy might. The major plays of Tennessee Williams fall into this category of drama.

Mystery Drama. This reconstructs the mechanical and psychological steps involved in a crime. A leading figure is usually some detective figure—whether a professional or gifted amateur—who puts a series of confounding clues together to track down a lawbreaker of some kind. Mystery dramas usually have a greater emphasis on a complex plot than is evident in, say, a psychological drama.

Social Drama/Thesis Plays. The world of drama is frequently used to direct attention to current social problems. The plays of Ibsen and Shaw are good examples of works whose primary aims include bringing serious social problems to the attention of audiences. Their work might be called *social dramas*. However, if a playwright goes beyond simply identifying and describing a problem, if he or she actually recommends a solution, either directly or by strong implication, the work could be called a *thesis play*; that is, a play which is written to support a particular social or political action. Many of the most popular plays of the late 19th century were written as thesis plays and strongly advocated such social programs as reform of the inheritance laws, better public health, prison reform, and labor unions.

The rise of drama as we know it parallels the rise of realism as a way of describing the world. As a result, the world of drama looks very much like the contemporary world of the playwright. It is a world of drawing rooms and offices, of city streets and country lanes, of tenements and prison cells. It is highly unlikely to contain throne rooms and temples of doom. In the same way, the characters are usually ordinary folk—or at least recognizable ones. Their speech is prose—frequently

George Bernard Shaw used the realistic format to create fascinating dramas—which just happen to crackle with ideas. This production of his *Candida* was mounted by the North Carolina School of the Arts.

idiomatic or written in regional dialects. In short, we feel at home in the world of the drama.

A DOLL'S HOUSE *(1879) BY HENRIK IBSEN*

Henrik Ibsen (1828–1906) is frequently credited with having given Western drama a whole new direction. This is certainly an overstatement, but it is true that with a series of realistic problem plays beginning in 1877 he captured the attention of critics and audiences alike. His plays, unlike the melodrama, bedroom farces, and stodgy poetic verse pieces dominating the commercial stages of the time, forced society to deal with them. His work became the subject of scholarly treatises and heated dinner party conversations. His plays served warning that in a rapidly evolving Western society, theatre was going to be a change-agent.

Nothing in Western society was changing so rapidly as the family, so it is not surprising that Ibsen's realistic plays are domestic dramas. They deal with relations between men and women, husbands and wives, parents and children, and how those fundamental relationships are influenced by those institutions that give structure to society: the church, business, education, and the traditional family. One theme to which Ibsen turned again and again was the position of women in European society of the time. All during the 1880s and beyond, the name of Ibsen was associated with feminism, and one could hardly carry on even a moderately literate conversation in polite society without having an opinion about his play *A Doll's House*.

The fame of *A Doll's House* does not rest on the form of the play at all: other realistic, domestic plays had preceded it, and Ibsen's relentless use of the devices of the "well-made play" breaks no new ground. However, the characters, particularly Nora, are incisively drawn and entirely recognizable. The interaction of the characters is rich, particularly in subtext—which invites audiences to exercise some psychological skill as they watch the carefully crafted drawing-room scenes develop. But, most of all, it is the ideas which gave—and still give—*A Doll's House* its impact. Ibsen is saying that there are some situations in married life that are so degrading, that even an intelligent, morally-upright woman like Nora will choose to leave the security of her home and the love of her children rather than submit. If Ibsen had chosen to describe those conditions as including physical and sexual abuse, insanity, rampant criminality, and the like, he would have received a far more sympathetic hearing. Instead, he portrayed a household filled with traditional, middle-class European values—a household such as most of the audience members either had or aspired to have. This was an outrage! His indictment was so general—and at the same time so penetrating—that society was forced to react. And it is said that the sound of the front door slamming at the end of this play is the sound of the door opening for women's suffrage.

A Doll's House takes place entirely in the home of Torvald Helmer, an attorney, and his wife Nora, in a medium-sized Norwegian town. The entire action transpires between the day before Christmas and Christmas Day itself.

Nora Helmer has just arrived home from some last minute shopping for her husband and three children. Early in the first scene we see evidence of the relationship she has with her husband. He has forbidden her to eat sweets, so she secretly buys macaroons and hides them from him; she has no money of her own and must seduce money from her husband even for Christmas gifts. Nora receives a caller, an old girlhood friend named Kristine Linde, whom she has not seen for nearly ten years. We learn a great deal about both as they bring each other up to date. Kristine was married for most of that time but her husband died, leaving her destitute and without any marketable skills to help support herself, her invalid mother, and younger brothers. Now she has come to her old friend because she knows that Torvald has been named the new director of the local bank, and in his new position may be able to find a job for Kristine. Nora promises to do what she can to influence Torvald.

Next, Nora begins to brag a bit; she, too, has weathered a very difficult period. Early in their marriage Torvald had gotten very sick and needed a change of climate to regain his health. However, the doctors did not tell him how serious the situation was, and left it to Nora to convince him to spend an extended period of time in Italy. She dealt with the financial problems by telling Torvald that a gift from her father had made the trip possible; actually, the money had come from a loan Nora had negotiated—using her father's signature on the note since women are not allowed to borrow money without their husband's knowledge—and Nora's father died shortly afterward. Torvald does not know any of this. In fact, Nora has secretly paid off the loan by systematically scrimping on the household expenses and wheedling small gifts from Torvald. Now she has paid off the loan and, with Torvald's new appointment sure to bring them prosperity, life looks rosy indeed. Nora laughs off Kristine's suggestion that it was foolish to allow this major deception into their marriage.

A Mr. Krogstad arrives to talk with Torvald, and it is apparent from Nora's reaction that she does not wish him around. While Krogstad is talking with Torvald in his office, we meet another of the Helmer's friends—the family physician, Dr. Rank, who also takes the opportunity to comment unfavorably on Krogstad's character. When Torvald emerges from the meeting he meets Kristine and, responding well to Nora's pleading, says that he thinks he has a job for her at the bank—implying that a position has just become vacant.

Nora is playing with her children when Krogstad returns to speak with her in private. It develops that Krogstad is the person from whom Nora borrowed the money for the trip to Italy. Now he is being fired from his minor post at the bank, the post Kristine is going to take. Krogstad urges Nora to use her influence to help him keep his job; if not, he is prepared to reveal the whole matter of the loan. Nora is defiant; what does she care if, now that the loan is paid back, the whole world knows what she has done? Krogstad reminds her of one little problem: when she secured her father's signature for the note, her father was, in fact, dead. Nora forged her father's signature on the note and is, therefore, as morally tainted as Krogstad is for an earlier "indiscretion" of his—the lapse for which Torvald now wants him out of the bank.

Nora tries to speak on behalf of Krogstad, but Torvald will hear none of it: he lectures Nora to the effect that moral corruption of that kind ruins everything it touches. Nora is left with the clear impression that she is a threat to her own children.

The second act is filled with preparations for a costume Christmas party which Nora and Torvald will attend the next night. Nora will go as a Neapolitan peasant and will dance the tarantella for the guests. Kristine is in and out, helping her prepare her costume. Nora tries again to speak for Krogstad, but succeeds only in arousing Trovald to the point of actually sending the letter of dismissal. Dr. Rank comes visiting and, in a scene in which Nora pretends to not understand the seriousness of what he is saying, tells her that he is dying of a congenital venereal disease. His last days will be particularly unattractive and so, to protect Torvald, he will be leaving a calling card with a black cross on it in the mail box when the final period begins, and will not see his old friends afterward. Nora then begins to enlist Dr. Rank's aid but, when he tells her that he always loved her, she is unable to seek help in that direction. After Rank leaves, Krogstad arrives to show Nora the letter he has written and to warn her again of the consequences if she does not convince Torvald to give him his job back. He leaves, placing the letter in the locked letter box—to which only Torvald has the key. Kristine finds Nora frantic with worry and gradually drags out of her the whole story of the forgery and the blackmail. Kristine then leaves to try to convince Krogstad to relent. In the meantime, Nora tries to keep Trovald from opening the mailbox by practicing her tarantella with such wild abandon that Torvald is quite amazed. Kristine returns; Krogstad had left town and will not be back until the following night, but she has left a note for him to contact her. Nora now faces the task of keeping Torvald away from the mailbox for another full day.

The third act begins with a scene between Kristine and Krogstad while the Helmers are at the party. It seems that they had been attracted to each other before Kristine married her first husband. Kristine suggests that they should get together and try to build new lives together; Krogstad is suspicious of her motives but Kristine assures him that she would not dream of "selling herself" once again for someone else's benefit. Indeed, when Krogstad offers to ask for his letter back from Torvald, Kristine urges him not to interfere; the miserable secret must come out into the open. In a stolen moment with Nora, she explains to her friend that she has nothing to worry about with Krogstad, but that she must have the matter out with Torvald. The Helmers return from the costume ball upstairs and, after some diversionary tactics have failed, Torvald finally opens the mailbox and finds, among other things, a card from Rank with the black cross. He also finds the letter from Krogstad. As he reads it, Nora considers suicide. It is clear that she expects Torvald to take the entire blame and does not want to ruin his career.

Instead, he is furious and berates her like a naughty child. He is concerned only for his reputation and begins to plan ways in which appearances can be saved. Just then, a second letter from Krogstad is hand-delivered, one in which he revokes any plan of disclosure. Torvald is almost comically relieved. As Nora goes into her room to change out of the Italian peasant costume, Torvald goes on and on about how things will return to normal and how he will protect his little bird, his little doll. But when Nora reappears, it is in a traveling dress. They have a serious conversation—the first one, Nora notes, in the eight years of their marriage. Nora goes on to say that she now understands that she has been treated like a plaything all her life, handed like a toy from her father to her husband. She feels that she has never been credited with having the power to make up her own mind, with having legitimate human needs, with having any worth except as a beautiful object. She reminds Torvald that only a few moments before, he had said that she was incapable of bringing up their children. She agrees with him: before she can bring up children, she herself must grow up, something she cannot do in an environment where she is treated like a child. And she is leaving home to do just that. She says that she cannot spend another night in a stranger's room. She gives Torvald his wedding ring back and demands hers in return. Then, with a small bag containing only her own belongings, she exits, leaving Torvald desolate. We hear the front door slam behind her.

COMEDY

Many of the functions of theatre associated with serious drama can also be achieved through comic means. Attitudes can be changed, achievements celebrated, and social problems addressed in a comic mood as easily as in a serious one. In addition, other goals such as perpetuation of the art of theatre, or display of skills, or providing a public event, can be achieved regardless of the mood. Therefore, we should not be surprised to discover that the world of comedy has great diversity, more perhaps than any other world.

The original definition of the word *comedy* encouraged that diversity: comedy (or *commedia*) referred to any story—not even a play—with a happy ending. In the early Renaissance, dramatic literature was divided into two very rough categories: tragedy and comedy. (Opera and the now extinct pastoral play were considered not to be categories of literature at all.)

Besides their inevitable happy endings, the subcategories of comedy—the subdivisions of the single world, as it were—share a general commitment to eliciting laughter from audiences. Laughter can range from the warm grin of empathy with an eccentric character, through the chuckle of appreciation at a witty turn of phrase, to the uncontrolled howl of an audience abandoning itself to the surprise of an impossible reversal in the plot. In view of this range, it is not surprising that the world of comedy contains several distinct subtypes.

Comedy of Character.   In this kind of comedy, the emphasis is on an examination of the character of the major figures. The comic potential grows out of the recognition of the contradictions and eccentricities both within and between individual characters. A good example of a

The Misanthrope by Moliere, for its comedy, depends on the careful development of the character of Alceste, a man who believes in plain speaking in an age of glittering hypocrisy.

comedy of character is Molière's *The Misanthrope.* The central character in this play, Alceste, is an intense young Parisian who professes to believe that all people should be honest in their dealings with each other. This conviction is a serious social liability among his glittering, hypocritical circle of friends. In fact, Alceste compounds his problems by falling desperately in love with Celimène, a woman as two-faced as she is beautiful. Alceste expects human beings to be hypocrites and, again and again in the course of the play, he has his worst expectations confirmed. Thoroughly embittered at the conclusion, he decides to leave behind the company of all humans—apparently by becoming a hermit. The play is extremely witty and filled with devastatingly funny examples of human hypocrisy. But, as one can see, the definition of *The Misanthrope* as a comedy is called into question by the ending (unless you see the confirmation of his expectations as being a happy ending for Alceste). In the final analysis, however, most critics categorize *The Misanthrope* as a comedy of character because Alceste shows the kind of personal inflexibility which audiences find amusing.

TARTUFFE (1664) *BY MOLIÈRE*

Tartuffe is famous for a number of reasons: it may be the most popular French comedy ever written; it is perhaps the best example of Molière's mature work; and it is a play which puts to rest the idea that comedy is the form of drama for playwrights who do not want trouble with the authorities.

The play's continuing popularity with both French-speaking and foreign audiences is easy to understand. The themes of hypocrisy and self-delusion are universal; the domestic setting is familar to anyone; the characters are well-drawn and accessible; and the comic situations are sure-fire. Molière has balanced his wonderfully witty language with plenty of physical comedy. He has also used his life-long experience with the commedia dell'arte in a number of ways. His characters are variations on the commedia's stereotyped characters, but without their predictability and shallowness; the plot of Tartuffe is a familiar scenario made surprising by the addition of a new character, the hypocrite Tartuffe, whose presence changes the center of gravity of the play and adds a distinctly sinister note. These advantages, however, were not apparent to all members of the premier audience.

Tartuffe was the first played at Versailles in 1664 and was well received by Louis XIV. But religious zealots in the court were severely offended by Molière's title figure, whom they took to be an attack on all religion. They prevailed upon the king to suppress all public performances until 1667. In that year, Molière tried the play again with several major changes, including a new title—*The Imposter*—and changes in the costume of Tartuffe intended to minimize his religious connections. Still, the bigots attacked him and his play with undiminished ferocity. It was not until 1669 that the king would allow Molière to present the play in its original form. *Tartuffe* quickly became Molière's biggest success, but the criticism continued. The zealots could not understand that the dramatist was criticizing only false piety and credulity. Their vicious attacks, coupled with the Church's traditional disdain for actors, prevented Molière from being buried in sanctified ground. Today, the gravesite of France's probably greatest dramatist is unknown.

Tartuffe carefully observes the unities of action, time, and place. There is only one plot, the action transpires in a single day, and the play is set entirely in a room of Monsieur Orgon, a middleclass Parisian, and his wife Elmire. The play begins during Orgon's absence; his mother, Mme. Pernelle, is visiting. But the domineering Mme. Pernelle is ending her visit abruptly because she is disappointed with the moral climate of her son's household. To hear her tell it, Elmire, her grandson Damis, her granddaughter Mariane, and Elmire's brother Cleante, are all on the road to perdition because they like such worldly things as entertaining friends, singing, pretty clothes, and an unobtrusive piety. Even the maid, the outspoken Dorine, comes in for a tonguelashing. Mme. Pernelle advises them all to follow the example of Tartuffe, a man whom the old woman—and her son—see as the very model of sanctity. It seems that Tartuffe is a very convenient model, too; Orgon has him living in their house. When the family objects that Tartuffe is nothing but a self-serving hypocrite, Mme. Pernelle departs in high dudgeon.

No sooner has she left than Orgon returns home from a two-day business trip. His first thought is for the welfare of Tartuffe. In a classic scene, Orgon does not even hear reports of his own wife's fever, but responds with "Poor fellow!" to evidence of Tartuffe's exuberant good health. Orgon goes on to explain to his brother-in-law how it was that he met Tartuffe and the man's pious acts and sayings since then. It is obvious that Orgon has fallen into the hands of a truly shameless con artist.

Mariane is engaged to the worthy young Valère, but now Orgon wants to break off the engagement and, instead, marry her to—Tartuffe. Mariane is so stunned by the news that she cannot even defend herself, so—in another famous scene reminiscent of commedia—the maid Dorine speaks for her, using every device ever employed by insolent servants. But Orgon is determined that Mariane shall marry Tartuffe.

Valère has heard the news and rushes to confirm it with Mariane. He thinks it is a match which Mariane wants and, before Dorine again saves the day, the two lovers nearly part in anger. Finally, under Dorine's leadership, the three begin to plot to foil the new marriage.

Finally, we meet Tartuffe. He is all that his detractors describe. Indeed, a new dimension to his villainy becomes apparent when Elmire tries to convince him to dismiss any thought of marriage to Mariane. He begins clumsily to seduce Elmire—all the time, of course, proclaiming that he has only her salvation at heart. But Damis has been hiding in a closet, and hearing proof of what he has suspected all along, he leaps out to confront Tartuffe. Orgon arrives and Damis, over his mother's objections, denounces Tartuffe to his father.

Tartuffe confesses! But he does so in such a way as to make Damis seem the unfair accuser. Orgon turns against Damis and, in a frenzy of religious zeal, disowns his son and makes Tartuffe his sole heir.

The time has come for Elmire to do what she can to reveal to Orgon Tartuffe's true nature. She prevails upon the reluctant Orgon to hide under a table whose covering hangs to the floor, and instructs him to reveal himself only when he has heard enough. She then invites Tartuffe into the room. Thinking they are alone, Tartuffe quickly resumes the seduction which was interrupted by Damis. Elmire skillfully leads him on until, in a passionate frenzy, the pious Tartuffe is nearly upon her. Finally, Orgon emerges to confront Tartuffe.

But Tartuffe is far from repentant. Indeed, he goes on the attack. It seems that Orgon has been holding a box of papers for an old friend, papers which are, he suspects, illegal. He has confessed his suspicions to Tartuffe who is, naturally, prepared to betray the sanctity of the confessional: Tartuffe claims Orgon's house as his own and orders Orgon and his family into the street.

Mme. Pernelle arrives and Orgon is in the unique position of trying to convince *her* that Tartuffe is a scoundrel. Even Mme. Pernelle is finally convinced when a bailiff, M. Loyal, arrives to physically evict them.

But matters grow worse. Valère arrives with the news that Tartuffe has denounced Orgon to the King; he begs Orgon to flee at once.

Too late! Tartuffe himself arrives with a very intimidating officer of the king. Tartuffe is insufferable as he denounces the man who lifted him from poverty and lords it over the whole family. Imperiously, he demands that the officer do his duty! The officer steps forward—and arrests Tartuffe. The officer explains that the King, always aware of the plight of his subjects, had spotted Tartuffe as a hypocrite from the very start. The sovereign had simply let Tartuffe attempt this last, dastardly act to see how far he would go. Tartuffe is taken away to prison; Orgon is forgiven by the King as reward for his service in the wars. Mariane and Valère will wed. The family is sustained.

But the audience is left wondering: What if the king had *not* been omniscient?

Comedy of Manners. That same inflexibility, this time in the social sphere, powers the *comedy of manners*. The situation always deals with the question of "manners" because the characters are always measured by the degree to which they are in or out of fashion. The most laughable figures in a comedy of manners are those who are unaware of the social graces and are therefore out of fashion through ignorance or stupidity; or they may be so excessively concerned about fashion that they overdo the matter. The great period of comedy of manners in English drama dates from the Restoration, roughly 1660 to 1700. In this period, the taste-makers were a relatively small, élite group of gentlemen and ladies who, because they had riches, power, and too much time on their hands, spent an amazing amount of energy in pursuit of that will-o'-the-wisp, fashion. Their favorite comedies mocked people who, like those raised in the country, might not be in fashion or—like the dandies of the day—were excessive in their clothes, speech, and behavior. Restoration comedy, as it is called, is peopled by an astounding mix of gallants, ladies, country bumpkins, fops, and caricatures of well-known London figures—all of whom are under the closest possible scrutiny for signs of being out of fashion. Of course, the possibility that one might find *one-*

self up there on the stage being mocked for some slight social gaffe was enough to make every opening night an intense experience for the aspiring lady or gentleman.

Comedy of manners illustrates very well one theory of comedy which has had currency since the Renaissance. The purpose of comedy, it says, is to act as a social corrective by making inappropriate behavior look ridiculous. According to this theory, an excessively jealous husband will be corrected by seeing a portrayal of jealousy ridiculed by an audience. Theatre, then, is one of the ways in which society goes about establishing the norms for correct behavior. And laughter is one important instrument by which society conveys its judgment. Critics of this theory, while allowing its truth in certain kinds of comedy—comedy of manners being a good example—reject its application to all forms of comedy. They point out that in certain periods the behaviors being ridiculed were the norms of the majority, not of an out-of-step minority. Still, the idea of comedy as a social corrective is an intriguing one and it explains a great deal about why a television series such as *All in the Family* can be enormously successful when its major comic figure, an exquisitely ignorant bigot, could not even have been interviewed on television a few years previously. Clearly, mainstream American attitudes had moved to a point where it was permissible to laugh at ideas which had previously been intimidating.

Situation Comedy.   Situation comedy is plot-centered and involves setting up new and interesting situations into which familiar characters move. Television comedy series are the best known examples; because it is a series, the producers assume that all viewers know the characters and very little time must be spent on character development. Instead, ingenuity goes into setting up intriguing situations. One can almost hear the minds of the producers and writers clicking over: "What happens if Ricky and Lucy Arnaz inherit a farm?" "What if Hotlips Houlihan thinks she's pregnant?" "What happens if the Beverly Hillbillies decide to go to the races?"

Of course, television did not make up the general formula of the situation comedy. For equally good examples of situation comedies, we can return to the *commedia dell'arte*, a vibrant form of popular theatre which got its start in 16th-century Italy—but based both its plots and characters on popular theatre forms dating from the pre-Christian era. For the next century and a half the stock characters of *commedia dell'arte* were seen on stages all over Europe. They included such figures as Arlequino (Harlequin), a clever parasite who could be counted on to dream up tricky ways for a young lover to win his beloved; Pantalone, a suspicious, scheming old man; Dottore, a pedantic fool who loved to impress others with his empty scholastic Latin; Capitano, a blustering braggart soldier who could be counted upon to flee at the first sign of real danger; and a set of suitably inexperienced young lovers. With these stock characters, augmented by others where necessary, *commedia*

Razullo.   Cucurucu.

Two fanciful characters from the commedia del'arte are captured in this engraving by Callot. In the background can be seen the simple outdoor stage that a traveling commedia del'arte company might have used. (B-13, 852 BALLI DI SFESSANIA: RAZULLO AND CUCURUCU, Jacques Callot; National Gallery of Art, Washington; Rosenwald Collection.)

The modern interest in improvisation has led many, many contemporary groups to attempt to recreate and update the commedia del'arte format. Here we see such a production: *The Strolling Players,* presented by a Canadian company.

troupes could improvise plays on a huge range of topics: Arlecchino Gets Drafted into the Army, Dottore Buys a Magic Potion, Pantalone Wants to Conceive an Heir, and so on. To be sure, whole sections of these plots were in fact stock scenes which could be dragged into any play with minor adjustments. But audiences never tired of seeing Arlecchino do his comic business with an imaginary fly—whether he was on his way to visit the Turks or on his way home from studying with the Magician of Prague. In just the same way, it appears that audiences never tire of seeing Corporal Klinger try to convince the U.S. Army that he is crazy and should be sent home.

Before we leave the world of comedy, some attention should be paid to a provocative idea concerning the meaning of laughter, an idea which has rich implications for comedy in the theatre. Henri Bergson, a French philosopher (1859–1941), suggested that laughter signaled the fact that we had detected "the mechanical encrusted on the living." Briefly put, his theory is that humans are constantly on the alert for situations in which people are not interacting smoothly and effectively with the world around them. When we see a person who is somewhat rigid or preprogrammed in his or her interactions we laugh. Comic situations frequently have such a pattern to them: a person continues talking to someone who has already left the scene; the driver who continues steering the car although the steering wheel has become detached; a comic misunderstanding which continues on and on because, once having made up their minds, the characters refuse to recognize evidence to the contrary. The list is endless. Bergson's theory fits comfortably into a larger theory of the social utility of theatre: our species must always stay responsive to its social and physical environments. Furthermore, we have a social obligation to either correct those who are not interacting effectively—or avoid them altogether. Comedy in the theatre gives us a laboratory in which we can develop the skills needed to identify those noninteractive individuals and groups.

FARCE

This is a cartoon world, a world of primary colors and primary motivations, a world in which the audience can work out its fantasies—and where inconvenient physical laws have been suspended accordingly.

One of the most memorable features of farce is the speed with which things happen. Increasingly complex plots—sometimes several

Because of his "classic" status and wealth of ideas, some critics hesitate to call Aristophanes a farce writer. However, the structure of his plays is vintage farce—as are the looney premises. In *The Frogs*, seen here in a Yale Repertory production employing a real swimming pool, the god Dionysus sets out for the underworld to bring back to Athens a good playwright.

plots—are crammed into too little time. The result is a growing frenzy in which people make wildly improbable decisions with no reflection at all and then follow those decisions through with inhuman intensity. By the end of a farce, the characters can be running about the stage, shouting, and out of control. In fact, the general dynamic of farce is a gradual loss of control as the characters grow more and more desperate.

Desperate? Desperate about what? Oddly enough, the major characters in farce are almost always desperate to protect their reputations. The typical modern farce is aptly named the "bedroom farce" because in the huge majority of cases the leading characters are either involved in or trying to consummate an extramarital affair. The spouse is in danger of discovering the infidelity and, to avoid a scandal, the would-be malefactors will try *anything*. Of course, each absurd explanation demands an even more difficult coverup until, late in the play, the lies have become so complex, the plot so circuitous, and the situation so preposterous that a normal human would gladly settle for a clean confession and a nice simple scandal.

But not farce characters! They tend to be compulsive in their drives and extravagant in their personalities. The major characters always seem to opt for the most complex solutions to the problem at hand and not to be discouraged when that solution has to be bolstered by something even *more* ridiculous. As you might expect, this pattern does not encourage subtle character development; farce characters are simple and exaggerated. In some cases, the eccentricities are simply bizarre. In Georges Feydeau's *Hotel Paradiso* there is one character who stutters severely—but only when it rains. In another of his plays a character barks—yes, "bow wow"—when excited, because his mother was frightened by a dog. Feydeau, perhaps the greatest of the farce writers, was especially intrigued by communication disorders and his plays are full of people who are deaf, or foreign, or have cleft palates, or who can only concentrate on some exotic special interest. These disorders help perpetuate the misunderstandings which are at the heart of farce.

HOTEL PARADISO *(1910)*
BY GEORGES FEYDEAU AND MAURICE DESVALLIÈRES

The name of Georges Feydeau (1862-1921) is almost synonymous with farce. During his long and productive career he refined the form, all the while keeping his subject matter fresh enough to keep three decades of Parisian audiences howling with delight. It is testimony to the universality of his work that Feydeau's plays remain in the repertory of the Comédie Française and continue to be produced by foreign companies.

But in another sense, his plays live forever in the turn-of-the-century Paris which Feydeau knew so well. It was a world in which a breezy, urban sophistication collided with the stuffy values of the French middleclass. It was a world loaded with lively examples of hypocrisy, self-delusion, and a social innocence which made for soaring misunderstandings. Farce is fueled by misunderstanding; Feydeau's best scenes are those in which more than half the people on stage think they know exactly what is going on—but don't. The remainder have no idea at all.

To get this kind of confusion airborne, Feydeau created characters endowed with a lovable pigheadedness: they get an idea into their head and—no matter how ridiculous it may seem to an objective observer—they cannot be dissuaded. Indeed, it often seems that the closer Feydeau's characters come to seeing the truth, the more desperately they cling to their delusion. Thus, the rising level of frenzy in his plays. The plots become more and more complicated, probability is stretched farther and farther, until chaos is held at bay only by frantic energy.

Like most of Feydeau's plays, *Hotel Paradiso* defends thoroughly bourgeois values. Otherwise stable marriages are endangered by the threat of adultery— but are saved only by luck: the bad luck of the adulterers. Boniface and Marcell are dogged by the worst kind of bad luck. The early reversals are not enough to discourage them; instead, this malevolent misfortune lures them deeper and deeper into threatening disaster. One can see in Feydeau the flip side of the benevolent justice in melodrama. His final message on this point is the worldly observation that adultery is a very silly human activity. It is never really consummated in his plays. And even if it were, the pleasure could not possibly be worth the trouble.

Hotel Paradiso has three acts. The first and third are set in the home of Monsieur Boniface; the second takes place in the infamous hotel itself.

M. Boniface is a builder who lives with his wife, Angelique, in a suburb of 1910 Paris. In an adjoining flat live their good friends, Monsieur Cot, an architect, and his wife Marcelle. Boniface is timid and whimsical, while his wife is a true battleaxe. Marcelle is slightly panicky and vulnerable in contrast to her gruff and indifferent husband. Conflict is inevitable.

Cot and Marcelle have a quarrel which spills into the Boniface household. The row escalates until Marcelle threatens to find a lover—Cot tells her to go right ahead and he storms out. Boniface, who has always been attracted to Marcelle, sees his chance. He tells Marcelle that her honor as a woman has been challenged and that she has no choice but to call her husband's bluff. He, Boniface, will defend her honor by becoming her lover. Marcelle, her vanity wounded and her pride enflamed, agrees. They will meet that very night—but where? Boniface takes it upon himself to find a discreet hotel.

Cot's nephew, a young philosophy major named Maxim, must return to college that evening; he is so oblivious to the world, however, that Cot asks if Boniface's maid, Victoire, can be sent along to see that he finds his way. The worldly Victoire accepts her assignment with enthusiasm, though it is clear that she hopes to provide Maxim with guidance of a very different sort.

Just then, Angelique receives some junk mail filled with fliers for the seedy Hotel Paradiso. Boniface and Victoire each take one. Trouble is foreshadowed in another way: because of a dispute over a lease, Cot has been asked by the court to check into reports that some cheap hotel is haunted. He is sceptical; he believes that the ghostly sounds are the result of poor plumbing, but to satisfy the court he must spend the night there. The hotel proves to be, of course, the Hotel Paradiso.

A further complication is added. M. Martin, an acquaintance from the country, arrives unexpectedly for a visit with the Bonifaces. He has mistaken a social pleasantry for a formal invitation and expects to stay a month. Worse, he has brought his four young daughters to Paris with him. Communication with Martin is difficult: he stutters badly, but only when it is raining. Amid the confusion of porters delivering and retrieving trunks, he is firmly told that it will be impossible for him and his family to stay at the Boniface home. He is asking about a possible hotel when he happens to overhear Boniface telling Marcelle that they will meet at the Hotel Paradiso and—thinking it a recommendation—he sets out for the hotel with his daughters.

Angelique is going to spend the night with her ailing sister. Not trusting Boniface, however, she locks him in the house. But he is prepared for such eventualities and uses a rope fireladder to climb out the window. So, like nearly everyone else in the play, Boniface leaves for the Hotel Paradiso and the event for which the whole first act has been preparation—the night in the hotel.

The Hotel Paradiso lives up to its worst expectations. It is a rundown flea bag managed with a relaxed hand by the Italian Anniello and his bumpkin apprentice, George. His hotel does not have many long-term guests and every room was, to hear Anniello tell it, the favorite of the "crown princess of Poland when she spent her honeymoon with the Lord Chamberlain." To keep tabs on everyone, Anniello has a brace and bit with which he bores holes in the walls to spy on the guests.

The first to arrive is Cot who is to spend the night in room 11, the large dormitory room in which the ghosts have appeared. He leaves his cigars, nightdress, and slippers in the room while he goes out for a glass of beer before bed.

Then Boniface and Marcelle, both extremely nervous, slip furtively into their room, number 10, just across the hall from Cot. Boniface begins immediately to express his love for Marcelle, culminating in a playful chase which smashes the only chair in the room. George, the bellboy, ever curious, decides to bore a hole through the wall and succeeds only in poking Boniface.

The Martin family arrives and George, not knowing that the room is already rented, puts them in Cot's. Martin immediately spies Marcelle, whom he knows from the Boniface home. She makes up some flimsy excuse for being in the hotel—an excuse which becomes even more ridiculous when Boniface barges back into the room from taking air on the balcony. Nothing will do but that the whole group must have tea with Marcelle in the tiny room with no chairs.

Victoire and the uncertain Maxim arrive and take a room on the same hallway as the other couples.

The Martins have returned to room 11 and are in the bathroom changing when M. Cot returns. After he has calmed down from discovering that someone has smoked his cigars and made off with his nightclothes, Cot goes to sleep in the curtained bed. The Martin girls return to bed and begin singing a scary song by the dim light of their curling iron heaters. Cot awakes and is terrified. He exits shouting that there are ghosts. Naturally, in the excitement, Cot runs into both Boniface and Marcelle—but does not recognize either one because Boniface is covered with soot from having tried to hide in the fireplace, and Marcelle has pulled a top hat down over her head. Cot escapes in

A moment of chaos occurs in Feydeau's *Hotel Paradiso* when the police raid the hotel of the title. This scene is from the American Conservatory Theatre production directed by Tom Moore.

the general panic. Some order is achieved when the police arrive to haul all the residents of the hotel to jail. Boniface and Marcelle are questioned separately. In an effort to protect Boniface, Marcelle says she is Mme. Boniface. For the same reason, Boniface says he is M. Cot.

The third act begins with Boniface climbing back up the fireladder into the locked room which is his perfect alibi. Angelique returns home after a harrowing night. It seems that the horses on the carriage in which she was riding had bolted, she had been thrown into a pile of rotten potatoes, and had spent the night unconscious in a peasant cottage. Boniface is sympathetic. Just then, however, a letter from the police arrives in which Mme. Boniface is requested to appear at headquarters to explain why she was at the Hotel Paradiso with M. Cot. Boniface pretends to be outraged. How could his wife be deceiving him with his best friend? M. Cot, too, has received such a letter, and it is Marcelle's chance to pretend anguish. The matter is not helped when the Police Inspector arrives to interrogate M. Cot and Anglique. He is not sure of the identification because of all the confusion—but he will never forget the dress that Mme. "Boniface" was wearing. Marcelle hurriedly assures Boniface that she has already given the dress away.

M. Martin has arrived to say goodbye; he is returning to his home in the country. Now the Inspector asks him to identify the couple at the hotel. All seems lost. But as he opens his mouth to utter the words which will ruin Boniface and Marcelle, a thunderstorm begins outside, precipitating the stutter which prevents him from saying a word. Just then, Victoire enters with Maxim. She is wearing the dress which Marcelle has given to her. Victoire readily admits that she was at the hotel—and everyone is pleased to identify her as the woman at the hotel the night before, and Maxim as the man! In fact, the Police Inspector returns to Maxim the 20,000 franc bail which Boniface had paid! Martin is hustled off to the train before the rain stops. And the play ends with the characters turning to the audience and explaining, "What a night!"

The audience can only agree.

Scenically, farce can become very complicated. At the very least, there has to be provision for the many entrances and exits. The mental image most people have of farce is a bedroom with lots of doors—and someone hiding behind each one. Some farces require several rooms on stage together, secret panels, trapdoors, disappearing beds, and special props and mechanical devices. To make matters worse, the physical world of farce is booby-trapped. It is constructed of banana peels to slip on, doors to run into, neckties that will not tie, and endless other hazards to frustrate the characters.

But why go to all the trouble? If the plots are contrived, the characters shallow and unrealistic, and the ideas considerably less than profound, what value has farce?

Eric Bentley, the American critic, playwright, and director, has suggested that the power of farce lies in its ability to act as a safety valve for fantasies which, if worked out in real life, would prove socially destructive. He cites the violent action of farce as an example: people slap one another, slam doors on their hands, fall down, and get physically assaulted by any number of environmental hazards—including pies in the face—without any serious harm. This, he notes, is fantasy life at its peak. But more important than the physical violence is the social violence. On every side, the world of farce violates the most sacred social relationships—especially the pair bond. Every husband and wife considers the possibilities of infidelity—but usually they do not follow through. If Bentley's thesis is correct, their chances of actually becoming unfaithful could be reduced by experiencing a farce. Not only would they have the vicarious experience of the illicit affair, but they would be reminded again of the danger of scandal.

The displacement of social violence is not limited to sexual matters, of course. Everyone who has ever wanted to throw a cream pie in the boss's face gets a chance in farce. These forbidden actions all play themselves out—and with only trivial consequences for the character and none at all for the audience. Once again, we see a theatrical world which allows us to experience what would be too painful or destructive in ordinary life and, as a result, to return enriched to the daily life of our familiar world.

All of the genres described above—tragedy, melodrama, drama, comedy, and farce—are familar literary realms. Each has been an alternative open to theatre artists and audiences for at least a century, and most have been around for far longer. Of course this list is not exhaustive; in a vital art such as theatre, critics are always ready to create combinations, a tendency which Shakespeare parodies when he has Polonius extoll the virtues of a touring theatrical troupe as:

> The best actors in the world, either for tragedy, comedy, history, pastoral, pastorical-comical, historical-pastoral, tragical-historical, tragical-comical-historical-pastoral, scene individual, or poem unlimited . . . (*Hamlet*, act II scene 2)

However, in the 20th century there have been several genuinely new models proposed, theatrical worlds which had not previously existed. Gradually each is moving toward acceptance as a separate genre of dramatic literature. In the meantime, at least three of these proposed worlds already have currency in the theatrical universe. They deserve description here.

THEATRE OF THE ABSURD

This theatre is one in which many of the accepted laws of reality and behavior have been purposely repealed—or, more properly, are shown as never having been in force.

The first to go are those having to do with causality and sequence, with the result that normal characteristics of plot are radically changed in theatre of the absurd. Information provided in the first act may or may not be in force in the third; the idea of coincidence is ridiculed by providing events which are so unlikely as to be impossible—and doing so repeatedly. Climaxes, if they are included at all, may be purposely undercut by some totally unexplained appearance of new information.

The dénouement may intentionally leave loose ends—frequently important ones—dangling. For example, in probably the most famous play of the theatre of the absurd, Samuel Beckett's *Waiting for Godot*, there is a single plot whose pattern is faithfully reproduced twice—once in the first act and once in the second: Two tramps wait at a desolate place for the arrival of someone called Godot. As they wait they speculate about a range of things, they squabble, make up, visit with some travellers who pass by, and—finally—are told that Godot won't be coming today. Maybe tomorrow. There is no detectable inciting incident, only a minor dramatic question (will Godot come today?), no rising action, and no climax. Yet the play can be a fascinating experience—even as it rejects most of the tradition of good plotting.

Beckett is rejecting the traditional plot for a good reason: he rejects the assumptions about the universe implied by the very logical pattern of a traditional plot.

At the conclusion of Ionesco's *The Chairs*, the "orator" arrives to deliver the long-awaited address. Note the doll-like quality of these characters from a Paris production of the play.

In the theatre of the absurd, the treatment of character also rejects some of theatre's traditional assumptions about human nature and psychology. For example, the question of human communication arises again and again: do humans ever truly communicate? In his one-act play *The Chairs*, Eugene Ionesco takes a very gloomy view: an elderly couple spend nearly an hour arranging chairs and greeting an (invisible) audience in preparation for a speech by "the orator." They are convinced that the orator will explain everything to the audience. So, just as he is about to begin his talk, their work of preparation well completed, they hurl themselves into a lake from a window in the meeting room. But, when he does begin to speak, the orator can only utter the inchoate growls and the meaningless roars of a mental defective. So much for communicating ultimate truth!

What about our assumed ability to "know" another person? In another one-act, *The Bald Soprano*, Ionesco places two people, already introduced as husband and wife, together in a parlor. After a strained silence they begin a conversation:

(Mr. and Mrs. Martin sit facing each other, without speaking. They smile timidly at each other. The dialogue which follows must be spoken in voices that are drawling, monotonous, a little singsong, without nuances)

MR. MARTIN: Excuse me, madam, but it seems to me, unless I'm mistaken, that I've met you somewhere before.

MRS. MARTIN: I, too, sir. It seems to me that I've met you somewhere before.

MR. MARTIN: Was it, by any chance, at Manchester that I caught a glimpse of you, madam?

MRS. MARTIN: That is very possible. I am originally from the city of Manchester. But I do not have a good memory, sir. I cannot say whether it was there that I caught a glimpse of you or not!

MR. MARTIN: Good God, that's curious! I, too, am originally from the city of Manchester, madam!

MRS. MARTIN: Isn't that curious!

MR. MARTIN: Isn't that curious! Only, I, madam, I left the city of Manchester about five weeks ago.

MRS. MARTIN: That is curious! What a bizarre coincidence! I, too, sir, I left the city of Manchester about five weeks ago.

MR. MARTIN: Madam, I took the 8:30 morning train which arrives in London at 4:45.

MRS. MARTIN: That is curious! How very bizarre! And what a coincidence! I took the same train, sir, I too.

MR. MARTIN: Good lord, how curious! Perhaps then, madam, it was on the train that I saw you?

MRS. MARTIN: It is indeed possible that is, not unlikely. It is plausible and, after all, why not!—But I don't recall it, sir!

MR. MARTIN: I travelled second class, madam. There is no second class in England, but I always travel second class.

MRS. MARTIN: That is curious! How very bizarre! And what a coincidence! I, too, sir, I travelled second class.

MR. MARTIN: How curious that is! Perhaps we did meet in second class, my dear lady!

MRS. MARTIN: That is certainly possible, and it is not at all unlikely. But I do not remember very well, my dear sir!

MR. MARTIN: My seat was in coach no. 8, compartment 6, my dear lady.

MRS. MARTIN: How curious that is! My seat was also in coach no. 8 compartment no. 6, my dear sir!

MR. MARTIN: How curious that is and what a bizarre coincidence! Perhaps we met in compartment 6, my dear lady?

MRS. MARTIN: It is indeed possible, after all! But I do not recall it, my dear sir!

MR. MARTIN: To tell the truth, my dear lady, I do not remember it either, but it is possible that we caught a glimpse of each other there, and as I think of it, it seems to me even very likely.

MRS. MARTIN: Oh! truly, of course, truly, sir!

MR. MARTIN: How curious it is! I had seat no. 3, next to the window, my dear lady.

MRS. MARTIN: Oh, good Lord, how curious and bizarre! I had seat no. 6, next to the window, across from you, my dear sir.

MR. MARTIN: Good God, how curious that is and what a coincidence! We were then seated facing each other, my dear lady! It is there that we must have seen each other!

MRS. MARTIN: How curious it is! It is possible, but I do not recall it, sir!

MR. MARTIN: To tell the truth, my dear lady, I do not remember it either. However, it is very possible that we saw each other on that occasion.

MRS. MARTIN: It is true, but I am not at all sure of it, sir.

MR. MARTIN: Dear madam, were you not the lady who asked me to place her suitcase in the luggage rack and who thanked me and gave me permission to smoke?

MRS. MARTIN: But of course, that must have been I, sir. How curious it is, how curious it is, and what a coincidence!

MR. MARTIN: How curious it is, how bizarre, what a coincidence! And well, well, it was perhaps at that moment that we came to know each other, madam?

MRS. MARTIN: How curious it is and what a coincidence! It is indeed possible, my dear sir! However, I do not believe that I recall it.

MR. MARTIN: Nor do I, madam. (A moment of silence. The clock strikes twice, then once.) Since coming to London, I have resided at Bromfield Street, my dear lady.

MRS. MARTIN: How curious that is, how bizarre! I, too, since coming to London, I have resided in Bromfield Street, my dear sir.

MR. MARTIN: How curious that is, well then, well then, perhaps we have seen each other in Bromfield Street, my dear lady.

MRS. MARTIN: How curious that is, how bizarre! It is indeed possible, after all! But I do not recall it, my dear sir.

MR. MARTIN: I reside at no. 19, my dear lady.

MRS. MARTIN: How curious that is. I also reside at no. 19, my dear sir.

MR. MARTIN: Well then, well then, well then, well then, perhaps we have seen each other in that house, dear lady?

MRS. MARTIN: It is indeed possible but I do not recall it, dear sir.

MR. MARTIN: My flat is on the fifth floor, no. 8, my dear lady.

MRS. MARTIN: How curious it is, good Lord, how bizarre! And what a coincidence! I too reside on the fifth floor, in flat no. 8, dear sir!

MR. MARTIN: (Musing) How curious it is, how curious it is, how curious it is, and what a coincidence! You know, in my bedroom there is a bed, and it is covered with a green eiderdown. This room, with the bed and the green eiderdown, is at the end of the corridor between the toilet and the bookcase, dear lady!

MRS. MARTIN: What a coincidence, good Lord, what a coincidence! My bedroom, too, has a bed with a green eiderdown and is at the end of the corridor, between the toilet, dear sir, and the bookcase!

MR. MARTIN: How bizarre, curious, strange! Then, madam, we live in the same room and we sleep in the same bed, dear lady. It is perhaps there that we have met!

MRS. MARTIN: How curious it is and what a coincidence! It is indeed possible that we have met there, and perhaps even last night. But I do not recall it, dear sir!

MR. MARTIN: I have a little girl, my little daughter, she lives with me, dear lady. She is two years old, she's blonde, she has a white eye and a red eye, she is very pretty, her name is Alice, dear lady.

MRS. MARTIN: What a bizarre coincidence! I, too, have a little girl. She is two years old, has a white eye and a red eye, she is very pretty, and her name is Alice, too, dear sir!

MR. MARTIN: (In the same drawling, monotonous voice) How curious it is and what a coincidence! And bizarre! Perhaps they are the same, dear lady!

MRS. MARTIN: How curious it is! It is indeed possible, dear sir. (A rather long moment of silence. The clock strikes 29 times)

MR. MARTIN: (After having reflected at length, gets up slowly and, unhurriedly,
              moves toward Mrs. Martin, who, surprised by his solemn air, has
              also gotten up very quietly. Mr. Martin, in the same flat, monot-
              onous voice, slightly singsong) Then, dear lady, I believe that
              there can be no doubt about it, we have seen each other before
              and you are my own wife . . . Elizabeth, I have found you again!
(Mrs. Martin approaches Mr. Martin without haste. They embrace without expression. The clock strikes once, very loud. This striking of the clock must be so loud
that it makes the audience jump. The Martins do not hear it.)
MRS. MARTIN: Donald, it's you, darling!
(They sit together in the same armchair, their arms around each other, and fall
asleep. The clock strikes several more times. . . .)*

Interestingly, the physical world of the theatre of the absurd is usually quite ordinary, as if a recognizable environment gives greater impact to the unexpected things happening within it. There are, of course, some exceptions. Occasionally, spectacular effects are called for, such as the dead body which one of Ionesco's plays assumes to be in the next room; the body continues growing throughout the play until its gigantic feet and legs completely fill the acting area.

Language, too, tends to be deceptively prosaic in the theatre of the absurd. It is as if the peculiar and the extraordinary are hidden behind a veil of the commonplace. Harold Pinter, whose early plays are usually included in the theatre of the absurd, uses this tension between text and subtext with great skill. The laconic speech, the long and frequent pauses, the carefully scripted nonverbal communication, creates a mood of often unbearable tension. Indeed, his plays are sometimes referred to as the theatre of menace because of his capacity to suggest that something simply awful is about to erupt out of the superficially commonplace.

The playwrights and other artists who created the theatre of the absurd do so with the clear recognition that the *form* of theatre conveyed a message as clearly as the *content*. In this case, the form which we experience in the theatre of the absurd clearly describes a view of our everyday world:

1. No one is in charge; God, if He or She ever existed, is either dead or immamaterial to human existence;

---

*Eugene Ionesco, *The Bald Soprano* (translated by Donald M. Allen), in *Four Plans* (New York: Grove Press, Inc. 1958). Reprinted by permission.

2. There is neither justice nor injustice in human life; systems of art or religion which suggest otherwise are either wishful thinking or transparent frauds;
3. Human communication is so difficult as to be impossible;
4. People can never really understand each other—especially their motivations for action;
5. Cause and effect are another example of people imposing on a disinterested world an order which it does not naturally have.

So what is left? Does the theatre of the absurd have any positive position? Most writers and artists who choose to create this world would find the question itself tiresome: it is a positive contribution, they might answer, to clear away the rubbish of humankind's self-deception and to recognize directly and coolly the ultimate fact that the individual is of no consequence in the face of the universe's implacable disinterest.

Sound familiar? In one of the richest and most instructive ironies, the nihilist position of the theatre of the absurd seems to come full circle to parallel that of the most essentially religious one: tragedy. In fact, as Martin Esslin neatly puts it, tragedy teaches audiences to recognize and value a tragic hero; theatre of the absurd teaches audiences to *be* a tragic hero.

EPIC THEATRE

Seldom in the history of any art does a single individual so persuasively advocate a whole kind of theatre that he or she ends up naming it. Bertolt Brecht (1898–1956) is such a figure in the history of modern theatre. He called his vision *epic theatre* in an effort to distinguish it from *Aristotelian theatre*, his term for nearly all theatre which predated his work. His reasons for choosing the word *epic* are of less importance here than describing it. In fact, today many people give him the backhanded compliment of ignoring the name *epic* altogether, preferring to refer to it as *Brechtian*.

The world of epic theatre is the world of the laboratory, the operating theatre, the courtroom. It is the theatre of analysis and demonstration. It is a place where, in theory, the audience is presented with evidence and left to form its own conclusion.

For Brecht, the Aristotelian theatre, the traditional theatre, creates a world in which everything is inevitable. The plot moves forward with machinelike inevitability toward a predetermined conclusion; characters are locked into psychological states which are shaped before the play begins and, consequently, choose to act only in those ways which will advance the plot; the form of the play itself rests upon assumptions about the world which, by and large, support the status quo. Even the audience is locked into a predetermined, ritualistic event; they sit passively in their seats "like people who are having something done to them," and are never encouraged to think for themselves. The reason for all this was simple to Brecht: as a convinced Marxist, he subscribed to the theory that all art—theatre included—was a part of a system for enforcing the power of the ruling classes over the proletariat (workers). Hence it was only natural that theatre should attempt to continue the status quo by all means at its disposal.

The answer, for Brecht, was to create a theatre which subverted traditional theatre. Its goal was to allow audiences to see the dynamics of human history in such a way as to make clear the underlying structure. (Again, as a Marxist, Brecht was sure that once the audience could see the principles of human history at work, they would understand those principles to be Marx's idea of dialectical materialism. The matter turned out not to be so clearcut.)

At first, Brecht suggested little learning pieces (*lehrstucke*) which presented parables with alternate outcomes. In some cases the audience actively voted for the ending which seemed most reasonable. His preference for parables continued throughout his career; even his later plays are set in exotic countries (China, the Ukraine, India) and involve mythic characters—usually from the working class. At every step, his goal was to make the familiar world strange, to create instead a world in which audiences would look in wonder at things which had always seemed ordinary and predictable.

Fairly early on, Brecht came to see that he was working at cross purposes with traditionally trained actors. A traditional actor, after all, tries to make the most extraordinary situation seem perfectly natural. He or she can take the most artificial language, the most ridiculous coincidences, the most unlikely character relationship, and convince an audience that each is perfectly reasonable. Brecht tried to subvert this tradition. He trained his actors to develop a sense of detachment from the character. To some degree, the Brechtian actor stands outside the character so that everything the character does becomes hypothetical rather than inevitable; at every decision point the actor allows the audience to see that a character has many options—and that the decision taken at this junction is only because of circumstances which are clearly understood by actor and audience alike.

Bertold Brecht liked to do radically, new adaptations of the classics. Here his Berliner Ensemble carries on the tradition with a production based on Shakespeare's *Coriolanus* with Ekkehard Schall as Coriolanus and Helene Weigel as Volumnia.

This novel approach to acting is only one of a number of "distancing devices" which characterize epic theatre. Other devices include reinterpreting classic plays in ways which would force a better understanding of the sociological forces at work. In Brecht's production, for example, *Hamlet* became a struggle between the feudal forces of Claudius and the promise of reform and industrialization represented by Prince Hamlet and his father. Brecht and his followers exploit the blatantly theatrical staging devices of oriental theatre to assure that audiences always understand that they are in the theatre: narrators may accompany mime passages; the use of masks and the symbolic changing of masks underscores the use of roles in everyday life; signs and loudspeakers may comment on the action. Finally, audiences are never allowed to forget that this experience is taking place in a theatre; lights may be left exposed; house lights may remain up, and stage rigging might be openly used, all to restate the fact that a theatre is a machine for demonstrating scientific facts. The aim always is to prevent the audience from becoming emotionally involved in the dramatic action.

Instead, they should adopt an attitude of scientific detachment which allows intellectual analysis.

The fact that Brecht was himself a Marxist should not confuse the issue. He felt, as most people do who have embraced a comprehensive worldview, that any audience left to discover the truth would come to share his convictions. But his techniques could be used to help discover truth anywhere. So, the epic theatre could be characterized as the ultimate human laboratory, a world created specifically to investigate the dynamics of human interaction.

THE THEATRE OF CRUELTY

Another single name is associated with this theatre: Antonin Artaud (1895–1945). His vision was most influentially expressed in a collection of essays published in 1938 as *The Theatre and Its Double*. The world it suggests is one in which the audience is confronted with a harrowing experience. Traditional theatre, Artaud felt, has been too narrowly interested in individual psychological problems and group dilemmas. It has not dealt with the real problems of alienation and violence, both of which are spiritual problems having their roots in the deepest levels of the subconscious. He proposed theatre experiences which would plumb those depths and purge society of those blocks by evoking them.

The chief villain in theatre is, in Artaud's view, language. It represents the ultimate cognitive activity and activates those areas of the brain responsible for the problems in the first place. Therefore, he proposes a world of striking theatrical images which bypass the cognitive mind altogether. This is achieved by shock and surprise; by a direct assault on the physical senses; by a "language of theatre" which activates the most primary visceral responses—horror, alarm, disgust, ritual ecstasy, and relief.

Since the '60's and early '70's a number of theatre troupes have made serious efforts to put Artaud's theories into practice. Their work is designed to confront the audience. Physically this is achieved by interpenetrating acting areas and audience space, thus forcing the audience to become "part of the action." This has been taken to the point of assaulting the audience physically: touching them, squirting water on them, forcing them to answer questions, kissing them, and so on. The dramatic setting for such plays are often shocking in themselves (death camps, insane asylums, prisons) and the characters people who are in extreme situations (junkies in withdrawal, condemned prisoners).

Plot is relatively unimportant in this world; what counts most is a series of striking theatrical images, and the linking of them into a coherent plot is secondary. Indeed, the unpredictability of the plot is often just one element of shock. Other elements of shock include loud noises, harsh language, screams, bright lights, and an overall sense of dread. Some examples are in order.

The Living Theatre, founded by Julian Beck and Judith Molina, began one of their productions with a single actor seated on the stage. In the course of perhaps fifteen minutes of snorting and hacking, he managed to clear his nasal passages—down his face. Many audience members objected and stalked out of the theatre rather than deal with an evening which began with that level of social violence. The theatre company, however, simply saw this prologue as one demonstration of the power of social conventions, social conventions which enslave us with a hidden tyranny. The Living Theatre also sees nudity as a social statement: many of their productions in the late '60's ended with the actors exiting through the audience and out of the theatre nude.

A theatre company with the highest levels of training and disci-

Akropolis, created by the Polish Laboratory Theatre under the direction of Jerzy Grotowski, comes close to realizing the goals of the Theatre of Cruelty: a shattering emotional experience from which the audience emerges like a survivor.

pline was *The Polish Laboratory Theatre* founded and directed by Jerzy Grotowski. In the 1960s, this company employed many of the techniques advocated by Artaud. Grotowski, however, believed strongly in a stripped-down, minimal theatre, which he called a "poor theatre." The emphasis in productions of the Polish Laboratory Theatre in this period was on his exceedingly well-trained actors. They could, and did, adopt grotesque physical characterizations which they maintained for long periods of time; their vocal training enabled them to make vocal sounds which one would have thought beyond the range of humans. The fact that the actors were *really doing* these difficult, uncomfortable, even painful activities (as opposed to actors in traditional theatre who *pretend* to do them) gave the experience an immediacy and intensity which some audience members found especially moving. In many respects, being a member of the very small audiences allowed to witness their work became an ordeal rather akin to being an official witness at an execution. Audiences who witnessed such works as *Akropolis*, which recounts the last hours of people in a Nazi death camp, left the experience shaken but cleansed.

And this is how one should return from the world of the theatre of cruelty. Like survivors of some catastrophe, audience members should be acutely aware of their own mortality, sensitized to the suffering of others, and yet with a sense of something like comradeship with all those who face the same dangers.

Discussion Questions

1. Think of a play you know (or, barring that, a movie or television drama) which combines the qualities of both tragedy and drama. List and explain the points of confusion.
2. Discuss the ways in which music can be included in tragedy, melodrama, drama, comedy, and farce. Does its function remain the same in each?
3. Have you ever seen a play (or movie or television drama) which you would consider a "thesis play"? Explain.
4. Explain in your own words what Bergson meant by "the mechanical encrusted upon the living." Give some examples from your own experience.
5. Brecht's epic theatre is frequently called a didactic or teaching theatre. Is that idea invalidated if an audience member comes away from the experience believing something different from what the playwright intended?
6. Let us hypothesize that somewhere there is a very warlike and violent society. Should this society be attracted to the theatre of cruelty?

13

Theatre Extended

INTRODUCTION

It is a central theme of this book that the most "artistic" theatrical performance is based upon principles of behavior which are detectable everywhere in human culture. Furthermore, we have suggested that there is an unbroken spectrum of behavioral elaboration from such apparently simple acts of communication as enactment in storytelling through to productions in the most elevated of high-art traditions. Everywhere in this book we have tried to point out the step-like connections between the principles which govern the art and those which we all employ in ordinary life.

With this spectrum in mind, it is useful to consider the branching routes to other human experiences. After all, not every dramatic impulse leads to the creation of a new play; not every empathic impulse leads to professional acting; not every attempt to understand the dramatic structure of human experience makes one a theatre critic. Indeed, even the twelve possible functions of theatre listed in chapter 2 can—and often are—achieved by people in other ways. Some of these alternative ways involve behaviors which are theatrical—at least in the broader definition which we have been using.

It is worth taking some time to look at activities which fall under this extended definition of "theatre."

THEATRE AND GROWTH*

The universal formula for growth and development is trial-and-error. An animal, a plant, a young human tries to do something—to reach for food, perhaps, or to enter an attractive space—and lives with the consequences. These consequences may be success, or frustration. Sometimes they are catastrophic. And that is the problem with development through trial-and-error; sometimes the learner does not survive the lesson. Or else he or she passes the final exam with such physical or emotional scars that the lesson cannot usefully be applied elsewhere.

Humankind long ago "decided" that we could not be so profligate with our individual members. There are easier, more efficient ways to teach our young the dangers of life, to explain that rewards attend certain activities, to pass on the values which have aided the species in the past and may enrich its future. And to do so without risking life and health in the process. The method involves a special gift: we call it the imagination. And those who possess imagination are singled out above all creatures. It blesses us at the same time that it curses us with a pervasive ferocity which the Greeks could only blame upon the gods.

Imagination is the gameboard of the mind in which A plays against B in a maze of balancing options. This is where contingencies collide and possibilities taunt the real world. It is life at only the slightest remove. But, through the imaginative manipulation of imagined concepts, humankind has developed the ability to compress into only a few generations the selective response which takes eons in other species.

"Imagine," says some effective teacher, some village elder, some shaman. "Imagine that you are in such-and-such a place." "Imagine that

*Much of this material is reprinted with permission from Brian Hansen, ed., *Theatre as a Teaching Tool*, (Washington, D.C.: American Theatre Association, 1978), unpublished.

you are someone else." "Imagine that someone else is doing thus-and-so to you." "What might you say?" "What should you do?" "What would happen if you did?" And the student responds.

But not simply in words. The power to imagine oneself in different times, different places, different circumstances is uniquely human; but so is the capacity to act on that imaginative leap. Never content, our species has not stopped at the mental activity of imagination, but has pushed on to the next step: the actual performance. Nothing sears home the point of a vicarious experience as well as seeing another enact it—or, better yet, enacting it oneself. The impact is more powerful, the remaining memory more complete, because even the simplest enactment is filled with sensory details which cannot be duplicated in other forms. It may be this engagement of the senses which is the hallmark of any meaningful experience; in any case, the more total the involvement of the senses, the greater the impact of the experience.

These then are the key elements in the extended range of theatrical activities: imaginative involvement and enactment within that imaginative world.

ENDS AND MEANS

Extended theatre techniques can help achieve a number of goals which are generally considered desirable. For simplicity's sake, these goals and the activities which promote them can be described in ten categories, each based upon a different skill which one hopes to develop.

1. To develop powers of concentration. Theatre activities—especially those associated with acting—demand the capacity to focus one's attention on the immediate environment and to exclude distractions. There are numerous exercises which actors and actor trainers use to develop those skills; some can easily be modified for children.

Example: A classroom game which can be used to build powers of observation divides the group into partners. The partners study one another for one minute. Then they turn their backs to one another and change one aspect of their appearance—a shoelace untied, a shirttail untucked, hair pulled back, etc. The partner is then to identify the subtle change. As people improve, the number of changes can be expanded to two or three at a time.

2. To develop imagination.   Imagination is the capacity to join concepts in novel ways—especially in ways which are not immediately consistent with objective reality.

Example: Beginning acting students are sometimes asked to form a circle. The first student is handed a mimed glob of "unidentifiable space substance" and told to shape from it some identifiable object; he or she then passes it to the next person who then reshapes it into a new object—and passes it on. The substance can be sticky or slippery, heavy or light, odorless or pungent, and the characteristics can change as needed. When everyone feels comfortable with it as individuals, the exercise can be expanded to include the whole group simultaneously. A gigantic glob of substance is shaped by the group into a single, fantastic environment or object—which the group then puts to use.

3. To develop awareness and control of the voice and body as expressive instruments.

Example: The advent of slow motion photography has allowed an appreciation of movements which could not previously be seen. In this exercise, the participants recreate a sports event or a fight in complete slow motion—including slow-motion speech! Everyone quickly learns how much control is needed to do anything smoothly and slowly. This activity also gives the opportunity to analyze and appreciate movement which is sometimes ignored.

4. To reflect upon and express emotions.   Many of us in the Western tradition are deeply distrustful of emotions in general and will avoid emotional display at all costs. There are a number of exercises which allow people to deal with emotional states—especially when the character is someone other than themselves.

Example: By random choice of slips of paper the participants match characters with activities. A participant might draw a slip with "an old man" and another "buries a pet dog." Or, "a young girl" plus "opens a birthday present." Or, a "teenage boy" plus "investigates a deserted cabin." At first, the participants may want to discuss the situations and the feelings they evoke; but eventually they must act them out. At a later level of development, two students may begin to improvise scenes together—always dealing with the emotional states which surround each dramatic situation.

5. To develop communication skills. This category is very popular in school settings; dramatic activities are widely believed to help students share thoughts and feelings in groups, to develop both verbal and non-verbal skills, to overcome blocks to communication and to operate as both a follower and a leader. As a result, there are a large number of theatre-based activities designed to increase communication skills.

Example: To illustrate the degree to which we can "force" roles on others through the group's expectations of them, the following activity can be used while the class is going about other activities—preferably noncritical tasks. As each student enters the classroom, the teacher affixes to the forehead of each a piece of masking tape with a word written on it. (The student wearing the label must not be allowed to see the word.) These descriptors can be such words as *stupid, funny, clumsy, leader,* or *genius.* The aim of the exercise is for the student to come to know the word with which he or she has been labeled as a result of the reactions of others; this is not a guessing game. As the student thinks he or she understands the label, the student simply adopts the role. Frequently students find that they have adopted the proper role without knowing the precise word on their foreheads.

6. To increase capacity to perceive dramatic form. People can learn to become more sensitive to those elements of dramatic form which are common in the theatre: the nature of conflict, the most effective location of climaxes, the sense of dramatic unity, the possibilities of theme, and so forth.

Example: Subtext is at the very heart of much drama. In this exercise, the participants explore that concept by trying to pursue hidden objectives. An improvisational scene is set up in a situation which would not normally allow relaxed communication (e.g., witnesses waiting to testify in a trial have been told not to discuss the case). However, each participant has been assigned some other, hidden objective (e.g., to steal a piece of jewelry, to arrange a date, to stretch out on the couch, etc.). Following the scene both participants and observers would discuss whether the hidden objectives were detected and convincingly portrayed.

7. To develop awareness of the environment. Specifically, this category of activity allows the participants to understand how interaction between people and the environment causes changes in both.

Example: To give emotional force to the term *endangered spe-*

cies," participants (usually younger children) are told that they are the last of their species and, because they are, unknown predators find them very valuable. They are to awake from a nap and fully explore an imaginary environment with all the stealth and cunning at their command. What frightens this animal? What gives it security? What kinds of dangers does it have to avoid? What happens to it?

8. To develop esteem for self and others. This class of activities helps to build a sense of personal value, to understand individual differences, to appreciate courage and assertiveness, to trust, and to appropriately adjust one's individuality when necessary.

Example: Participants work in groups of four; each team of two is made up of a "person" and an "alter-ego." A simple conflict situation is set up between the "persons." However, as the scene is being improvised, the "alter-egos" speak what the "person" cannot. The "person" may, if the situation warrants, argue with his or her "alter-ego." (It is usually better if the "alter-egos" do not communicate directly with one another.) In discussion, the participants can reflect on the conflicting internal values which make up each person, the degree to which statements to others are sometimes shaped to conceal true feelings, and the difficulty of asserting oneself effectively.

9. To develop the ability to think and act clearly and logically. Traditional Oxford debates and courtroom presentations by attorneys are based on an essentially theatrical premise: clarity, logic, and justice can be served if individuals *pretend* for a time that they firmly believe that an assigned point of view is the correct one. By arguing as forcefully as they can in favor of a position which may or may not be their own, debators can serve the interests of logic and truth, and attorneys can seek justice. In a less obvious way, participants in a theatre-based activity can develop these same skills. Here is a remarkable example exercise developed by a schoolmaster in a small village in Japan.

Example: A student considering a proposed action kneels on one side of and facing a large square pillow. For this position, she argues that the proposition is good, marshalling every argument to support her position. Then, she moves to the opposite side of the pillow and argues that the proposition is all bad. These completed, she moves to a third side to argue that it is *neither* good nor bad. Finally, she moves to the fourth side to argue that it is *both* good and bad. At the conclusion, she puts her hand on the center of the pillow and silently experiences the Tao, the great oneness, the harmony of all things.

10. To develop social, political, and ethical sensibility. This category is very broad indeed. It is also subject to very emotional responses: what one person considers as developing an ethical sensibility another person calls indoctrination. Yet it is possible to set up situations in which individuals clarify their own values without inappropriate influence from others. Theatre techniques are particularly effective for education of this kind.

Example: To provoke a class studying population pressures, Alvin Toffler, the futurist, simulated the future condition of the world by arranging for the physical size of a classroom to shrink each day. So many additional square feet of the room were roped off, so many desks

The San Francisco Mime Troupe builds on the tradition of the commedia del' arte to provide highly satirical pieces with a strong political point of view. This scene is from their anti-Viet Nam War piece *L'Amante Militaire* (1967).

and chairs removed each day until students had to physically deal with overcrowding and diminishing resources.

Example: Students exchange homes with the understanding that, for a given period (three days to a week), the exchanged students be treated *exactly the way the originals were treated.*

Example: Guerrilla theatre. The aim of guerrilla theatre troupes is to take a didactic (or at least provocative) piece *to* an audience—preferably when they least expect it. The act of preparing a guerrilla theatre production and presenting it for unprepared—and sometimes hostile—audiences forces a clarification of values. Some interesting guerrilla theatre productions have been:

— The *actos* presented by the Teatro Campesino (Farmworkers Theatre) which were intended to raise the spirits of striking farmworkers in California's Salinas Valley and to rally consumers' support for a strike.

— The pieces attacking U.S. involvement in Viet Nam during the demonstrations which marked the late '60's and early '70's. One college class in human sexuality devised a guerrilla piece called "Skin Flick" which they performed by flashlight during pornographic movies.

ORGANIZED USES OF THEATRE TECHNIQUES

The techniques categorized and described above represent only a small fraction of the techniques which can be used by anyone who wishes: parents, clergy, teachers, counselors, recreation leaders, psychologists, human potential facilitators, and many more. Some, however, are used more or less regularly by professionals whose disciplines have continuity and organization. Naturally, each of these fields addresses certain goals and believes in specific principles of operation. Moreover, in most fields, there are professional organizations which attempt to monitor the profession and upgrade the quality of practitioners.

Creative Drama. The Children's Theatre Association of America defines creative drama as follows:

> Creative drama is an improvisational, non-exhibitional, process-centered form of drama in which participants are guided by a leader to imagine, enact, and reflect upon human experiences. Although creative drama has traditionally been thought of in relation to children and young people, the process is appropriate to all ages. (1977)

In America, Winifred Ward, a teacher, is generally credited with giving the creative drama movement definition and credibility with a number of influential books in the 1930s and 1940s. Today, the general position of the field is that creative drama is an integral form of learning which can achieve many of the ten learning goals described earlier in this chapter. Leaders in the field maintain that creative drama is as important as music education or art education, and like those other arts activities, should be included as a regular part of the general education of all schoolchildren.

In Ward's original work it was a matter of faith that creative drama was almost never aimed at public presentation and that any audience at all was a negative influence. Today, the stand on this issue seems to be relaxing: few if any creative drama specialists would support public performance for strangers, but many would allow informal sharing of work with invited and supportive groups. And all agree that the comments of classmates who are not immediate performers are a valuable addition to the essential discussion following each creative drama presentation.

Creative drama should not be confused with children's theatre. The latter is the presentation, by either child actors or adults, of theatre pieces especially intended for children.

Psychodrama. Although there may be great benefit to psychologically healthy individuals who participate, psychodrama is generally considered a therapeutic system. The majority of the work in psychodrama is done in an institutional setting; there are several centers devoted to research and training in psychodrama. The most famous of these is New York's Psychodrama Institute founded by the father of the field, Joseph Moreno.

The benefit of psychodrama is the self-discovery which results from patient-improvised scenes involving key figures in their lives— including themselves. These may be recreations of scenes which they actually lived through or fictitious scenes in which parallel situations arise. The process involves three steps—preparation, the enactment, and discussion. The patient may begin as no more than a member of a discussion group following an enactment by others. But ultimately the patient must assume a role and play through the situation presented to the characters. Very personal work is, naturally, kept very private; but psychodramatists have no general objection to the presence of an audience—indeed, involvement of the audience in the discussion phase is often very useful.

Still, the crucial interaction in psychodrama is not audience/actor, actor/actor, or character/character; it is actor/character. The feelings aroused in the patient as he or she is forced to deal with imaginary situations give the psychodramatist and any attending psychologists or psychiatrists a good indication of what may be troubling him or her. Once the problem is diagnosed, crucial scenes may be repeated—usually with variations—in such a way as to allow the patient to deal with new, but similar situations spontaneously. This last point is central to psychodrama: disturbed people cannot be spontaneous because they are still responding to some previous experience, not the one which they are in at the present time. In psychodrama, improvisation is both a means and a goal.

Sociodrama.   A variation on the psychodrama model, sociodrama is not interested in dealing with disturbed patients. Instead, sociodrama uses many of the same techniques to solve problems within groups. The groups can be work groups, teams, even whole communities. The basic technique is role playing. People who may have never thought of a problem from another participant's point of view may be asked to adopt the role of someone else. Hence, in a sociodramatic exercise during a labor dispute, the president of the union may be asked to play the role of the president of the company. In the course of the experience, the labor leader who may have considered the company president a powerful figure with absolute freedom might discover how responsible the president is to others—the board of directors, the chair of the board, the government's regulatory bodies, the stockholders. The final aim of sociodrama is not, however, human empathy; the union leader's understanding of the company president's plight is useful only if it allows the two to work together to solve the labor dispute. And, fortunately, the technique can work effectively.

The techniques of sociodrama, especially role-reversal exercises, are often part of the armory of techniques employed by professionals involved in conflict resolution: Labor mediators, social workers, clergy, and group psychologists.

Human Potential Activities.   Theatre-based exercises have become a standard instrument among human potential facilitators and systems. For example, such programs as est, Arica, and gestalt psychology often employ techniques which are familiar to theatre professionals. Participants may be involved in imagination exercises identical to those used in actor training. Blocks to verbal and nonverbal communication can be addressed and overcome in improvisations. Gestalt psychologists are particularly famous for using a technique in which an important figure, living or dead, is imagined sitting in an empty chair; the participant then talks with the "person," sharing with the substitute figure thoughts which could not be said in the presence of the original one.

It is important to note in closing that the extended theatre techniques are not the property of any group. They are freely available to any person—and they are readily adapted to many different situations. Some of the best human potential exercises were developed by parents for use in the family; ministers are perfectly capable of using these techniques where appropriate; and creative classroom teachers almost always have a few theatre games up their sleeves for when the going gets rough.

A few of these techniques have some danger if employed carelessly by people who have no training or common sense. There is some danger that some of the more probing techniques—especially when used with young or otherwise vulnerable participants—may uncover or stimulate processes which can only be brought to conclusion by a health professional. With this in mind, psychodramatists who are not themselves psychologists usually work closely with a team of psychologists and psychiatrists. Anybody who would use theatre-based techniques to expand their growth environment owes it to everyone concerned—himself or herself especially—to learn all he or she can about techniques which have such powerful potential.

CONCLUSION

The theatre-based techniques described in this chapter have a familiarity to them that some may find a trifle disarming. One can almost hear some readers protesting: "But my third-grade teacher used to do that." Or "My children and I play that game." Or "We do that in our therapy group all the time." And it is true. These techniques are familiar because the forces which make theatre are so familiar.

That has been a recurrent theme of this book: the art of theatre is an elaboration of ordinary impulses and activities which all cultures share. The value of theatre reflects the value of those everyday activities; it becomes more important than everyday life to the degree that artists are able to extend, enrich, and amplify those ever-present values on special occasions. In the understandable desire to celebrate and improve the best in any art form, it is an error to forget the art's basis in life, to ignore the roots in pursuit of the flower.

And yet, finally, the dynamics of theatre work against that separation. No matter whether we perceive it as such, the art of theatre and the life of any culture are in an interactive relationship that defies division. Without so much as a by-your-leave, the forces at work in society drive people to imagine what does not exist. For some, their minds, bodies, and voices are driven to make their fantasies manifest and to share them with others. As they do, the largest feedback loop is closed and the individual imagination becomes the collective one. The realm of human options is expanded, decisions are made, and the course of history is changed. In small ways or large, for individuals or for nations, things can never be the same.

And somewhere in that mix, both responding to and influencing the forces that shape human destiny, stands the art of theatre.

Discussion Questions

1. Can you imagine ways in which even the professional theatre might benefit from the techniques described in this chapter?
2. What element of a usual "theatre experience" is sometimes missing in these techniques?
3. Many of these techniques are sometimes referred to as "theatre games." Is this term useful? Why? Why not?
4. What is the difference between creative drama and children's theatre?
5. Describe in your own words why acting as a participant in a theatre-based activity can be such a powerful teaching/learning experience.

Index